Mary Shelley and the Rights of the Child

Political Philosophy in *Frankenstein*

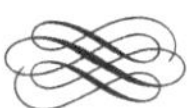

Eileen Hunt Botting

PENN

UNIVERSITY OF PENNSYLVANIA PRESS

PHILADELPHIA

Haney Foundation Series

A volume in the Haney Foundation Series, established in 1961 with the generous support of Dr. John Louis Haney.

Published by
University of Pennsylvania Press
Philadelphia, Pennsylvania 19104-4112
www.upenn.edu/pennpress

Printed in the United States of America on acid-free paper
10 9 8 7 6 5 4 3 2 1

Library of Congress Cataloging-in-Publication Data
Names: Botting, Eileen Hunt, 1971– author.
Title: Mary Shelley and the rights of the child : political philosophy in *Frankenstein* / Eileen Hunt Botting.
Other titles: Haney Foundation series.
Description: 1st edition. | Philadelphia : University of Pennsylvania Press, [2017] | Series: Haney Foundation series
Identifiers: LCCN 2017012493 | ISBN 9780812249620 (hardcover : alk. paper)
Subjects: LCSH: Shelley, Mary Wollstonecraft, 1797–1851. Frankenstein. | Shelley, Mary Wollstonecraft, 1797–1851—Political and social views. | Children's rights—Philosophy. | Children's rights in literature. | Parent and child in literature.
Classification: LCC PR5397.F73 B676 2017 | DDC 823/.7—dc23
LC record available at https://lccn.loc.gov/2017012493

CONTENTS

Mary Shelley and the Rights of the Child

PREFACE

Welcome to the *Creature Double Feature*

Growing up in suburban Massachusetts in the 1970s, I spent my Saturday afternoons, like most kids in the Boston area, watching the *Creature Double Feature* on Channel 56. The double feature consisted of two monster movies—usually beloved B-movies made by Universal Studios of Hollywood, Hammer Studios of London, and Toho Studios of Tokyo from the 1930s through the 1960s. In the matinee lineup, there was typically a giant monster movie, such as *Mothra vs. Godzilla*, paired with a small monster movie, such as *Frankenstein Meets the Wolf Man*. Battles between monsters (usually of the same size) were common, but these battles derived their interest from the original Universal monster movies of the 1930s, which centered on a single creature of supranatural (and typically malevolent) powers.

In this ménage, Dracula, the Wolf Man, and Frankenstein's Creature loomed large in my imagination. They were the archetypal monsters from which all other monsters were made—though small compared to Godzilla and the radiation-spawned mutants of the Pacific Rim. The Japanese giant monster movies, in fact, all seemed to mine from the core theme of the Frankenstein story: humans could use the power of science to create or alter life irresponsibly, thus causing their own destruction. In the aftermath of Hiroshima, this lesson from fiction felt all too real.[1]

To my childhood self, however, Dracula was the scariest monster by far. The Count appeared human yet used his supernatural powers to deliberately and emotionlessly do inhuman things to his vulnerable human victims, who were usually young women. By contrast, werewolves were frightening if only because a completely innocent person could become one by chance, as when bitten by a wolf in the middle of the night. After that stroke of bad luck, all it took was the light of the full moon to trigger one's transformation into a bloodthirsty animal ruled by instinct. Dracula was scary for his intentions, but the Wolf Man was frightening for his lack of them.

The real puzzle to my young mind was why Frankenstein's Creature was even considered a monster. The Frankenstein films were simply not scary in the way that the blood-soaked vampire and werewolf flicks were. Most of the time, I could not even watch the opening credits of a Hammer Studios vampire movie without running out of the room as soon as their signature special effect—Technicolor blood—dripped down the neck of a maiden victim of the Count. Unlike Dracula and the Wolf Man, Frankenstein's Creature commanded a spooky fascination and awe but not horror. Although he was assembled from the parts of human and other animal corpses, then animated by electricity, his oversized, even clumsy frame—grotesque as it was—elicited more sympathy than fear. The Creature was not evil incarnate like Dracula, nor an animal gone haywire like the Wolf Man. The Creature was more like an orphan child, made and abandoned by his scientist father and abused by nearly everyone he encountered as he strove to survive in the world on his own.

The Universal Frankenstein films of the 1930s reinforced this view of the Creature as a child who was not born evil but rather made monstrous as a result of mistreatment. In the 1931 classic *Frankenstein*, directed by James Whale, the reanimated Creature first greets the light with the sensitive eyes, inarticulate sounds, and inquisitive hands of a newborn. This innocent moment is soon disturbed by his sadistic abuse at the hands of Dr. Frankenstein's servant Fritz, who tortures him with a stick set on fire. Once he escapes, the Creature roams the countryside looking to satisfy the basic needs denied him by his father and Fritz: food, water, shelter, security, care, companionship, and love. He instead finds villagers who respond to him with violence due to his strange appearance. Seeking a respite from this abuse, he encounters a little girl, who has been let outside to play by her parents. In a striking cinematic image, the towering Creature and the tiny child sit together contentedly, tossing daisy petals into a sunlit pond. When the petals run out, the Creature assumes the girl, pretty like a flower, wants to be thrown into the water. Unaware that she will not float like the petals, he unintentionally causes her to drown. Horrified, the Creature runs away, as a child does when he cannot face the consequences of what he has done. In fact, the actor Boris Karloff wanted to underscore the Creature's innocence by laying the girl in the water gently like a flower, but Whale directed him to pick her up roughly and throw her in the pond. Either way, Karloff ingeniously interpreted the Creature as an affectionate and playful child who, without the guidance of a parent or any other adult, does not know his own strength or how to reason the consequences of his actions. Sensing the childlike quality of Karloff's Creature, the actress Marilyn Harris—who played the girl by the pond—felt a strong sympathy for the "Monster" on set. She developed a fond relationship with Karloff, perhaps because she had suffered abuse and physical torture by her sadistic stage mother since infancy.[2]

Whale's 1935 sequel, *The Bride of Frankenstein*, manipulates the image of the Creature as a child to both comic and tragic effect. In an almost slapstick scene, the Creature proves himself to be an amiable companion to an old blind man living alone in the woods. Unafraid of his guest because he cannot see him, the hermit unwittingly spills soup on the grunting Creature but cheerfully bonds with him over shared wine and tobacco. "Mmmmm good!" the Creature blurts to his "phwend," as a toddler would happily babble to a parent who feeds him. Some villagers stop by the cottage and disrupt this brief domestic idyll, attacking the Creature on sight. Later, the Creature learns more words under the tutelage of Dr. Pretorius. He uses the power of language to demand that his father furnish him a companion. Dr. Frankenstein makes him a bride despite his reservations about Dr. Pretorius's plan to use the so-called monsters to create a new species. When the bride unexpectedly rejects her intended mate, the Creature does not seek revenge against his father or his wife, Elizabeth. All grown up, yet truly alone, he chooses to immolate himself, his bride, and Dr. Pretorius in the flames that consume his father's laboratory in order to prevent further harm that they (or his father's science) could do to others. Watching these films directed by Whale, my young self sympathized with the Creature more than anyone. As Stephen King cogently remarked, "We see the horror of being a monster in the eyes of Boris Karloff."[3]

Paying homage to Whale's classics in his 1974 dark comedy, *Young Frankenstein*, the director Mel Brooks even used the same sets, similar scenes, black and white film—and, most crucially, the image of the Creature as a child. Like *Bride*, Brooks's adaptation sardonically played with the absurdity of the Creature's predicament as a stitched-together, electrified, hulking orphan, even as it recognized its tragedy. In one of the most evocative scenes, Gene Wilder—in the role of the great-grandson of Dr. Frankenstein—enters a cell that contains the wailing Creature, thinking he will be killed by the supposed monster. But when his friends break in to save him, the doctor is found cuddling the giant Creature like a baby, promising to love and care for his child forever.

Young Frankenstein thus responds to a comic counterfactual that cuts to the heart of the tragedy of Mary Shelley's original story: what if the Creature had been given a hug by his father, instead of being exposed to suffering by him? Even the seemingly facetious title *Young Frankenstein* suggests that the deeper meaning of Shelley's story is rooted in the intense, yet perhaps insatiable, demands of parent-child relationships. Imagining the impact of a hug between Dr. Frankenstein and his Creature is no joke, even as it makes us laugh at Wilder.

I was in high school in the late 1980s when I first read Shelley's 1818 novel, *Frankenstein; or, the Modern Prometheus*. I picked it up partly out of curiosity to see the genesis of all those *Creature Double Features* that had mesmerized me not so long ago on Saturday afternoon television. What I found in Shelley's text was a story that resembled, in themes and symbolism, its many film adaptations. Yet the novel—with its three-tiered, Chinese box–like structure—was far more complex, mysterious, and compelling than any of its cinematic versions.[4]

Plot points also differed in important ways across the novel and the films. Unlike the 1931 *Frankenstein*, the Creature's major wrongdoing was not the accidental drowning of a girl.[5] For his first and worst crime, Shelley had the Creature kill Victor's Frankenstein's little brother, William, in a fit of vengeful and jealous rage against his maker's family. The Creature recounts how the murder was a deliberate attempt to avenge his father's abandonment of him: "I gazed on my victim, and my heart swelled with exultation and triumph: clapping my hands, I exclaimed, 'I, too, can create desolation; my enemy is not impregnable.'"[6] The Creature's joy in causing the death of the young boy is child*ish*, as he claps his hands with glee for his evil deed, but it is not child*like*, for it marks the end of his innocence. To compound the gravity and intentionality of this offense, Shelley had the Creature frame the servant girl, Justine, for the murder of William, the child she helped to raise.

The Creature's growing sense of desolation in the wake of these crimes drives him to demand of his father the provision of a basic "right" to "live in the interchange of those sympathies necessary for my being."[7] Because Victor had failed as a parent to provide the Creature love, he as a parent must arrange for a loving substitute. Since his monstrous features cause people to fear him, the Creature reasons that this substitute must be a female companion who is equal to him in every respect, including ugliness, so that they may live together in sympathy and peace, alone in a South American desert far away from the hostility of human beings. Unlike the 1935 film by Whale, Shelley had Victor begin but then abruptly terminate the making of the equal female companion—not a "bride." Robbed of any hope of finding friendship and community in this life, the Creature responds with gruesome violence of the most calculated kind: he murders Victor's best friend, Henry Clerval; frames his maker as the killer; and then strangles Victor's wife, Elizabeth, on her nuptial bed. Through these dark episodes, Shelley consistently stressed how the Creature's cruel intention to do evil for the sake of vengeance made him into the immoral monster that society had originally, tragically, mistaken him to be.

In college, I was fascinated enough with the story to read it for fun during summer breaks—along with my other (quirkily chosen) favorite books, Augustine's *Confessions*, Marlowe's *Dr. Faustus*, and Dickens's *Great Expectations*. Coincidentally, the Creature taught himself to read with three books—Milton's *Paradise Lost*, Plutarch's *Lives*, and Goethe's *Sorrows of Young Werther*—before he deciphered the story of his own creation in his father's journal. With more of a literary background, I was able to appreciate the philosophical richness of Shelley's story, especially her reworking of the narrative of the fall of once innocent creatures into sin, death, and tragedy. In this light, *Frankenstein* looked like a *bildungsroman* gone wrong.

What kept drawing me back to Shelley's novel was the sympathetic aspect of the character of the Creature, despite all of his crimes. Growing up in the security of a loving and prosperous family, the story confronted me with a truly terrifying thought experiment: what would it have been like to be brought into this world only to be immediately rejected and exposed? Contemplating this worst-case scenario, I came to see the Creature's double identity as a superhuman avenger and a hideous monster to be a dangerous psychological fiction, foisted upon his self-image by his father's and society's horrified reaction to his features. Once his two-faced mask of inhuman mutant and righteous nemesis was removed, one could see the Creature for who he really was: a stateless orphan, abandoned by family, abused by society, and ignored by the law.[8] A product of circumstances beyond his control, yet ultimately responsible for his own actions, the unnamed Creature deserved sympathy from other people, even when he had behaved very, very badly.

Even—perhaps especially—a child could see that.

INTRODUCTION

Frankenstein and the Question of Children's Rights

Alone in his secret laboratory, without the support or knowledge of his family, friends, or chemistry professors, Victor used untested scientific techniques to elicit life and consciousness in a previously dead body made of parts of humans and other animals. This living Creature looked monstrous and inhuman to his creator because his gigantic size and alien visage challenged the received notion of the human. Horrified, Victor rejected his Creature rather than caring for him. Through this act of hubris and irresponsibility, Victor arguably became the most important literary figure to use science to play God in modern Western thought. Unlike the ancient Prometheus, who rebelled against the gods to give fire to humanity, this modern Prometheus acted without a sense of responsibility to humanity, including the queer-looking person he made. The ethical consequences of this action are extremely tragic: the Creature's murder of several innocent bystanders, including virtually all of Victor's family; the questioning of Victor's sanity (by himself and others); and finally, the untimely death of the young protagonist somewhere near the North Pole, before he could stop and punish his monster.

Most readers will recognize this story as *Frankenstein; or, the Modern Prometheus*, the 1818 novel by Mary Shelley, even if they have never read her book. This is because the story of Victor Frankenstein and his Creature has become a kind of "script" familiar to almost everyone. The deep resonance of its mythological symbolism has driven the global success of its publication, translation, and adaptation in theater, film, art, and literature since the nineteenth century. In his study of the impact of Shelley's story on modern conceptions of biological science, Jon Turney argued, "Once a script has been laid down, a single cue can evoke an entire story, as an interpretive frame or context for what is being discussed. In this sense, the *Frankenstein* script has become one of the most important in our culture's discussion of science and technology. To activate it, all you need is the word: *Frankenstein*."[1]

Certainly the story of *Frankenstein* has become such a framing script for the public view of science, especially the as yet unrealized idea of the artificial creation (not simply the technologically assisted reproduction) of human life with the aid of biology and chemistry.[2] Without a doubt, there is also a real power to reading Shelley's novel through the lens of science. The novel projects many insights for engaging the ethical question of the scope of human responsibility for the consequences of scientific research. Yet there is also much to be learned from the Frankenstein story by shifting the interpretive lens from science (or the ethics of science) to *politics*. Indeed, Mary Shelley had initially provided such a political frame for reading the book when she dedicated it to her father, the anarchist political philosopher and political novelist: "TO WILLIAM GODWIN, THE AUTHOR OF POLITICAL JUSTICE, CALEB WILLIAMS, & [et]c."[3]

Since the earliest reviews of the book, readers have unearthed the political meanings of *Frankenstein*. Underscoring the Rousseauian and Godwinian themes of his wife's first novel, Percy Shelley in 1817 argued that *Frankenstein* had at its core a moral and political concern with the vicious cycle of injustice. Injustice was not natural or an act of God. Rather, injustice originated in society, especially in its unequal economic and political orders. Building upon the central thesis of Rousseau's *Second Discourse* (1755), Godwin argued in *Political Justice* (1793) that such unequal economic and political orders established institutional frameworks for systematically and unjustly discriminating against some people in favor of others. Ascribing this Godwinian view of injustice to *Frankenstein*, Percy Shelley contended that the novel illustrated how the perpetuation of political injustice against people tragically made the victims capable of doing further, even greater, injustice to others. In so doing, he wrote one of the first and most enduring political interpretations of the novel: "Treat a person ill, and he will become wicked . . . too often in society, those who are best qualified to be its benefactors and its ornaments, are branded by some accident with scorn, and changed, by neglect and solitude of heart, into a scourge and a curse."[4]

Alongside Godwin's anarchistic political philosophy, disruptive political events of the 1810s—such as Luddite riots against dehumanizing factory work in Britain—were also likely sources for the radical political subtext of Shelley's story.[5] During the Victorian era, a political frame for reading Frankenstein's so-called "Monster" as a product and perpetuator of injustice came to dominate even the popular representations of the Creature for the public eye.[6] Beginning with debates about the 1832 Reform Bill concerning the enfranchisement of working-class men in Britain and extending through transatlantic nineteenth-century debates about abolition and imperialism, political cartoons regularly deployed reimaginings of Frankenstein's massive "Monster" as symbols for public fear of the revolt and uprising of the masses against injustice.[7]

I follow Mary and Percy Shelley in training the mind's eye on the profound political questions generated by the structure and sources of the novel. While accepting Turney's view of "Frankenstein" as a framing script for science, this book argues that the Frankenstein story, as rooted in Shelley's novel, also functions as a framing script for politics—especially the still radical idea of rights for children. While a variety of compelling political readings of *Frankenstein* have been made, particularly after literary criticism on the novel has boomed since the 1970s, critics have typically interpreted the early nineteenth-century novel through the lens of a more recent school of thought—such as psychoanalytic feminism, Marxism, critical disability studies, or critical race theory. Through their attention to the ways that the novel resonates with contemporary debates on gender, class, race, colonialism, imperialism, disability, and other issues of identity politics, these readings have helped scholars, including myself, to see the Creature as a child who has been subjected to political injustice through his abandonment, abuse, and neglect by a society that ostracizes him due to his differences from other people.[8] What distinguishes my political reading is its insistence that the very architecture of the novel—its narrative structure and its foundational philosophical sources—puts the question of children's rights at the very heart of the text. Thus, even as it can be productively read from myriad political perspectives, the text of *Frankenstein* itself functions as a framing device for philosophical consideration of the idea of children's rights.

Frankenstein is a profound work of speculative fiction designed to engage philosophical questions concerning children's rights to the means for their healthy development and well-being—fundamentally, rights to warmth, food, water, clothing, shelter, care, education, family, community, and, most crucially, love. Shelley structured her novel around a series of five interconnected thought experiments, which press readers to think through a core set of moral problems related to the definition, purpose, and ethical scope of the rights of children in relationship to parents' and other adults' duties toward children.[9] These thought experiments picture Frankenstein's Creature as a stateless orphan, abandoned by family, abused by society, and ignored by the law. The Creature's bleak political predicament and the social tragedies that result from it provoke readers of Shelley's novel to consider whether fundamental rights for all children can be justified.

This new political reading of *Frankenstein* does not discount the value of other interpretations of Shelley's richly symbolic and multisided modern myth but rather positions itself alongside them as an innovative and fresh perspective. Mine is not the one "true" reading of the novel—for there is no such thing. Yet it is a valid reading of *Frankenstein*, which demonstrates the novel's enduring relevance to children's rights by examining the story's connections to political philosophy, past and present.

The Familial and Philosophical Background for the Frankenstein Myth

As the daughter of the political philosophers Mary Wollstonecraft and William Godwin, Shelley was well schooled in seventeenth- and eighteenth-century moral and political thought. Blending her familial background in political philosophy with her youthful love of fanciful storytelling, Shelley developed one of the most powerful myths in modernity.[10] *Frankenstein* ostensibly rewrites the ancient myth of Prometheus, but like all good myths, its central metaphor has taken on "a life of its own."[11] The image of the "Monster"—a motherless and nameless Creature made by his father-scientist only to be abandoned to a cruel education in hardship and a subsequent life of crime—has become iconic and mimetic, spiraling out from early nineteenth-century Britain into new Western and non-Western iterations. "There is no such thing as *Frankenstein*," Paul O'Flinn wrote in 1983, "there are only *Frankensteins*, as the text is ceaselessly rewritten, reproduced, refilmed, and redesigned."[12]

As Paul Cantor has argued, *Frankenstein* is a modern myth, and like all myths, its psychologically powerful symbolism can be interpreted in many ways.[13] Although the most common way to read the meaning of the myth is through the lens of science, it is as productive to interpret it through the lens of politics. The "monster" was a powerful symbol within seventeenth- and eighteenth-century Western political thought because it could obliquely address the stark moral problems of the age: the Hobbesian choice between a brutal state of nature or an absolute sovereign Leviathan, the severing of humanity from its religious moorings as represented by the fall of Milton's Satan, and the fear of mob violence and total democratic revolution expressed by Burke in his *Reflections on the Revolution in France* (1790).[14]

By unleashing the tragic myth of Victor Frankenstein and his "Monster" upon modern culture, Shelley's novel raised moral questions about the European Enlightenment's interest in conducting (real or imagined) social experiments with children and their education in order to theorize and justify new models of political organization premised on the idea of human equality.[15] The Frankenstein myth calls into question the moral and political value of Enlightenment-era perfectionist models of understanding humanity and its potentially limitless development through science, politics, or experimental models of family life and education.[16] The problem of bad education, for girls and boys, preoccupied thinkers of the long eighteenth century.[17] Many proposed practical solutions to the varied instances of the problem, with Locke and Rousseau favoring private, family-based education and Wollstonecraft favoring free, coeducational, public, primary, day schools provided by the state. The rise of modern, empirically tested and verified natural science led to attempts to systematize the analysis of society and politics along similar lines—in part through the application of the concept of scientific experiment to the study of education and communities. Although he was on one level a critic of modern science's corrosive influence on morals, Rousseau presented in his *Emile* (1762) the most influential example of a theoretical social experiment: the imagining of the private education of an orphan boy by a male tutor, separated almost entirely from society, in order to hypothesize the positive effects of such private education in contrast to the known bad effects of formal, public, and communal forms of education in the eighteenth century.[18]

Partly inspired by Rousseau, experiments in social life, especially in marriage and family, became common among intellectual elites, such as Wollstonecraft and Godwin, in both their theories and their lives. The negative consequences of their real-life social experiments (such as having children outside of the institution of patriarchal marriage) were often unforeseen or unintended but nonetheless did harm to themselves and others in the short and long term. This dark dimension of her parents' experimental ethics, her biographers agree, was one inspiration for Shelley's tale in which a man experiments with reproduction without a woman, only to abandon his "hideous progeny" to a bad education that makes him into the "monster" he appears to be.[19]

Seeing Shelley's Creature as a Child

Since the first stage adaptation of *Frankenstein*, which portrayed the "monster" as having "the mind of an infant," it has been standard in theater, film, and literary criticism to represent Frankenstein's Creature as a child.[20] Mary Shelley watched with approval the 1823 play *Presumption: or, the Fate of Frankenstein* and even revised aspects of the 1831 edition of her novel in light of its themes.[21] What stayed constant across her two editions of 1818 and 1831 was her own representation of the Creature as a child—not in his "superhuman" mind and body but, more profoundly, in his needy and emotionally insecure psychology.[22] A genealogy of the Creature's infantilization in the visual arts can be traced from Victorian-era stage productions to the 1927 London play by Peggy Webling that inspired James Whale's iconic 1931 film *Frankenstein*.[23] As I recalled in the Preface, Whale's classic film has shaped virtually all of the subsequent cinematic images of the Creature, especially his childlike qualities.

Beginning in the 1970s, feminist scholarship on *Frankenstein* developed an influential line of interpretation of the novel that returned to many of Shelley's original themes.[24] To critics such as Ellen Moers, Sandra M. Gilbert, Susan Gubar, and Anne K. Mellor, Victor's usurping of the reproductive power of women through science signaled Shelley's recognition of the vital importance of women for human life and development. According to this feminist reading, the Creature was not only a child but also, more profoundly, a motherless and abandoned baby. Shelley herself may have identified with the Creature due to the loss of her mother from a childbirth infection. She may have even felt guilt for her mother's death—to the point that she fictionalized herself as a monstrous infant in her first novel, written at the age of nineteen. On a deeper level, the father-scientist's flight from his "miserable monster" tapped into the teenage Shelley's own traumatic experience of pregnancy and birth—especially the loss of a premature infant just months before she conceived the story of *Frankenstein*.[25] Shelley's conflicted relationship with her father, who disowned her when she eloped with Percy Shelley, has also been cited as a source for the emotional tug of war between Victor and his Creature. In this biographical light, the novel's emotional power lies in its treatment of the psychological experience of motherlessness, fatherlessness, and the horrors of teenage motherhood.[26]

The personal and familial subtext of the novel is built into its three-tiered structure. The frame story is a collection of letters by Captain Walton, telling the astounding tale of Victor Frankenstein and his Creature to his sister, who has the initials "M.W.S." As Mellor argued, the first (and perhaps ideal) audience for *Frankenstein* and for seeing the Creature as a child is the mother of the story herself—Mary Wollstonecraft Shelley.[27] Elaborating this parent-child analogy, Shelley's 1831 introduction to the third edition described *Frankenstein* as her "hideous progeny" and "offspring of happy days," which she bid to "go forth and prosper."[28]

While seeing the Creature as a child has become a canonical reading of the Frankenstein story in all its forms, it is new to argue that Shelley's original novel provokes the philosophical question of whether children have rights. A skeptic might say that this reading of the novel is not only new but also as preposterous as the premise of the novel itself. For one, the word "right" is only used a handful of times in the entire novel—and without the modifier "children's." Second, Shelley chose to write in the genre of the novel, not political philosophy, due to her exceptional literary talents. As she confided in her 1838 journal, she thought she lacked the "argumentative powers" to write a nonfiction defense of her privately held political views, which in many ways aligned with the liberals of the time: "I see things pretty clearly, but I cannot demonstrate them." "Besides," she concluded, "I feel the counterarguments too strongly."[29] Her gifts of imagination, insight, and empathy made her a great fiction writer, not a philosopher. These gifts would have also enabled her to write a "good tragedy," she thought, if her father had not discouraged her when she expressed interest in becoming a playwright after seeing *Presumption* in 1823.[30]

Fiction afforded Shelley a wider berth than philosophy in which to safely test her perhaps dangerous moral and political ideas. In the aforementioned 1838 journal entry, she suggested that she chose fiction over nonfiction because the former genre was more open-ended and therefore more conducive to wide-ranging philosophical thought on difficult questions such as feminism: "besides on some topics (especially with regard to my own sex) I am far from making up my mind." This productive resistance to making up her mind may have been cultivated in the summer and fall of 1816, when she was an unmarried teenage mother, the youngest in her male-dominated commune of writers, composing a draft of her first novel. As a fiction writer, she felt she had greater freedom to explore ideas for the benefit of others without making the philosophical mistake of committing too early or rigidly to a particular position: "When I feel that I can say what will benefit my fellow creatures, I will speak,--not before."[31] But without a treatise to convey her ideas in a more straightforward way than the novel, it is difficult, perhaps even impossible, to know what her answer to the question of children's rights was.

To answer the skeptic: the task of this book is not to uncover a philosophy of children's rights within the novel *Frankenstein*, nor is it to make historical claims about Shelley's true views on children's rights. It is rather to explain why and show how Shelley's *Frankenstein* has the intellectual and imaginative power to spur readers to wonder whether and, if so, why children—the most vulnerable and powerless of persons—have rights, even when they are denied enjoyment of them by parents and leaders of states. One of the benefits of Shelley's choice of the novel over the treatise is that the novel form allows for this sort of big and open-ended philosophical question to be entertained by readers from a variety of temporal contexts, cultural backgrounds, and political perspectives. This is perhaps why the book was ranked, in a 2016 survey of college syllabi, among the top five most commonly assigned books at universities around the world.[32] Such widespread reader responses to the text, across time and place, bring new insights not only to the interpretation of *Frankenstein* but also to philosophical consideration of the question of children's rights.[33]

Frankenstein's Five Thought Experiments on the Rights of the Child

All fiction is imaginative and, hence, contrary to fact. Speculative fiction employs what philosophers call counterfactual scenarios, which are contrary to fact in a more complicated way. Such speculative or philosophical fiction imagines alternate worlds that could have existed if something had happened differently. This is technically called a counterfactual conditional: if X (which does not obtain), then what would follow from X? A speculative fiction asks the reader to think through the psychological, moral, and political consequences of that counterfactual premise as if it happened to be true.

A paradigmatic work of speculative fiction, *Frankenstein* begs its audience to reason through the ethical consequences of an uncanny counterfactual: what if a man had used science to create an (at least partly) human life without a woman? This counterfactual derives its imaginative force from positing an altogether new form of reproduction. Even in the early twenty-first century—with all of the recent advances in assisted reproductive technology, such as the womb transplant, artificial gametes, and three-parent in vitro fertilization—a human, or even a close human relative, has yet to be made without an egg and a womb of at least one female and sperm from a male. Although nonhuman animals such as chickens, sheep, and cows are regularly cloned and artificial gametes have been generated from stem cells of humans of the opposite sex, neither biotechnology has yet been used to create a human or close human relative.[34] Moreover, the eggs and wombs of females have not yet been eliminated from the process of reproduction. An enucleated egg is used in most reproductive experiments, including cloning of nonhuman animals. Scientists continue to discuss the possibility of making artificial wombs, but there is no working model as of yet for the incubation of any species to the point of live birth. Two centuries after Shelley wrote *Frankenstein*, humans and other animals can be made from a variety of biotechnological interventions, but females still play a crucial part in the reproductive process.[35]

From the counterfactual premise of a father-scientist's making an (at least partly) human life without a woman, Shelley crafted a set of interconnected thought experiments that constitute the basic narrative structure of the greatest work of Gothic literature and the source of all science fiction since:

1. What if a man had sole parental responsibility for a child due to using science to create him without a biological mother?
2. What if the child was totally abandoned because the lone parent (and other people) did not love him due to fear and disgust of his hideous form?
3. What if the newborn child had the ability to survive on his own due to his eight-foot frame, extraordinary strength, and incredible capability for language acquisition and independent learning?
4. What if the child was not only abandoned and neglected by his parent but also hurt or abused by every human he encountered due to his monstrous appearance?
5. What if the neglected child claimed a fundamental right to share love with a sympathetic and equal female companion, thereby forcing his father-scientist to choose to either (a) make a female companion for his child (risking the development of a new species that could destroy the human race) or (b) suffer the angry revenge of his child who had become truly monstrous in behavior?

These five thought experiments are nested together in the novel like a Chinese box. The reader opens the top of one box, only to find another box inside.[36] Each box contains a counterfactual scenario that prompts the reader to ask a series of moral and political questions about children and their rights. Reading the novel as this cascade of thought experiments on the rights of the child is my original contribution to both the interpretation of *Frankenstein* and theories of children's rights.

It is interesting to note that in this series of thought experiments, science plays only an instrumental and conceptually nebulous role. Victor's unspecified—even shady and dubious—knowledge of alchemy, anatomy, chemistry, and electricity gives him the means for the creation of a motherless child who has the size and strength to survive, but not thrive, in the most extreme conditions of social deprivation. Shelley's lack of attention to the specifics of how the Creature was made through science distinguishes her novel from its many film adaptations, which have been obsessed with speculating detailed scientific techniques for the creation of life. Moreover, Victor's combination of the medieval "science" of alchemy with the modern science of chemistry in making the Creature discredits any simplistic reading of the novel as a morality tale about the dangers of modern science. When we look at *Frankenstein* through counterfactual and political lenses, science takes a back seat, serving only as a mechanism in a set of thought experiments that push us to consider the moral and political relationships between parents and children, children and other adults, and children and broader communities. David Collings has wonderfully summed up this point in his own political reading of the novel: "The key contrast in *Frankenstein* is not between good and bad science but between a factual and counterfactual scenario."[37]

Peter Swirski has contributed the important insight that literary thought experiments are not much different from scientific or philosophical thought experiments. Whether it is Galileo's theorization of the feather and the stone falling at the same rate, Judith Jarvis Thompson's hard case of a person who wakes up to find she is life support for a virtuoso violinist, or Shelley's story of a scientist who makes an (at least partly) human life without a woman, all thought experiments work basically the same way and serve similar functions. Thought experiments are examples of armchair theorizing, in that they take place entirely in someone's mind.[38]

Thought experiments require the experimenter to entertain a counterfactual premise, such as "What if a child had been made without a biological mother?" Leaning back in the proverbial armchair, the experimenter has the imaginative chance to think through the consequences of accepting that false premise as true. There may be the possibility of empirically verifying the results of the experiment, as was the case with the astronauts of Apollo 15 testing

Galileo's theory about falling objects in the vacuum of outer space. With literary or ethical thought experiments, the process of empirical verification is less exact but still involves an interchange between theory and experience. The ethical or literary experimenter has the opportunity to compare the results of her armchair theorizing with her experiences or the experiences of others, in order to refine the experiment and eventually draw out the relevant moral and political conclusions for application in the real world.[39]

According to Swirski, what ultimately makes any thought experiment an *experiment* is its cognitive power to ask the armchair thinker to isolate and manipulate the variables that determine the consequences of the counterfactual scenario. The thought-experimenter should be able to identify the independent variable (or causal premise) and the dependent variable (or causal outcome), as well as any underlying cause behind them. The thought experiment is designed to alter the independent variable for the sake of reasoning through the consequences of accepting that false premise as true.[40]

By looking at *Frankenstein* through the lens of Swirski's criteria for a thought experiment, we can see how the novel operates as a kind of mental incubator for some radical moral and political ideas on children, family, and society as a whole. In the first counterfactual scenario that frames the novel, Victor's decision to make a baby without a woman pulls the reader's attention toward Shelley's manipulation of a key variable: the role of a woman in reproduction. The idea of a man generating life without a woman brings about the idea of an altogether motherless child. The underlying cause of the child's lack of a mother is his father's hubristic or irresponsible use of his knowledge of the science of life and death.

The first thought experiment of *Frankenstein* thus tweaks the variables of who performs reproduction and how reproduction happens in order to spur moral questions on the roles and duties of men and women in childrearing. Ultimately, the tragic outcome of the novel leads readers to wonder if the child would have been better off without such a father or never to have been made or born. More provocatively, it prods us to query whether all children, especially infants, have a right to be mothered, whether by a biological mother or another person who has taken on the intensive caregiving and loving practices of mothering a child.

The second thought experiment of the novel turns on the idea of the creation of a child so hideous that the father-scientist abandons him on sight. While parents typically adore their babies for their perfection and beauty, this counterfactual scenario supposes the father-scientist's revulsion and even fear toward his corpse-like Creature. Victor's flight from the child follows from this supposition.

Shelley modifies the variables of how a parent feels toward a newborn and what the newborn looks like in order to direct the reader's mind to the issue of the role of the affections in motivating the practice of parental duty toward children. Even if parents have felt fear, revulsion, or ambivalence toward their newborns in real life, their feelings (and memories) of love toward their infants typically help them to overcome any urge to abandon or otherwise harm them and to fulfill their duties to care for them. By changing the variables of parental emotions and infant features, Shelley's second thought experiment tests the hypothesis that parental love plays a vital role in establishing the affective and practical basis for the moral relationship between parent and child.

Without parental love, children's right to parental care does not seem to stand a chance of satisfaction. This demanding idea—that parental love is necessary for children's proper care, healthy development, and well-being—in turn generates a series of thorny moral and political questions. Do children have a right to love? If so, what does a child's right to love entail—merely passive receipt of love from another or a shared and active relationship of love and "interchange . . . of sympathies?" Does this right only pertain to the parent-child relationship? If not, who (or what) might responsibly arrange for or fulfill it?

In the novel's third thought experiment, the Creature's tragic predicament as a stateless orphan stirs readers to consider why children deserve rights. While the Creature is not a de jure orphan, or technically lacking a family altogether, he is a de facto orphan (an exposed child in fact living without the love and care of his family). In addition, he can be read as either de jure stateless (technically lacking a state altogether) or effectively stateless (a child with an unregistered birth in the country of origin).[41]

Even when they are not stateless or orphaned, newborns and infants often fail to thrive and even die without the loving care of parents or parental figures because they are fundamentally dependent on such loving care for their healthy development and well-being.[42] *Frankenstein* deliberately runs counter to these facts. The novel shows us what would happen if a baby had the physical and cognitive abilities to survive at birth completely on its own.

Shelley thus elaborated a counterfactual found in the opening pages of one of her favorite books, Rousseau's *Emile*: "If man were born big and strong, his size and strength would be useless to him . . . in that they would keep others from thinking of aiding him."[43] Rousseau did not tease out the implications of this counterfactual for his own theory of the family. However, Shelley used this brilliant idea of a giant baby as a premise for *Frankenstein*. The size and strength of the Creature, paired with his incredibly swift cognitive development, allows him to survive without the provision of basic rights to warmth, clothing, food, water, shelter, care, education, family, community, and even love. By playing with the variables of how strong and how smart a baby could be, Shelley tested the hypothesis that infants need provision of basic rights, not merely conditions of survival, in order to thrive or develop well and feel happy. By switching from Victor's to the Creature's point of view, she enabled readers to see from a young child's perspective the painful results of the deprivation of rights, especially the right to love, during one's infancy.

In the penultimate thought experiment of the novel, the Creature survives his abandonment by his father only to be totally abused by society. By exposing the Creature to the worst conditions of vulnerability, without any social support, the fourth thought experiment leads readers to reason through the broader political implications of extreme child neglect and abuse. The failure of parents and families to fulfill a child's basic right to love indicates the need for some other responsible body, beyond the family, to arrange for the provision of this right. Thus, the injustice of the Creature's experience of total abuse provokes readers to consider the justice of legal and political institutions that provide a support system for children and their families, especially the most vulnerable among them.[44]

The fifth and final counterfactual scenario of the novel is cleverly construed as a pair of thought experiments entertained by the main protagonists, the first by the Creature and the second by Victor. Perhaps the prime example of the ingenuity of Shelley's speculative fiction, this pair of thought experiments conducted within a broader set of thought experiments has become the basis of all science fiction. First, the Creature speculates that if he had an equal female companion who was made to be as ugly as him, then she would love him. This experience of being loved by a companion like himself would enable him to leave human civilization and live in peace with her in the remote wilds of South America. The creature tests the theory that it is his "unearthly ugliness" that stands in the way of his experience of love by imagining his ideal companion to be just as ugly.[45]

By running the Creature's thought experiment in one's own mind, one comes to question the ethics of his proposal to satisfy his right to love through the creation of a being solely for this purpose. His proposal fails to respect the equality and freedom of the prospective companion by imagining her as a mere instrument for the satisfaction of his passive and consumptive right to be loved, not a partner in the sharing of a loving relationship. The Creature's thought experiment thus exposes the limits to a child's right to love. Even when the total deprivation of rights has created what Costas Douzinas calls an "insatiable desire" and demand for rights, the victims of such deprivation nevertheless face moral limits on the scope of the rights to which they are entitled.[46]

Victor responds to his child's demand with a two-pronged thought experiment. In the first prong of his decision tree, Victor counterfactually reasons that *if* he made such a female *and*, he further posits, she could reproduce with his Creature, he would risk the evolution of a new species that would have the power to destroy the human race. On the other prong looms the possibility of suffering the angry revenge of his Creature for refusing to make him such a companion. His ultimate decision to deny his Creature a companion in order to be a benefactor of humanity in fact instigates the Creature's violent revenge against him.

In refusing to make the female creature, Victor raises the question of whether moral and political concern for the well-being of future generations trumps not only self-interest but also parental responsibility for the well-being of one's own children. Given its tragic ending, the novel itself remains open to the possibility that Victor should have resolved this moral dilemma differently. Its cascade of thought experiments furnishes readers with the philosophical tools to determine what the relative weights of self-interest, parental duty, and humanitarian responsibility ought to be in the ethical provision of children's right to love. It sparks the question of whether humanitarian responsibility ought to be framed more broadly than a duty to assist the human species so that the idea of "humanitarianism" cannot be used to justify the exclusion of marginalized persons, nonhuman or posthuman life forms, or any so-called monsters from considerations of justice. It also provokes one to ask whether the concept of the human is too narrow and ought to be supplemented or perhaps replaced with broader concepts such as person, being, or creature.

The moral point of Shelley's cascade of literary thought experiments is not as straightforward as that of some strictly philosophical thought experiments, which seek only to rule out or disprove certain theses. In ethics, Robert Nozick famously imagined an "experience machine" that could give people the chance to experience a simulation of total hedonistic pleasure indistinguishable from the real thing.[47] Through this thought experiment, Nozick guided his readers to realize that it would be wrong to live under the sway of such a pleasure-making machine and, consequently, that a purely hedonistic view of the value of life is false. Like Nozick's experience machine, one point of Shelley's cascade of thought experiments is to rule out certain routes of conduct or action as morally wrong or false. *Frankenstein*'s five thought experiments on the rights of the child lead readers to see that the abandonment of any child ought to be avoided in order to protect that child's fundamental rights, especially to share love with a parent or fitting substitute. By following her cascade of thought experiments to their logical conclusions, we find that she does not ethically rule out the artificial creation of life but rather the loveless treatment of children, however they are made. Beyond this moral outcome, her series of thought experiments pushes readers to think beyond *what not to do to children* toward *what to do for and with children*, including those made by artificial means. In this way, Shelley's thought experiments move beyond the negative formulation of simple moral rules (refrain from X) and look toward the complex contemplation of positive social and political obligations (do Y).

Shelley's thought experiments also bring to mind questions that are at the fore of debates on children's rights today. The philosopher S. Matthew Liao has argued, quite contentiously, that all children have a right "to be loved" by biological parents or, if they are not available, then adoptive or foster parents. He has appealed to an array of social scientific and medical-psychiatric evidence to support this claim. Based on this evidence, he has powerfully reminded readers that human infants will often fail to thrive and even die if not loved by parents or parental figures.[48] I follow Liao in appealing to the strong empirical evidence for the justification of a child's right to love, but I also employ Shelley's literary thought experiments to develop the moral and political argument for the right to love in new directions.

Ultimately, I derive from my reading of *Frankenstein* distinctive support for some of Liao's views on children's right to love while pushing forward a more robust and relational understanding of children's right to share, not simply receive, love. Artificially created then abandoned, the Creature demands of his father-scientist the fulfillment of a "right" to "live in the interchange of those sympathies necessary for . . . being." Soon thereafter, he reframes this claim as a right to experience "love of another" with someone to whom he is closely "attached," even if that person is not his parent.[49] The Creature's claim for a child's right to share sympathy and love with a parent or someone with whom he shares a similarly deep emotional attachment is broader in ethical and political scope than Liao's narrower formulation of a child's "right to be loved," preferably by biological parents. Most crucially, the Creature's formulation of this right to love is active and relational, not merely passive and receptive. By arguing for the right to share love, not merely to be loved, the Creature avoids the conceptualization of children as passive receptacles for the love of parents and mere instruments for the successful performance of adult moral duties. From the Creature's perspective, children are rather active rights-bearers who exercise the right to love in relation to others—first and foremost, with their parents (who need not be biological or genetic relatives, as Liao prefers) but also with fitting substitutes (who need not be parental figures, as Liao prefers). Shelley's literary thought experiments give us a broader conception of a child's right to love and the ethical parameters for its fulfillment than does Liao. At the same time, her thought experiments reinforce many of his compelling conclusions as well as those of contemporary social science and medicine on the vital significance of love, especially parental love, for children's well-being and healthy development.

Shelley's imaginative and bold representation of the child as an active and relational rights-bearer has serious ethical implications for theories of children's rights. Theories of children's rights—beginning with John Locke—have often treated children as unequal to and lesser than adults, not as persons who are moral equals to adults as rights-holders (even if they do not hold the same slate of rights). By looking at the question of a child's right to love through the lens of Shelley's literary thought experiments, readers have the mental opportunity to overturn certain prejudicial assumptions about children that have presented obstacles to the public recognition of their fundamental rights, such as sharing love, which are, in the Creature's words, "necessary" for their very "being."

Frankenstein; or, a Novel on the Rights of the Child

Through a cascade of thought experiments and the ethical questions it spawns, the novel *Frankenstein* performs a philosophical function: pushing readers to consider why children have rights and how such rights are related to parental and other adult responsibilities. Shelley thus followed in the footsteps of her mother. Wollstonecraft built on the ideas of Locke and Rousseau to develop the first systematic theory of children's rights in her *A Vindication of the Rights of Woman* (1792)—a book her daughter read extensively around the time she conceived and composed the story of *Frankenstein*.[50]

In her parents, Shelley had some impressive role models for how to write a philosophical novel. Godwin's *Things as They Are; or, the Adventures of Caleb*

Williams (1794) was the premier work of political fiction of the time. In it he aimed to translate the abstract arguments of his 1793 treatise *Political Justice* into a concrete story that was compelling for a broader audience. Putting the anarchist ideas of *Political Justice* into narrative form, the novel exposed the hypocrisy of the legal system and the destructive power of society and government to corrupt and ruin even the most virtuous individuals. Borrowing elements of *Caleb Williams*, Wollstonecraft began to compose a philosophical novel that would illustrate her political ideas on women's oppression and women's rights. Written in the last year of her life, the manuscript of *Maria: or, the Wrongs of Woman* was left unfinished as a result of her death from a childbirth infection in September 1797. She died, at the age of thirty-eight, only two weeks after bringing her daughter Mary Wollstonecraft Godwin into the world. Although the *Rights of Woman* had set forth an extended moral justification for universal human rights, including the rights of slaves, women, children, and the poor, Wollstonecraft used her novel *Maria* to focus on the political problem of women's lack of access to rights in a patriarchal society.

Perhaps Shelley did not feel the need to write a straightforward justification of children's rights because her mother had already accomplished that task in her *Rights of Woman*. Another reason may be that Shelley saw herself as different from her mother—in talents, ideas, and political actions. In 1835, she wrote to her mother's friend, Maria Gisborne, that Wollstonecraft "had not sufficient fire of imagination." In the same letter, Shelley challenged her mother's view of the equal intellectual capabilities of the sexes: "In short my belief is—whether there be sex in souls or not—that the sex of our material mechanism makes us quite different creatures—better though weaker but wanting in the higher grades of intellect. —"[51] In her 1838 journal, Shelley described herself as a vindicator of the rights of women, but one who chose to consistently act on her feminist principles of social justice rather than to write about them: "If I have never . . . written to vindicate the Rights of women, . . . I have ever befriended women when oppressed—at every risk I have defended & supported victims to the social system."[52] While devoted to the memory of the mother she had barely met, Shelley still carved a distinctive identity for herself, personally, philosophically, and politically.

Building upon but not replicating her mother's work, Shelley's *Frankenstein* continued a family tradition of philosophical storytelling. Picking up where her mother left off, Shelley wrote a novel that engages the radical questions of whether, why, and how children have rights, regardless of how they are made or raised or how they behave. And yet, she did not use the novel as a blunt mouthpiece for her mother's views. Like all great fiction for a grown-up audience, *Frankenstein* is not a didactic tale with a clear moral to its story. The narrative structure of *Frankenstein* instead sets up an imaginative venue in which the still visionary political idea of children's rights can be repeatedly incubated and debated. This incubator for radical political ideas works with special force when read against the background of the philosophical sources of the novel: Shelley's own deep readings of Locke, Rousseau, and her parents' political theories.[53]

Like her parents, Shelley wrote philosophical fiction, but unlike them, she wrote speculative, not political, fiction. Political fiction like *Caleb Williams* or *Maria* was didactic in purpose: explaining and illustrating in layperson's terms the nuts and bolts of an abstract political philosophy, such as Godwin's anarchism or Wollstonecraft's feminism. Speculative fiction like *Frankenstein* took the abstraction of the philosophical novel to a whole new level. Essentially, speculative fiction makes readers ask questions about the unknown or even the unknowable, rather than teach or persuade them of what is already known. By contrast, political fiction incites readers to imagine something that did not happen in order to illustrate a philosophical point about politics. Speculative fiction, on the other hand, invites readers to consider "what if" something had happened that has not occurred (or could not occur) in order for them to reason through the moral and political consequences of that counterfactual.

In his 1818 review of *Frankenstein*, Sir Walter Scott made an interesting distinction between two types of "marvellous" fiction. Romances began with an untrue, usually supernatural, premise, which had no other aim but to inspire delight, wonder, or awe in the audience. There was another "class of fiction," however, that used a marvelous premise for a more intellectual purpose: "the author's principal object . . . is less to produce an effect by means of the marvels of the narrations, than to open new trains and channels of thought, by placing men in supposed situations of extraordinary and preternatural character, and then describing the mode of feeling and conduct which they are most likely to adopt."[54] The cognitive power of such fictions, like *Frankenstein*, was to invite the reader to think through what would have happened if that marvelous premise happened to be true. How would it affect the people involved in that (seemingly preposterous) situation? Scott went on to argue that the latter class of marvelous fiction involved a kind of epistemological exchange between audience and author: "we grant the extraordinary postulates which the author demands as the foundation of his narrative, only on condition of his deducing the consequences with logical precision."[55] Pulled into a surreal or hyperreal alternate reality, readers follow along the author's counterfactual chain of reasoning to understand "the mode of feeling and conduct which they are most likely to adopt," as if the story were true and they were the characters themselves. Scott's great insight is that *Frankenstein* is built around "rules of probability" despite the "extraordinary circumstances" in which its characters are placed. In taking this scientific approach to fiction, Shelley created a marvelous yet emotionally believable novel that speculates the "probable consequences" of a child's making without a mother and abandonment by his father-scientist to an uncaring world.[56]

The ultimate moral consequence of Victor Frankenstein's irresponsibility toward his Creature is the child's persistent, pathetic, impassioned demand for the provision of a basic right to love, without which he does not have a chance to thrive—or even a reason to live. In the final scene of the novel, the Creature hovers over the dead body of his father, uttering "exclamations of grief and horror."[57] Although he has not murdered him, the Creature takes responsibility for his father's death: "That is also my victim!"[58] Yet he does not take total responsibility for the tragedies that have befallen the whole Frankenstein clan. The Creature draws a causal link between his father's refusal to care for him and his own insatiable need for love that had grown dangerously out of control: "For whilst I destroyed his hopes, I did not satisfy my own desires. They were for ever ardent and craving; still I desired love and fellowship, and I was still spurned. Was there no injustice in this?"[59] While owning his own guilt for the terrible crimes he has committed, the Creature puts the blame not only on himself and his father but also on society at large: "Am I to be thought the only criminal, when all human kind sinned against me?"[60] Again, he summons the idea of "injustice" to describe his predicament: "I, the miserable and the abandoned, am an abortion, to be spurned at, and kicked, and trampled on. Even now my blood boils at the recollection of this injustice."[61] This cri de coeur of a stateless orphan makes a plea to the reader to ponder how child neglect and abuse is a political injustice on the scale of a crime against humanity. Yet some of the Creature's last words, before his intended suicide, still recollect the happier moments of his early infancy: "when I felt the cheering warmth of summer, and heard the rustling of the leaves and the chirping of the birds, and these were all to me, I should have wept to die."[62] Despite the horror of his abuse at the hands of humanity, the Creature ultimately gives the reader a reason why children's rights ought to be protected by society at large: the meaning of life—happiness itself—would otherwise be extinguished.

Which *Frankenstein*?

Thus far, I have referred to the 1818 text of *Frankenstein*. It was the first published version of the text. Shelley went on to revise this text twice: in 1823, with unpublished annotations to a copy of the 1818 text she gave to her friend Mrs. Thomas in Genoa (now known as the "1818 Thomas copy," housed at the J. P. Morgan Library), and in 1831, with the publication of the third edition of the novel. Her father, William Godwin, revised the text and published it in a second edition in 1823 (which the publisher likely reissued in 1826). Mary Shelley had no authorial or editorial control over this version, so it is now placed outside of her corpus.[63]

Despite the fact that Shelley was the sole editor of the 1831 edition, most scholars today consider the 1818 text to be the preferred version of the novel, because it is closest in time and milieu to the story that Shelley first conceived and wrote in the summer and early fall of 1816.[64] I do not take a stand as to which of the published editions of *Frankenstein* is better. Rather, I follow Shelley in her sense of the story as one so compelling to the imagination that even the author herself can profitably revisit it. Her introduction to the 1831 edition made this point about creative revision with an evocative reproductive metaphor: "And now, once again, I bid my hideous progeny go forth and prosper."[65] Given that she revised the text in light of the first stage production of *Frankenstein*, which she enjoyed in London in 1823, Shelley welcomed the way that the story itself seemed to generate new iterations.[66]

In Chapter 1, I refer to Charles E. Robinson's scholarly reconstruction of the earliest manuscripts of the novel from 1816 to 1817 in order to underscore the "fluid" origins of the story of Frankenstein not in one but several texts. I accept Robinson's judgment that Mary Shelley was no doubt the original and primary author of the novel, as well as the creative source and force behind it. I also accept his view that Percy Shelley was an important contributor to the novel in adding around 5,000 words in the process of editing her 67,000 words, especially in the frame story of Captain Walton in the Arctic and in the Creature's story-within-a-story about Felix and Safie.[67]

In the remaining chapters of the book, I reference the 1816–17, 1818, 1818 Thomas Copy, and 1831 texts of *Frankenstein* according to the insights each version brings to the arguments at hand. I focus on the 1818 text, however, like most scholars of the novel. Ultimately, the differences between the texts of *Frankenstein* are ones of nuance and peripheral to the unchanging core of the story. Shelley (and Percy, her editor) kept the narrative structure of the tale intact while playing with some of the details. As she wrote in her 1831 introduction, "I have changed no portion of the story, nor introduced any new ideas or circumstances. I have mended the language where it was so bald as to interfere with the interest of the narrative . . . leaving the core and substance of it untouched."[68] It is this narrative "core" of the novel that is my primary source material, alongside the philosophical texts that informed her writing of *Frankenstein.*

Chapter Summary

Chapter 1 explores the philosophical background for the novel's treatment of the question of children's rights. Between 1814 and 1818, Shelley recorded in her journals an intensive self-directed reading program. She immersed herself in the works of the social contract thinkers, especially Locke and Rousseau, as well as prominent critiques of them by Hume, Burke, Wollstonecraft, and Godwin. Following her parents, Shelley directed much of her attention to Locke's influential theories of the mind, child development, and education, plus Rousseau's elaborations and permutations of them. Wollstonecraft and Godwin took inspiration from Locke's and Rousseau's theories of the mind, child development, and education yet did not rely on the device of the social contract to formulate their own theories of rights.[69]

The theories of rights that evolved across the works of Hobbes, Locke, Rousseau, and Kant and even their critics, Wollstonecraft and Godwin, all relied, in varying ways, on haunting images of the stateless orphan. The stateless orphan served as a foil for the social contract tradition's conception of the adult male citizen, safely inscribed within a legitimate political community, as a rights-bearer. The social contract tradition presupposed a binary relationship between nature and society that placed women, family, and children outside the bounds of the formally political realm. Standing out in the cold of nature, children had either no or few rights in social contract theory.

With the Creature's murderous quest for the rights to parental care, love, and education that he should have been afforded at birth, Shelley dramatized the dark implications of the image of the stateless orphan for modern political theory. If adults marginalized children in the community or banished them beyond the protective bounds of law, then children's claims to even the most basic of rights would not be heard by those with the power to fulfill them. If adults denied children their fundamental rights—especially to parental care and love and a beneficial education—then there would be bad consequences for both their families and society at large.

Moving well beyond even Wollstonecraft's defense of children's fundamental rights to parental care and a nontyrannical education, Shelley used the voice of the Creature to raise the provocative question of whether children have a right to share love with parents or, if parents or parental figures were unavailable, with a loving substitute. In giving the Creature a sympathetic voice and an astounding story of survival of exposure at birth, she transfigured the image of the stateless orphan within modern political thought. No longer hovering, alone and almost invisible, at the margins of the social contract tradition and its critics, the "spectre" of the stateless orphan staked a large, looming, and loud presence at the narrative heart of *Frankenstein*.[70]

Chapter 2 pinpoints the immediate source for Shelley's engagement of the question of children's rights in her reading of her mother's oeuvre, especially Wollstonecraft's greatest political treatise, the *Rights of Woman*, and posthumous novel, *Maria*. In these and other works, Wollstonecraft set forth an unprecedented theory of the universal and fundamental rights of children. Children, both female and male, had these rights solely by virtue of their moral status as human creatures made in the rational image of God. Children's rights were human rights understood as "moral rights," which obtained solely by virtue of a metaphysical/ethical conception of humanity.[71] The fundamental rights of children were both *negative*—to not be abused by adults—and *positive*—to receive parental care and rational (nontyrannical) education.

These fundamental human rights of children together generated a civil right to free and equal public coeducation. Wollstonecraft conceived the right to public education, without discrimination as to gender, class, or other social status, as a formative process of moral and civic education, distinctive from parental education but not a replacement for it. Children's exercise of their civil right to public education would teach them the value of respecting oneself and others as moral and political equals, even if their parents had failed—at times or at all—to model these values. As they grew up, schoolchildren would soak in the egalitarian values necessary for growing into the exercise of the full slate of civil and political rights afforded to adult citizens of a modern representative republic. Two centuries before democratic theorists of education such as Amy Gutmann, Wollstonecraft envisioned public education as a kind of school for citizenship.[72]

Also anticipating a trend in contemporary theories of children's rights, Wollstonecraft conceived of children's rights in deontological or duty-based terms—namely, as corresponding to parental and other adult duties. Unlike Onora O'Neill and other Kantian theorists who delimit children's rights due to a narrow view of parental and adult duties to minors, Wollstonecraft offered a deeper and more demanding conception of parental and adult duties to children and, correspondingly, a more expansive set of children's rights.[73] This pivotal innovation in human rights theory was due to Wollstonecraft's justification of a truly universal set of human rights via a theological and metaphysical conception of the human being as an equal moral and rational being, regardless of age, gender, class, race, or any social status.

Chapter 3 "runs" the five thought experiments that constitute the narrative core of *Frankenstein*: (1) What would it mean for a child to be made absolutely motherless? (2) What would happen if the child were so ugly that no one loved him, including the father-scientist who made him without a woman? (3) What if the child had the physical and mental strength to survive exposure at birth? (4) What if the child suffered total abuse by society in addition to his utter motherlessness and lovelessness? (5) What enduring obligations would the child's father have toward the abused and abandoned child, and what would be the limits of those obligations and the child's corresponding rights? By running this cascade of thought experiments, I show how Shelley critically received the principles of her mother's theory of children's rights to construct a speculative fiction that would invite further consideration of the rights of the child.

Running Shelley's thought experiments on the rights of the child reveals that she had different moral and political concerns than Wollstonecraft. Unlike her mother, Shelley never took a stand on political issues such as the value of free, state-provided education versus private, family-based education. Instead, *Frankenstein*'s exposure of the flaws in Victor and the Creature's solitary educations prods readers to consider the importance of the social dimension of the education of young people, regardless of how such schooling is formally implemented in any given time period or culture.[74] While Wollstonecraft had idealistically argued for the value of coparenting by mothers and fathers in partnership together, *Frankenstein* focused the reader's mind on the special value of the practice of mothering—or intensively loving care by a parent, regardless of sex or gender—for children's healthy development.

Unlike Wollstonecraft, Shelley steered away from using a metaphysical conception of the human being as the basis for justifying the rights of the child. Indeed, she avoided any reference to religion or theology in *Frankenstein* (except the title page's epigraph from *Paradise Lost*, which indirectly alluded to

God as Adam's "Maker").[75] Its glaring lack of religion triggered some of her contemporary readers to think it an atheistic, even blasphemous, text on the idea of creating life without God.[76] Rather than base her thinking on children's rights on a questionable metaphysical conception of the human being, Shelley illustrated the fundamentally contested definition of humanity with her counterfactual story of a "monster" made from human and other animal parts. Because no one—not even the Creature himself—can settle on whether he is human or not, he symbolizes the plight of all those people, including children, who stand outside the bounds of the social contract tradition's and the modern liberal state's idealized conception of the human being and citizen as an independent, rational, male adult.

Following her mother's criticisms of the social contract tradition, Shelley's thought experiments in *Frankenstein* do not rule out infants from consideration for moral rights due to their lack of moral agency or some other trait of adult human beings deemed by philosophers to be essential to the exercise of such rights.[77] Unlike her mother, however, she did not outline general definitions of humanity and human rights under which infants and other children fit. Shelley rather employed the literary technique of "negative capability"—or what her contemporary and acquaintance, the poet John Keats, coincidentally defined, in a private letter in December 1817, as the creative process of dwelling on what was lacking, strange, or disturbing.[78] Applying this poetic principle of negative capability to the story of *Frankenstein*, Shelley led the reader to consider what children deserve and need by deducing the dire consequences of what the Creature lacked. While Wollstonecraft primarily defended a child's right to parental care and rational education, Shelley took this argument a step further in suggesting what the Creature lacked and desired the most was not only care and education but also love from a parent who would take the time and energy to mother him.

Shelley's *Frankenstein* ultimately resonates with Wollstonecraft's foundational argument that children's rights correspond to parental duties. Thought Experiments 1 through 4 speculate the reasons why Victor remains responsible for the provision or, at minimum, the arrangement of his own child's enjoyment of the right to love, even after his exposure of the Creature to a cruel and abusive world. Yet the novel's fifth and final thought experiment submits that parental duties must address not only a child's legitimate needs or demands, such as fulfillment of the right to love, but also the moral limits of those rights claims. Even the most abused and vulnerable child, like the Creature, faces limits to the satisfaction of the right to love.

The ultimate limit to a child's right to love is not only moral but also physically inevitable: over time, the aging process turns children into adults who are no longer dependent on sharing love with a parent or appropriate substitute for their healthy development and well-being. Children "grow out" of the right to love because the right to love does not apply to romantic and other adult partnerships. As Wollstonecraft argued, such adult partnerships presume the freedom and equality of both parties in order for love to be shared in a fully egalitarian way. An adult cannot morally expect—as the Creature childishly did—that a projected companion or friend will dutifully fulfill one's desire for love as a parent or fitting substitute ideally does.

Through the exploration of the moral relationship between duty and love, Shelley pushes the reader beyond the Kantian philosophical assumption that love, as an involuntary expression of irrational feeling, cannot endow an action with moral worth. For Kant, only duty (as freely chosen by a rational will) can be the basis for an action with moral worth. While love might accompany duty in the performance of a moral action, it is duty that gives the action moral worth, not love. This view of love as irrational, involuntary, and unproductive of moral worth still informs contemporary theories of children's rights. Philosophers typically take a position of skepticism toward the idea of a child's right to love by pointing out that "parents cannot choose to love their child."[79] In contrast, the tragic story of Victor and the Creature leads the reader, via the principle of negative capability, to consider a new, two-way, bilevel view of parent-child love. This alternative view allows for love to be freely and lovingly performed as a duty toward children by parents and for children to hold a corresponding right to share love with parents or with fitting substitutes when parents fail to fulfill their duty to love them.

Ideally, parent-child love is a two-way street with emotional, physical, and moral benefits to both parties. Borrowing the Creature's words, such love is best understood as the "interchange of sympathy" between parent and child. It should be a sympathetic and affectionate relationship in which parents foster the healthy and happy growth and development of children, and children in turn learn to reciprocate love and related virtues with their parents and, ultimately, with other people. A child's right to love is thus the *right to share love with*, not merely the *right to be loved by*, a parent or fitting substitute.[80]

On an abstract moral level, the parent has a duty to fulfill the child's right to such a loving relationship; on a deeper emotional level, the sharing of the feeling of love is the way in which the duty is fulfilled. If and only if a parent is unavailable or unfit to fulfill the child's right to love, then the parent retains a minimal duty to arrange for a fitting substitute to assume this parental duty. The lack of any parent or parental figure to even arrange for such a substitute suggests a broader political problem that ought to be rectified: because the child's right to love persists even in the absence of a particular duty-bearer to fulfill it, there must be some other responsible (likely extrafamilial) body to arrange for its fulfillment. Shelley leaves it open for the reader to contemplate the many forms such a responsible body might take—communal, national, international, transnational, and so on.

Although Shelley did not speculate what could have or should have happened if the Creature had been granted the conditions for enjoying his right to love during childhood, *Frankenstein*'s five thought experiments on the rights of the child open the door to such speculation by the reader. The reader might reasonably conclude, by applying and extending the explicitly political arguments of the *Rights of Woman*, that while children sometimes tragically "grow out" of the right to love before it can be fulfilled, they ought to "grow into" other rights, such as free and equal citizenship, that were unavailable to them in childhood.[81] In time, such free and equal citizens might seek to secure in law children's moral right to love by developing a social and political support system for parents and families who face obstacles to sharing love with their children. By ensuring each and every child's sharing of love with a parent or fitting substitute during childhood, such a support system would enable collective enjoyment of the most fundamental right to which each and every person is entitled due to their passage through childhood, the time of everyone's greatest emotional, social, and (except in the counterfactual case of the Creature) physical vulnerability.

The concluding chapter applies insights drawn from *Frankenstein*'s five thought experiments on the rights of the child to the analysis of three moral frontiers of children's rights: the rights of disabled children, especially those with birth defects or other mutations or physical deformities deemed "monstrous" by society; the rights of stateless orphans, especially those who migrate across borders without any adult support; and the rights of posthuman children, or children made, altered, or evolved through interventions in science and technology to be strikingly different in features and/or capacities from their human ancestors/creators. Through its uncanny and often futuristic engagement of the questions surrounding disabled, stateless, and posthuman children's rights, Shelley's novel productively challenges not only many of the assumptions about children's rights made by the leading political theorists of her immediate past but also those of the contemporary international legal standard for children's rights. While the preamble to the United Nations' Convention on the Rights of the Child (1989) goes so far as to recognize that "the child, for the full and harmonious development of his or her personality, should grow up in a family environment, in an atmosphere of happiness, love and understanding," it falls short of an explicit claim for children's right to love. Through the voice and story of the Creature, Shelley presses readers to consider whether we ought to recognize the moral right to love as a formal and legal right of the child.

Even more radically, the Creature's strange and counterfactual plight as a motherless, loveless, stateless orphan, bereft of even a niche in the ecosystem, pushes readers to explore the question of children's rights as continuous with the question of the rights of the most marginalized and vulnerable of sentient beings, including nonhuman and posthuman life forms. While the rights of the child are formulated as human rights in contemporary international law, the story of the Creature suggests that we ought to move beyond such a limited "humanitarian" and speciesist conception of justice to a truly cosmopolitan and posthuman(itarian) account of rights for children and other vulnerable "fellow creatures."[82] Otherwise, theorists of rights run the risk of making the same grave and small-minded mistakes as Victor Frankenstein: superficially yet perniciously discriminating against children on the basis of their looks; (dis) abilities; familial, cultural, or political origins; or even the manner they were made or born. By making these moral errors, theories of children's rights follow a long tradition of marginalizing the child, dating at least to the early modern social contract thinkers. Without transcending the limits of this philosophical tradition, theorists of children's rights will only contribute to the ongoing collective failure of society to adequately support the fundamental rights of the child—especially the most basic of rights, love.

CHAPTER 1

The Specter of the Stateless Orphan from Hobbes to Shelley

> "What terrified me will terrify others; and I need only describe the spectre which had haunted my midnight pillow."
>
> —Mary Shelley, "Introduction to *Frankenstein*" (Third Edition, 1831)

> I threw the door open as children are accustomed to do when they expect a spectre to stand in waiting for them on the other side.
>
> "Do not ask me," cried I, putting my hands before my eyes, for I thought I saw the spectre glide into the room. "He can tell! Oh, save me! Save me!" I imagined that the monster seized me; I struggled furiously and fell down in a fit.
>
> —Mary Shelley, *The Original Frankenstein* (1816–17 Draft)

On a "dreary night of November," Victor Frankenstein infused "a spark of being into the lifeless thing" that lay at his feet. Against his own expectations, he did not love whom he had made. He "rushed out of the room" at first sight of "the wretch whom with such infinite pains and care" he "had endeavored to form." In shock, Victor went to bed to seek a mental escape. Yet once asleep, he faced a nightmare about his fiancée becoming his dead mother. To his horror, he found himself kissing this gruesome visage of a rotting corpse. Even when the Creature awoke him like a baby would in the night—muttering "inarticulate sounds while a grin wrinkled his cheeks"—Victor "escaped and rushed down stairs."[1] The next morning, when he returned to his laboratory, he dreaded to see "the creature" walking around his room. As a child would expect to see a "spectre" on the other side of a door, Victor fearfully anticipated his reunion with him. He felt the polar opposite emotional response to how a new father would joyfully look forward to see the child he has helped bring to life.[2]

In this pivotal scene, Mary Shelley played with role reversals on two levels. In Victor, the reader encounters a parent fearfully exchanging roles with a child. In the Creature, the reader sees a child forced to switch roles with a ghost. As the nearly nineteen-year-old Shelley already knew when she first worked on this passage, the greatest fear of a new and devoted mother is the death of her baby. Through death, the infant becomes a ghost: a mere memory that haunts the imagination of the parents. At age seventeen, Shelley had experienced such terror when she found her first-born daughter, Clara, dead in her crib, only two weeks after her precarious birth, two months premature.

In her first novel conceived a little over a year after this loss, Shelley had the central parental figure of the story—Victor Frankenstein—behave as her husband, Percy, did in the wake of this personal tragedy. Both men run from the specters of their children instead of facing them. After Victor made and abandoned his Creature, he wandered in the nighttime streets of Ingolstadt until he happened to run into his best friend from home, Henry Clerval. In response to his friend's innocent query about his strange behavior, Victor hallucinated the presence of "the spectre" or "monster" he had created.[3]

Just three days after her firstborn's death, Shelley wrote in her journal, "Still think about my little baby—'tis hard indeed for a mother to lose her child." Four days later, she reflected, "S.[helley] H.[ogg] & C.[lary] go to town—stay at home . . . & think of my little dead baby—this is foolish I suppose yet whenever I am left alone to my own thoughts & do not read to divert them they always come back to the same point—that I was a mother & am so no longer."[4] As she further recounted in her March 1815 journal, Percy regularly went out on the town with her stepsister, Claire, while she mourned the loss of their baby alone at home.

Less than two weeks after she found their baby lifeless in her crib, Shelley had a waking nightmare. Her journal recalled a "Dream that my little baby came to life again—that it had only been cold & that we rubbed it by the fire & it lived—I awake & find no baby—I think about the little thing all day."[5] Shelley beheld her reanimated baby in a dream, only to find her dead, again, upon waking. A little more than a year later, she depicted Victor Frankenstein's feverish imagining of the presence of his Creature as a "spectre"—a mere ghost, image, or memory of the "man" he had hoped to make. Like Shelley's dead baby, the Creature is also a "monster"—a hideous "corpse" who is terrible to face.[6] She brought this imagery full circle in her 1831 introduction to *Frankenstein.* Recalling the night in June 1816 when she was possessed with the idea for a "ghost story," Shelley described her first vision of the Creature as "the hideous corpse," which his maker had thought would be "the cradle of life." She instantly knew that this image of a living corpse, unexpectedly rising from the "cradle" as it were, would "terrify others." She only had to find the words to describe to readers this "spectre which had haunted my midnight pillow."[7]

While Shelley's March 1815 dream may contain the psychic seeds of *Frankenstein*'s story of a scientist who brings dead tissue to life, it is also illuminating for understanding the novel's concern with the ethics of parent-child relationships.[8] Shelley's dream of her dead baby, reanimated by the warm touch of her parents, suggests her deep reverence for the power of parental love to bring life into the world and sustain it.[9] Her private record of grief in her journal—however abrupt, toneless, and slightly numb the entries might feel to a modern reader—are reflective of her willingness to confront her baby's death in all of its sadness rather than avoid it. In the wake of the loss of her firstborn, Shelley behaved as a parent, not a child—despite her mere seventeen years. In contrast, Percy and his fictional alter ego, Victor, behaved not as parents but as children by running from the specters for whom they were responsible rather than confronting them head on.

By representing the Creature not only as a (reanimated) child but also as a specter, Shelley drew upon her harrowing experience of grief for her dead baby. As U. C. Knoepflmacher and Anne K. Mellor have argued, she may have also drawn from a deeper psychological reservoir: her own experience of maternal loss and paternal neglect during her infancy.[10] Looking beyond her (in)famously tragic biography, it is less well known that Shelley also drew upon her deep reading in the social contract tradition, especially John Locke and Jean-Jacques Rousseau, to depict the Creature as a child who is at once both real and unreal, appearing and disappearing like a ghost at the outskirts of the imagination.

It cannot be proven that Shelley's loss of her mother and her firstborn baby made a deep psychological impression on the themes of *Frankenstein.* Likewise, it cannot be known beyond a shadow of a doubt that she used the story of the Creature to symbolically overturn the marginalization of children in the early modern social contract tradition. Just as scholars have seen the ghosts of her dead mother, dead baby, and distant father lurking in the shadows of the story of her first novel, I propose that much can be learned from treating the social contract thinkers as subterranean sources for her engagement of the question of children's rights.

Haunting the Margins: The Specter of the Stateless Orphan in the Social Contract Tradition

Haunting images of the stateless orphan—a child abandoned to survive or die on its own, without protection of family, society, or state—loomed at the perimeters of the theoretical social contracts drawn up by Thomas Hobbes, John Locke, Jean-Jacques Rousseau, and Immanuel Kant. A dark typology of the stateless orphan was implicit within the early modern social contract tradition. This typology moved beyond the simple concept of the de jure orphan as technically lacking a family altogether by exploring other, dire ways that children could lack love, care, and protection by adults. Hobbes's and Rousseau's state of nature theories posited scenarios in which children were de facto orphans who had family but lived without their love and care. Locke pictured a child who was either de facto or de jure orphaned in a state of war. Kant's theory of the state engaged the case of effective orphans who initially lived within families that did not (or could not) love and care for them. These early modern social contract thinkers also forebodingly imagined different types of statelessness for such orphans. The children of the state of nature were de jure stateless (technically lacking a state altogether). Thus, any orphans (de jure, de facto, or effective) in the state of nature were doubly deprived of the protection of either family or state. Kant went still further and argued that illegitimate babies ought to be effectively stateless (born into a state without entitlement to formal, registered legal status as a subject or citizen) and killed by their mothers with impunity while the state looked the other way. If neglected or abused in the family before death, such an illegitimate baby would have been effectively orphaned. If exposed by the mother before death, such an illegitimate baby would have been made a de facto orphan, if only briefly.[11]

The social contract thinkers consistently resorted to images of the stateless orphan to develop their justifications of the rights of adult white propertied men in opposition to those persons who were perceived as lacking the reason and independence to take on the responsibilities of rights-holders. Through this trope, Hobbes, Locke, Rousseau, and Kant defined rights-holders in terms of what they were not: children. In so doing, they strongly implied that children—like women, nonwhites, non-Protestants, the poor, the disabled, and other persons deemed inadequate for full membership in modern Western European conceptions of political community—should be excluded from formal legal provision and enjoyment of rights.[12]

The social contract tradition furnished unforgettable images of relatively powerless and isolated children exposed to violence and the cold of nature: Hobbes's stony defense of a mother's right to expose (and de facto orphan) her baby in the state of nature, Locke's stoic picture of the rather limited freedom of the child who is de facto or de jure orphaned by military conquest, Rousseau's disturbing hypothesis that savage mothers would release their crawling babies into the wild of the state of nature and de facto orphanhood, and Kant's greater sympathy for a mother who intends to kill her illegitimate child than for her victim, an effectively stateless and orphaned newborn. This iconic recurrence of the stateless orphan served as the ultimate conceptual foil for the justification of the rights of powerful adult men united together in the bonds of politics. According to the social contract tradition, men had rights because they had a share in power—whether it was property, the governance of the commonwealth, or the protection of the absolute sovereign as guaranteed by the communal social contract. Children had no or few rights because they had no or little power to share or because they were simply forgotten or ignored.

Although almost invisible on the fringe of the social contract tradition, the specter of the stateless orphan has been arresting, even frightening, and thus enduring because it forces adults to confront their worst fears: What would it be like to be so abandoned by parents and other adults, helpless and alone? How would one's own children feel if they found themselves in such a dire predicament? By eliciting these fears, the worst-case scenario of the stateless orphan positioned powerless children and powerful adults at opposite points in the Western social imaginary of the modern state.[13] In this theoretical vision, powerless children survived or died at the margins of politics, or even beyond politics, while powerful adult men had the power to protect (or not protect) children within the bounds of the political community. Worse, the patriarchal biases of modern European political thought meant that if children were construed as warranting protection under the law, it would typically be limited to firstborn boys who could potentially inherit the father's estate under the rule of primogeniture. Worst, this political theory often corresponded with legal practice. From the seventeenth through the bulk of the twentieth century, fathers were subjects or citizens with rights over their children and wives under the patriarchal systems of Western law. As a consequence, modern Western culture and law has tolerated, if not enthusiastically endorsed, the relative or absolute absence of children's (especially girls' and unprivileged boys') and women's rights.

The disquieting predicament of the abandoned Creature dramatized the problems with the social contract thinkers' exclusion of children from meaningful access to basic rights to care, love, education, and sometimes even life itself. Living without the care and love of his family, the Creature is a de facto orphan. As a child migrant surviving on his own without the protection of a state, he could be read as either de jure stateless (technically lacking a state altogether) or effectively stateless (lacking a formal birth record in his country of origin, Germany).

Responding in part to the social contract tradition, Shelley reframed the image of the stateless orphan in an unexpected way by changing the reason why it is fearsome. Conjured in the person of the Creature, her specter begs readers to consider the moral bankruptcy of justifying rights for adults on the backs of children. By chronicling the Creature's violent rampage for provision of the rights to care, love, and education that he had deserved as much as any newborn, she staged a profound critique of modern Western political theory. Her implicit target was the social contract tradition, particularly its assumption that children and women belong to the cold realm of nature, beyond the protective barrier of rights provided to adult men under the laws of the state.

Shelley's critical appropriation of the image of the stateless orphan is uncanny. It reverses the trope and its significance while retaining its eerie familiarity. Unlike the social contract thinkers, Shelley did not depict the stateless orphan as a phantom with the power to spook us into defending rights solely for privileged adult men. She rather transfigured the icon to subvert the idea that children lack rights when they are forced by their makers to haunt the margins of the political community. In this way, she built on her father's commitment to fighting political injustice on the broadest scale and her mother's interest in defending the rights of women, slaves, children, the poor, and other historically oppressed groups. She also paved the way for many a feminist reading of *Frankenstein* in which the Creature is seen as a woman (even Shelley herself) or any person who has suffered marginalization due to broader discriminatory norms that have privileged white, propertied, independent, able-bodied, and able-minded adult men above other members of a political community.[14]

Unlike the social contract thinkers, Shelley did not ignore the problems with the use of the image of the stateless orphan. She rather confronted them head on. The newborn Creature's brutal experience of neglect and cruelty at the hands of his father and society draws out the misopedia (or hatred of children) implicit in political arguments that rely upon imagery of children's abandonment, abuse, and death to buttress the notion of rights for adults. This is why the image, idea, or "spectre" of Shelley's Creature troubles audiences even to the present day: not so much because of his monstrous appearance but rather because of his monstrous treatment by his father and society. For it is the Creature's tragic predicament as a stateless orphan that generates a series of fatal plot points, which together trigger him to behave like the "monster" society originally mistook him to be.

Hobbes's Exposed Infants

First in his *De Cive* (1642) and then in his *Leviathan* (1651), Hobbes conducted a thought experiment that summoned the specter of the stateless orphan into the margins of the modern social contract tradition. The thought experiment sought to identify the rights of mothers in the state of nature before the establishment of a sovereign or any form of positive law. Hobbes hypothesized that such women would elect to "expose" their infants rather than "nourish" them, once the care of the children ran counter to their "right" or "Liberty" to use their "own power" for "the preservation" of their "own nature."[15] Hobbes's conception of a mother's right to commit infanticide in the state of nature was tied to his definition of power as the "present means, to obtain some future apparent Good" and his definition of liberty/freedom as "the absence of externall Impediments."[16] The mothers of the state of nature exercised the most extreme type of "right of Dominion over the Child" when there was no apparent good for them in the care of the dependent or any obstacle to committing infanticide.[17] Because the infants were utterly dependent on their mothers for nourishment and other means of survival, Hobbes deduced that they had no right to life independent of the wills of their mothers to provide the conditions for living. Cocooned in his attic laboratory, in a kind of self-made state of nature, Victor Frankenstein can be seen as illustrating this cold Hobbesian logic: he makes a selfish choice to use absolute parental power to expose his Creature rather than to care for him.[18]

In modern contractarian thought, Hobbes begat the image of the stateless orphan by dooming the exposed infant to languish and die at the borders of the state of nature, without a chance of gaining protection of a sovereign under a social compact. Without maternal nourishment or any adult care, the exposed infant must be presumed dead in the brutal world of the Hobbesian state of nature, where individuals are driven by self-preservation, not compassion for others. Like Shelley's actual firstborn, this theoretical dead baby becomes a memory or a ghost in the philosopher's political imagination. Hobbes's stateless orphan has absolutely no rights: not even the primordial right to self-preservation that he granted to all other humans, whether in the state of nature or under the commonwealth. In Hobbes's state of nature, the exposed infant has no freedom or power to defend his life and therefore has no right to live. Without instinctive or habituated maternal sympathy to trump self-interested survival, Hobbesian mothers of the state of nature are not too far from animals who eat their young. Callously discarded through the exercise of maternal freedom and power in the state of nature, the de jure stateless and de facto orphaned child is the afterbirth of Hobbes's thought experiment on the rights of mothers outside of government. Thus, Hobbes initiated a dark theme that reemerges in the works of Locke, Rousseau, and Kant: women's rights—however meagerly and hypothetically construed—entail the absence or near negation of children's rights, especially for the relatively powerless infant.

Locke's "Children of the Vanquished"

Arguing against the Hobbesian view that the only solution to war and anarchy is absolute sovereign government, Locke reconceived the state of nature to make life without positive law and government look more palatable—especially from the point of view of his adult readership. In the Lockean version of the state of nature, as outlined in his *Second Treatise of Government* (1690), families and other small communities enjoy peaceful relations until someone's private property is taken or otherwise violated by a criminal or a conqueror. Only once the state of nature became such a state of war, the people would have reason to consent to a social contract through which a limited government would be established to adjudicate their conflicts and maintain peace. Moreover, if that government ever acted tyrannically toward its people, the people had the right to revolt against it and return to the original, pacific, stage of the state of nature.

To his credit, Locke challenged Hobbes's desolate view of the state of nature as a constant state of war where even mothers are potentially at battle with their babies over scarce resources for survival. Against Hobbes's conception of a mother's natural right to expose her infant, Locke contended that all parents had a "Duty . . . to take care of their Off-spring, during the imperfect state of Childhood."[19] Locke never gave an explicit ground or reason for this parental duty but rather presented it as an inescapable moral consequence of reproduction. If they abrogated this duty, then the parents lost all power with respect to the child's life and upbringing: "when he quits his Care of them, he loses his power over them."[20] Legitimate parental power derived from the performance of the parental duty to care for one's own children. Thus, whoever cared for a child and preserved his life—say, by rescuing a foundling exposed to the wilderness—was in fact the true parent, regardless of whether there was a biological relationship to the child. Locke imagined such a scenario in which a "Foster-Father of an exposed child" has the same parental power as a "Natural Father" who cares for his biological child.[21] With this example, Locke clearly explained that parental duty means to practice primary caregiving for a child. Consequently, legitimate parental powers are derived not from biological relationships but from intensive and responsible caregiving relationships to children.

From the parental duty to care for one's own children, whether biological or adopted, Locke derived a child's right to be maintained by one's parents. His *First Treatise of Government* (1690) drew upon the Hebrew Bible's story of Adam in Eden to make a scriptural case for children's "Right to be nourish'd and maintained by their Parents, nay a right not only to a bare Subsistance but to the conveniences and comforts of life, as far as the conditions of their Parents can afford it."[22] Because God provided Adam with everything he needed for his nourishment and other forms of physical maintenance both in Eden and even after his expulsion from it, Adam and all of his descendants have an "equal Right to the use of the inferior Creatures, for the comfortable preservation of their Beings."[23] The problem with this scriptural example is that its male bias—or privileging of Adam over Eve, men over women, and boys over girls—limited the scope of Locke's argument for the rights of children from the outset. The rights of Eve and her daughters were not explicitly considered, so that the rights of children appeared to be focused on the sons.

Indeed, as Locke's argument unfolded in the *Second Treatise*, the scope of children's right to parental maintenance, or the material means for life, growth, and comfort, clearly applied more to the fathers and the sons than to the mothers and the daughters. Although he was at times critical of the concept and practice of primogeniture, or the automatic descent of family property through the eldest son, Locke gave a father the right to bequeath his estate to his favorite child.[24] Moreover, he repeatedly implied—through the use of masculine nouns and pronouns—that it was best for this heir to be a son.[25] Locke also assumed the value of a patrilineal and patriarchal line of descent for the conservation of a family estate over time. For example, Locke speculated that when "Fathers" died in a losing battle to a conqueror, the right to their estates passed neither to their conqueror nor to their "Wives" but rather to their "Children."[26] These children of conquest, he went on, were "Free-men" unlike the "Men . . . who were subdued."[27] While widows of conquest retained their original "share" in the family property, they served only as temporary caretakers of the father's (implicitly greater) share of the estate until an adult son could assume responsibility for it.[28] Favored sons appeared to stand first in line for inheritance of their fathers' estates. Practically speaking, they enjoyed a greater right to provision of basic needs essential to their development into self-sufficient caretakers of those estates.[29] A strong and troubling implication of this argument was that daughters retained the right to parental maintenance only secondarily to their brothers, whether in the state of nature, the state of war, or under government.

Locke also conceptualized the content of children's right to parental maintenance in a rather limited way. First, he defined maintenance primarily in material terms—as in providing the food, shelter, and other physical means of sustenance for a (preferably male) child's development and growth into adulthood, when he could be a fitting heir to the family estate.[30] Second, the right to parental maintenance led straight to the right to private property.[31] Under this rubric, children (especially boys) seemed only to serve as vessels for their father's material fortunes. Worse, they were vessels that required a lot of special upkeep until the ship could be safely sailed with the family property on board. Although they did not own their children as a kind of property, fathers retained a proprietary interest in their children's bodies, which they helped to make and had an obligation to preserve.[32] Yet sons (and, secondarily, daughters) had no right to parental maintenance independent of their father's proprietary interest in their bodies as vessels for the safe transport of the family estate across the generations. Whether in the state of nature or under a social contract, a child's right to parental (and, specifically, paternal) maintenance was tied to and subordinate to the father's right to have a suitable (preferably male) heir.

On Locke's account, children have less intrinsic value as individuals and more extrinsic value in terms of the function they may perform in carrying forward the paternal name and material legacy of the family. Younger sons at least kept the name of the father to match the name of the estate. The identity of girls was erased and redrawn in marriage. A girl lost her maiden identity and became what Wollstonecraft called a "mere cypher" in the act of taking the name of her husband.[33] According to Kate Millet, this change in name marked the "civil death" of her identity under coverture, the patriarchal legal code that subsumed the wife and children under the male head of the family.[34] Much like Frankenstein's Creature, Lockean girls went nameless in that liminal space between the provision of paternal care and the passage to adulthood and marriage.

It was within this theoretical framework that Locke unveiled a new specter of the stateless orphan for the social contract tradition: the "Children of the vanquished."[35] These children were rendered either de jure or de facto orphaned and de jure stateless by an aggressive military conquest of their homeland. They might still have physical access to their family's home and property or be "spoiled of all their Father's goods . . . left to starve and perish."[36] Locke's discussion of children's rights in the wake of conquest focused on the former case of the orphan whose family estate was not spoiled. Similarly to Hobbes's thought experiment on the exposed infant in the state of nature, Locke seemed to assume, bleakly, the inevitable death of the stateless orphan without his "Father's goods" to sustain him. Rights did not pertain to a dead child—and, in Locke's dismal estimation, the stateless orphan bereft of his "Father's goods" might as well be dead.

In his broader discussion of the problem of conquest, Locke argued, "The Aggressor put himself in a state of War with another."[37] As a result, no positive law obtained to adjudicate the conflict between aggressor and defender. Rather, only God's natural law of morality applied to their situation. Made in the image of their rational God, people had the potential to use reason to discern and apply God's law. According to Locke's derivation and application of the natural law to the case of conquest, any children rendered orphaned and stateless by a conqueror had a right not to be taken as captives.[38] At the same time, he argued that the conquering people could not rightfully take a "Man's . . . estate" even as they could rightfully take that "Man's Person" through death or capture.[39] In so doing, Locke set up a problematic analogy between children and family estates. He suggested that paternal proprietary interests—in the family estate and in favored sons as preferred vessels for the estate—endured beyond the death of the father. Like the ghost of Hamlet's father, the dead father manifested by vicariously exercising his rights to property and power through his favored son.[40] Although Locke denied that children were formally "property" of their fathers, he strongly implied that children were at least analogous to family property in terms of the father's proprietary relationship to them.[41] The (implied male) child of conquest had a right not to be taken as loot by a conqueror because he was the preferred vessel through which his dead father's estate would be preserved. Moreover, the estate provided the most obvious means for the child's subsistence in the meantime before he could formally serve as heir.

By addressing the worst-case scenario of the child who is bereft of both family and homeland in the wake of a military conquest, Locke unwittingly exposed the problems with his limited arguments for children's rights. This Lockean stateless orphan was left in a "state of war" because no government existed to protect either his life or his "right" to serve as an high-maintenance vessel for his dead father's estate.[42] His orphan status underscored the importance of parental, especially paternal, maintenance for a child's safety and security. Without a family, and especially without a father, the child of conquest had no way to ensure his enjoyment of the right to parental maintenance. Without a state, he had no way to function as a vessel for the intergenerational transport of his father's estate. In short, the stateless orphan—even if a favored son—had no real access to the right to parental maintenance that he supposedly had from birth.[43] Although Locke argued that the conquerors had no right to take the estates of the conquered, the stateless orphan could not exercise the right to hold the family estate if his parents and other adult relatives were dead or living apart from him, and he lacked the capability (maturity, independence, and reason) to serve as caretaker of the property himself.

Locke acknowledged again and again that the conqueror had greater power than the conquered. Although the conqueror had no moral "right" to take land, child captives, and slaves by force, he in fact had the power to use his greater force to do so.[44] Thus, the predicament of the stateless orphan only served to illustrate the inability of children to exercise rights and enjoy freedom without the protection of family (especially fathers) and a state. Although Locke insisted that the stateless orphan had no obligation to acquiesce to the conqueror, he did not present the child with any option beyond "consent" to the conquest.[45] Contradicting his earlier argument that minors lack the use of reason to meaningfully consent, whether tacitly or expressly, to property ownership or to political regimes, Locke problematically waived this restriction in the case of the stateless orphan.[46] He suggested that without family or a state, the child of conquest should and could exercise consent to become part of the conquering nation for the sake of his own survival and hopefully the security of the family estate too. The child who lost parents and a homeland by conquest, in theory, gained the freedom of an adult "Free-man" due to his lack of any guardian. In the same breath, Locke implied that the actual power differential between the conqueror and the child—including the child's lack of a fully formed faculty of reason—meant that the child's consent would be in fact extorted through force and hence not truly free.[47]

The extreme political predicament of Locke's stateless orphan thus dramatized a real problem for his social contract theory: the "Children of the vanquished" lacked both protection for their rights (gained upon the death of their fathers or both parents) and the ability to truly consent (like any child) to a new, legitimate protector for them. The children effectively became slaves to the conqueror, who took their family estates by force and extorted their obedience. Although it was his philosophical aim to refute Hobbes's view that moral or political consent was possible at the hands of force, Locke's own example of the stateless orphan ironically reinforced the Hobbesian view of exposed infants in the state of nature as effectively powerless and thus rightless. Even under the protection of a parent or a commonwealth, the Lockean child lacked direct access to rights, for his rights were derivative of and thus subordinate to the rights of the father or government to whom he was dependent for his care and maintenance. When pushed to their logical conclusion, Locke's meager arguments concerning children's rights to parental maintenance entailed that these rights were essentially meaningless without submission to a father, parental figure, or conqueror who had the power to protect that child's access to family property in the long term.

Rousseau's Wild Toddlers

Although Rousseau's 1762 novel *Emile* is more famous for its literary portrait of an orphan boy separated from society for the sake of an educational experiment, it was his 1755 *Second Discourse* that raised another specter of the stateless orphan for the social contract tradition. The orphan Emile lacked parents but was not technically, or de jure, stateless: he grew up to become an obedient subject of France, albeit one who preferred to marry and raise his family in the provinces.[48] In the *Second Discourse*, however, Rousseau had reimagined the predicament of the de jure stateless (and de facto orphaned) child in the context of his own—highly creative—reworking of the concept of the state of nature.

Rousseau's theory of the state of nature began with some Hobbesian premises when it came to situating children and women within this counterfactual prepolitical domain. Like Hobbes, he imagined the state of nature as largely asocial, but he took this premise to a different extreme. While Hobbes deduced that the state of nature would be a state of anarchy and war, Rousseau hypothesized that primitive people's preference for solitude would lead to peace or at least conditions of noninterference. Rousseau furthermore conjectured that men and women in the state of nature would live relatively solitary lives, only meeting periodically to copulate. Mothers would care for their infants only so long as the children lacked the capability to crawl or toddle into the wild on their own: "The mother suckled her children, when just born for her own sake; but afterwards when habit had made them dear to her, for theirs; but they no sooner gained strength enough to run about in quest of food than they separated even from her, and as they scarcely had any other method of not losing each other, than that of remaining constantly in each other's sight, they soon came to a point of not even recognizing each other when they happened to meet again."[49] Not only was there no society or government in the Rousseauian state of nature, but there were also no families beyond a temporary mother-infant dyad. Moving beyond even Hobbes, Rousseau assumed that all mothers would fail to establish a long-term bond with their children in the state of nature, to the point of exposing all toddlers to the wilderness rather than caring for them beyond infancy. *Contra* Hobbes, at least some of these exposed children somehow survive and grow up, alone, to eventually reproduce in the asocial manner of their parents: "Their need once gratified, the sexes took no further notice of each other, and even the child was nothing to his mother, the moment he could do without her."[50]

In her feminist reading of the *Second Discourse*, Penny Weiss argued that Rousseau followed Hobbes in conceptualizing "mother-child relations in the state of nature" as "no different from other animals."[51] Problematically, this primal model of the "natural woman" provides no moral guidance for how either mothers or parents in general ought to behave toward their children in actual society.[52] Together with his infamous public confession of abandoning his five children to an almost certain death in a Paris foundling hospital, Rousseau's view of natural woman as lacking any substantial affectionate or moral bond with her children may have provided an inspiration for the plot of Shelley's *Frankenstein*.[53] Scholars have traditionally emphasized the parallels between the tragic trajectory of Rousseau's "natural man" as he moves from the state of nature into the corruption of society and civilization and the (mis) education of the Creature through his mistreatment by his father and people in general.[54] If we accept that Shelley was at least indirectly aware of the argument of the *Second Discourse*, then we should be willing to entertain another provocative hypothesis: Victor Frankenstein bears an uncanny resemblance to Rousseau's natural woman, for he is not only an absent but also an utterly unloving parent—like Rousseau himself.

Later in the *Second Discourse*, Rousseau speculated that the invention of private property would ultimately change the pattern of asocial sexual reproduction in the state of nature. Only once copulating couples decided to make and reside in "cabins" would sexual reproduction lead to the establishment of stable families beyond the original, temporary mother-infant dyad.[55] Society was then born for Rousseau but with its two main woes: first, the problem of *amour-propre*, or competitive awareness of the differences between self and others, and, second, the unjust differences between rich and poor that arise from competition and the resultant accumulation of private property by some and not others.[56]

Building upon Locke, Rousseau famously posited, "Man was born free." Moving beyond both Locke and Hobbes, Rousseau speculated that man's natural freedom had been the least encumbered in the early, individualistic stage of the state of nature, where the "first law" was "to attend to his own survival." Yet Rousseau's wild toddlers of the state of nature had no realistic conditions for being free or defending their lives. Like Hobbes and Locke, Rousseau assumed that children's right to life itself must be derivative of and thus subordinate to their parents' rights to the same. The survival of Rousseau's wild toddlers—alone in the woods—must be by chance. According to the parameters of the thought experiment, the wild toddlers were not capable of defending themselves beyond their random search for food in the woods. Unless someone more powerful happened to hear the "cry of nature" when they were injured or dying and then, moved by pity, tried to help them, they had no protection of their right to life.[57] Given Rousseau's assumption that stable families only come into being with the building of private property in the form of a cabin, these de facto orphaned toddlers do not even have the protective parental and familial relationships and material conditions necessary for fully enjoying (let alone exercising) the right to life until a far later and social stage of the state of nature.

By portraying the stateless orphan as a toddler wandering alone into the wild, Rousseau offered the requisite human sacrifice for the contractarian justification of a strong, free, independent, and equal (yet implicitly patriarchal and ableist) political community. In his ideal republic outlined in his *Social Contract* (1762), adult men would rule themselves in free and equal union with one another, instead of being politically enslaved to rich overlords. Following Hobbes, Rousseau limited women's rights to two natural rights: self-preservation and child exposure. Also like Hobbes, he circumscribed the second—dark and terrible—maternal right within the hypothetical state of nature. Even so circumscribed, this formulation of a woman's right to expose her children inherently thwarted children's right to life.

Kant's Illegitimate Babies

For Hobbes, Locke, and Rousseau, children stood outside or at the periphery of the political realm or social contract—as signified by the recurring apparition of the stateless orphan at the margins of their political theories. A conceptual cost of using social contract theory to justify greater and more equal rights for men was the loss of rights for children. This trend crystallized in Kant, who brought to the center of his social contract theory many of the misopedic ideas hovering at the edges of his predecessor's works.

In his 1784 essay "What Is Enlightenment?" Kant framed the concept of modern citizenship—especially the citizen's right to free participation in public debate on political ideas—in terms of a binary between maturity and immaturity. Immaturity for Kant was "the inability to make use of one's intellect without the direction of another." Maturity, on the other hand, was the ability to make use of one's intellect independently, plus the courage to actually use it. Kant went on to argue that most people practiced a "self-incurred immaturity" in that they lacked the courage to use their intellects independently. Those who had reason and the courage to use it were mature, and those who lacked reason and/or the courage to use it were immature. Displaying his prejudices against the young, the disabled, and the elderly, Kant deployed the image of a walker to illustrate the latter distinction and its political implications. Those who were mature in their use of reason could walk on their own two feet, so to speak. By contrast, those who lacked (or lost) maturity in reason or the courage to use it relied upon a walker—metaphorically and sometimes actually. The political implication of this analogy was clear to Kant: only the mature—meaning, adults with full use of their reason—had the resources of mind and character to participate fully in a modern republic and its intellectual debates in the public sphere. The prevalence of childlike immaturity meant that the "largest part of humanity" (including the "entirety of the fairer sex") was not capable of true citizenship.[58]

Later, in his 1793 essay "Theory and Practice," Kant moved past such misopedic metaphors to explicitly exclude children from citizenship. He argued that a "paternalistic" government would be "the greatest imaginable despotism" because the citizens would be "passive" like "dependent children" in that they could not make decisions for themselves. In contrast, he justified a "patriotic" state as one in which all adult male members were equal rights-holders insofar as they had the capability to use reason to govern themselves. He explicitly argued that "neither woman nor child" is a "citizen" because they lacked, by nature, this rational capability for self-governance. Only adult men who owned "some property (which also includes any skill, trade, fine art, or science)" could be citizens because they earned their livelihoods on their own, not from childlike or wifelike dependency on others.[59]

Kant's *Metaphysics of Morals* (1797) brought the specter of the stateless orphan out of the state of nature and into debates on the morality and legality of infanticide in the modern state. Although his moral theory deduced that murder was always wrong, and his political theory concluded that "anyone who is a murderer . . . must also suffer death" by state execution, he quickly made a telling exception.[60] In the case of an unmarried mother killing her baby due to the shame of illegitimacy, Kant thought the killing not only justified but also desirable.

A mother's intentional killing or murder of an illegitimate baby was justified for Kant because the child had "slipped" into the commonwealth, as it were, without the legal sanction of marriage to legitimate his birth.[61] Hence, the baby had absolutely no legal status, let alone rights, under the commonwealth. Kant's illegitimate baby was effectively stateless despite his presence within the modern state. If exposed by the mother, rather than immediately killed by her, then the illegitimate baby was both de facto orphaned and effectively stateless. If neglected or abused in the family prior to being killed by the mother, then the illegitimate baby would be both effectively orphaned and effectively stateless.

This act of infanticide was desirable for Kant because the illegitimate child was a costly sexual mistake and thus never should have been born. The baby's very existence tarnished the mother's honor and presented an undue burden upon society's obligation to care for its young. It was better for all involved for the mother to quietly kill the infant as soon as possible, without the direct knowledge, intervention, or punishment of the state but, seemingly, with the state's implicit consent.

As with Hobbes's exposed infant and Rousseau's wild toddler, Kant's illegitimate baby does not meaningfully enjoy the right to life or self-preservation. Even worse, Kant explicitly justified infanticide under the positive law of the modern state, not the hypothetical state of nature without positive law. Kant legitimated the denial of the right to life to any baby born out of wedlock so long as the act of infanticide went unnoticed by the state. Although the state would have to punish the mother for murder if the crime was discovered, the "destruction" of the baby "can be ignored" if not.[62] Because the mother's honor would be permanently stained if the infant did not die in the shadows of society, Kant perversely reasoned against his own universalistic moral principles that such a murder would be justified if kept invisible to the public eye.

On a superficial level, Kant justified infanticide in cases of illegitimacy for the sake of protecting the mother's reputation. This may appear chivalric, especially in the context of his treatment of eighteenth-century conceptions of honor and their implications for women in this section of *The Metaphysics of Morals*. Whatever its motive, however, this move on Kant's part legitimates a patriarchal system of culture and law that considers women's value only in terms of their sexual reputation. In so doing, Kant conceptualized women of potential disrepute and their illegitimate offspring as something less than human—certainly not moral and rational beings capable of upholding absolute moral duties and bearing universal rights.

Kant transmuted the specter of the stateless orphan from a dark afterthought of state of nature theory into a shameful sexual by-product of a patriarchal social contract.[63] Yet Kant's victim of infanticide is not the only child who suffers from a lack of rights in his ideal republican polity. His broader view of children as incapable of rational and moral maturity meant that they must be explicitly and formally excluded from citizenship and, even more troublingly, from rights altogether.

Kant's view of children as belonging outside of the state has been influential in Western political thought and practice since the European Enlightenment. As Sana Nakata explains, "Kantian liberalism sets the boundaries between those who are legitimate members of a social and political community and those who are not. Children, defined against reason and maturity, are both necessarily and naturally excluded."[64] In this philosophical frame, children—even more than women—appeared as the ultimate "Other" or "monster."[65] With their lack of reason and capability for self-rule, it was as though children belonged to a world separate from adults. Worse off than their mothers, Kantian children were not subject to rights and, worst of all, not even seen as fully human subjects. Simone de Beauvoir explained how this dehumanizing view of children had a negative impact upon the psychology of children themselves. Children, especially those of the second, subordinated sex, grew up to see themselves as "monsters" who threatened the God-like power of their parents.[66]

Until recently, liberal states treated women and children the same—as minors incapable of citizenship.[67] Although Kant accorded women and children the same status as legal nonentities, he ultimately construed children as morally inferior to even women. The honorable women of a Kantian republic would at least have the dark and terrible right to kill their illegitimate offspring if they executed the deed while the state looked the other way. From the Kantian state's point of view, children were invisible. Ghastlier, this invisibility was "obliterative" for those children who were stigmatized by illegitimacy from birth. Like the disabled who have been euthanized and sterilized in order to erase their deformities from modern political communities, Kant's illegitimate babies had to be obliterated in order to keep these outcasts completely out of sight of the law that ruled out their very existence.[68]

The Problem of Bad Education: Shelley's Immersion in Locke, Rousseau, Wollstonecraft, and Godwin

The problem of bad education—or the problem of society's potentially corrosive influence on the morals and character of children—preoccupied the leading political theorists from the long eighteenth century, from Locke to Mary Wollstonecraft. It was a problem that faced all children, especially in their early years when they had little or no control over their environment, let alone their socialization and education. From the beginning of life, education could be very bad for children's minds and bodies, despite the good intentions of their parents, caregivers, and tutors. Shelley learned about the problem of bad education in practice from her own immersion in a hothouse education at home by her father, William Godwin. At the same time, her father trained her to grapple with the problem of bad education in the abstract by reading Locke, Rousseau, and two of their most prominent pupils and critics—her parents, Godwin and Wollstonecraft.

Locke and Rousseau set forth theories of child development that intended to remedy the problem of bad education through the isolation of children from corrosive social forces. In *Frankenstein*, Shelley staged a complex critique of these influential theories of child development.[69] Victor and the Creature experience two types of social isolation in their youth. Alphonse Frankenstein isolates Victor from the broader Genevan society and culture for the sake of his son's happy development at home with his small and tight-knit family. Victor in turn entirely isolates the Creature from family, society, culture, and the state when he exposes his child soon after his creation. Both Victor and his Creature meet bad ends due to their inability to socially interact with a sense of responsibility toward others, especially those closest to them. With these parallel storylines and character developments, the novel delivers a powerful critique of Locke and Rousseau's attempts to contain the problem of bad education by isolating children from broader social forces. The (mis)educations of Victor and the Creature confront readers with the question of whether such social isolation—no matter the degree, form, or cause—would be even worse for children than outright immersion in a broader culture of moral corruption.

Shelley's introduction to the problem of bad education, in theory and in practice, almost began in the crib. Godwin raised his daughter Mary to revere her dead mother and even become an intellectual substitute for her. A portrait of Wollstonecraft was the focal point of the library of Shelley's childhood home in London, even after her father had remarried. Educated largely at home by her father, the young Shelley had access to all of her mother's books, including the posthumous works that Godwin had edited and published alongside his biography of her life, *Memoirs of the Author of A Vindication of the Rights of Woman* (1798).[70]

Shelley's journal traces her reading of her mother's works in the years just prior to composing and publishing *Frankenstein*. In 1814, the year she eloped with Percy Shelley, she consumed Wollstonecraft's major literary works: *Mary, a Fiction* (1788); *Letters Written During a Short Residence in Sweden, Norway, and Denmark* (1796); and *Maria: or, the Wrongs of Woman* (1798). She also studied her mother's *An Historical and Moral View of the French Revolution* (1794) and *Elements of Morality* (1789), a translation of C. G. Salzmann's moral philosophy for children. In 1815, the year she suffered the death of her first baby, she read the whole of Wollstonecraft's *Posthumous Works* (1798). In 1816, the year she wrote the first, novella-length draft of *Frankenstein*, she tackled her mother's greatest political treatise, *A Vindication of the Rights of Woman* (1792). By the age of nineteen, Shelley had recorded her reading of virtually all of her mother's oeuvre.[71]

Since the early childhood of his daughter, Godwin had taught Shelley to debate the political philosophies of Locke and Rousseau with him at the dinner table.[72] Although he rejected the usage of the conceptual devices of the state of nature and the social contract for the justification of government, his *Enquiry Concerning Political Justice* (1793) was heavily indebted to Locke and Rousseau's educational theories. After she eloped with Percy, Shelley prioritized the works of Locke, Rousseau, Godwin, and Wollstonecraft in her self-directed reading program that she recorded in her journal from 1814 to 1818. She and Percy sometimes read and discussed these works, especially those of her parents, together. But she devoted more attention to studying all four of these political philosophers' literary, educational, epistemological, and political writings than her husband did.

Shelley kept returning to Rousseau's major literary/philosophical works—*Emile, or On Education* (1762); *Julie, or the New Heloise* (1761); and *Confessions* (1782)—as well as her father's treatise, *Political Justice,* and its companion novel, *Caleb Williams* (1794). She dove into the empiricist epistemology of Book I of Locke's *Essay Concerning Human Understanding* (1690). She examined contemporary responses to *Emile,* including one French feminist rewriting of it, *Adele and Theodore* (1782), by Madame de Genlis. She also engaged some of the most prominent criticisms of and philosophical alternatives to the social contract tradition by David Hume, Edmund Burke, and her parents.[73]

Shelley's interest in the social contract thinkers persisted through her twenties into her forties. She noted that she read commentaries on Hobbes, Locke, and Kant in 1819 and kept a nearly daily record of Percy's consumption of the entire *Leviathan* in her journal of March 1820. In 1821, Percy dipped into the works of Immanuel Kant, and she followed suit by picking up an Italian translation of Kant's *Physical Geography* in 1822.[74] She wrote a critical biography of Rousseau, chastising his coldhearted abandonment of his five children, for the *Cyclopaedia Lives of . . . Eminent Men* in 1839.[75] However, her early, indirect exposure to Hobbes, Locke, and Kant through her parents' political theories probably influenced her authorship and revisions of *Frankenstein* more than any of her direct encounters with their writings. Rousseau was the exception, of course. His stature as a literary giant, plus the influence of the radical strands of his educational and political theory upon her parents, made him regular and inspiring reading for Shelley. Hence, he is universally acknowledged as an important philosophical source for *Frankenstein.*[76]

But even the eccentric Rousseau had his influences. As we have seen, he borrowed elements of Hobbes to raise his own specter of the stateless orphan in the state of nature. Even more important for his broader conceptions of the child and childhood were Locke's *Essay Concerning Human Understanding*

(1690) and *Some Thoughts Concerning Education* (1693). *Some Thoughts* built on the epistemological framework of the *Essay* to advance the most influential theory of child development and education to arise from the European Enlightenment. In the *Essay*, Locke used the metaphor of a "white paper" to describe the infant's mind in the womb and after birth.[77] While blank at first, the child's mental "paper" was gradually filled with ideas, primarily based on the impressions of sensory experiences. Although most of these ideas were written on the mind after the child was born, a few "faint ideas" of "hunger, thirst, and warmth, and some pains" might originate in the womb.[78] As a result, it was morally important for parents and tutors to control which experiences formed a child's mind from birth—and to some degree even before it.

An ominous aspect of the Lockean theory of child development was its assumption that children, especially infants, were passive objects waiting to be written upon by experiences as dictated by parents and other adults. Even in the interior world of their minds, children had no real freedom from parental and adult intervention. As Locke conceded in the *Second Treatise*, they were not born "in" freedom or even "to" a right to freedom as children but rather only born "to" a right to be free once adults.[79] By tracing out the dire consequences of Victor Frankenstein's thoughtless cruelty toward his Creature, Shelley counterfactually reasoned that a parent could—*contra* the benevolent intentions of Locke's philosophy of education—abuse his or her power to write upon the "white paper" of the child's mind in a way that made the child not a model of virtue but the "hideous progeny" of the abuser.

Rousseau's *Emile* put into literary form an extreme version of what Locke had argued about child development. A male tutor takes responsibility for the orphan Emile and conducts a social experiment with his charge. Contrary to typical eighteenth-century parenting and educational practices, the tutor isolates Emile from the family, society, and culture as much as possible before he reaches adulthood. This isolation allows the tutor to circumvent broader influences and exert near-total control over the contents of the boy's mind, including his beliefs, desires, and preferences. Emile grows up to adopt his tutor's vision of the best life available for a man in modern society: married to a virtuous woman chosen by his teacher, living in the provinces away from the corruption of cities, and following the laws of the monarchical state in which he was born despite the lack of opportunity for true (republican) citizenship.

Book 1 of *Emile* had begun with the cautionary counterfactual: "Under existing conditions a man left to himself from birth would be more of a monster than the rest."[80] However, Rousseau did not use his philosophical novel to test the validity of this moral hypothesis. First of all, Emile is never truly alone due to his constant supervision by his tutor. His childhood transpires in a kind of socially controlled isolation. Second, even in this unusual though not total condition of social isolation, Emile grows up to be a virtuous (if reclusive) man, not an asocial and amoral monster. Yet Rousseau's idea of a "man left to himself from birth" recasts the specter of the stateless orphan, giving him for the first time the guise of a "monster." In leaving this tantalizing counterfactual untouched, Rousseau paved the way for thinkers such as Wollstonecraft and Shelley to explore more deeply how conditions of extreme social and educational deprivation could disfigure the character of anyone—even, or perhaps especially, a vulnerable child.

In her *Rights of Woman*, Wollstonecraft critically responded to both Locke and Rousseau's theories of child development and drew out their negative repercussions for the education of girls. Quoting from *Some Thoughts*, she agreed with Locke that "'if the mind be curbed and humbled too much in children; if their spirits be abased and broken much by too strict an hand over them; they lose all their vigour and industry.'"[81] Wollstonecraft gave Locke his due for his desire to prevent such stunting of children's minds and bodies through overly restrictive and authoritarian parenting. At the same time, she perceived the moral problems with his theory of the mind for the education of girls in a patriarchal society. If the minds of children were blank slates, then parents and other adults could easily manipulate their mental contents in a pernicious fashion. In a patriarchal society, girls were especially vulnerable to such manipulation due to the wider oppression of women. As Wollstonecraft observed, "Girls, from various causes, are more kept down by their parents, in every sense of the word, than boys."[82] She reasoned that girls in such a patriarchal society had no real chance of experiencing the mental or physical freedom necessary for developing the vigor and industry that, according to Locke, characterized a healthy and happy childhood. The long-term impact of such deprivation was equally bad: as a consequence of being "taught slavishly to submit to their parents, they are prepared for the slavery of marriage."[83]

As Alan Richardson and other literary critics have underscored, the "implicitly tyrannical relation of (male) teacher and (female) student is . . . 'pure Gothic.'"[84] The sinister (and sexual) aspect of pedagogy's power differential between the patriarch-tutor and vulnerable young woman made it an ideal subject for both feminist and Gothic literature. Wollstonecraft indeed made it a central theme of her final novel, *Maria: or, the Wrongs of Woman*. Trapped in an asylum by her abusive husband, Maria seeks refuge in the arms of a scoundrel. He beguiles her by reading Rousseau's famous tale of a girl seduced by her tutor, *Julie, or the New Heloise.*

Wollstonecraft applied her feminist critique of Locke's philosophy of mind to reveal the flaws in Rousseau's fictional model for female education: Sophie, the girl raised to be the wife of Emile. Against Rousseau's essentialist view that Sophie and other girls play with dolls and mirrors because they are vain by nature, Wollstonecraft reflected on the basis of experience that if girls are given the same opportunity to play outside as boys, then they tend to play the same games.[85] Unfortunately, these girls were the exception, not the rule. Rather than enjoy such freedom alongside boys, girls were "taught from their infancy that beauty is woman's scepter."[86] When subjected to such a superficial education from birth, "the mind shapes itself to the body, and, roaming round its gilt cage, only seeks to adorn its prison."[87] Bound by such a bad education, girls were unlikely to develop a sense of the value of intellectual pursuits versus mere bodily pleasure. With the whole of their conscious lives devoted to physical self-decoration for the approval of men, women's minds were consumed, as it were, by their bodies.

As Wollstonecraft ominously put it, a girl became an "irrational monster" as a result of the vicious cycle of bad education.[88] Tyrannized by parents under the broader system of patriarchal power, girls grew up knowing nothing but tyranny. They eventually lashed out against this injustice in the only way they knew how: by tyrannizing others, especially their own siblings, husbands, and children.

Perhaps to test her mother's idea that domination and isolation hurt everyone, regardless of gender or other social status, Shelley made Victor and his Creature struggle with a similar psychology of tyranny. When reunited with his Creature for the first time, Victor immediately tries to "extinguish the spark that I so negligently bestowed."[89] Easily falling into the role of father-overlord, Victor threatens to wield "the fierce vengeance of my arm wreaked on your miserable head."[90] Killing the child he made on his own would be the ultimate act of paternal tyranny, but the Creature's greater power prevents it. In their second encounter, the Creature seizes the role of tyrant when Victor fails to provide him a companion. To his father, he commands, "You are my creator, but I am your master—Obey!"[91] When Victor refuses yet again to make his child a female companion, the vicious cycle of tyranny comes full circle, with the Creature pledging his final revenge against his "tyrant and tormentor."[92]

In engaging the psychology of tyranny, Shelley also took inspiration from her father. She repeatedly read *Political Justice* in the years just prior to dedicating *Frankenstein* to its author. Following Locke's *Second Treatise* and Rousseau's *Second Discourse* and *Social Contract*, Godwin addressed the problem of tyranny in its political form, or what he called despotism. In the opening pages of *Political Justice*, Godwin sadly observed, "Despotism prevails over nine-tenths of the globe."[93] Quoting from the *Second Treatise*, he agreed with Locke that despotism was a "'vile and miserable'" form of government "'more to be deprecated than anarchy itself.'"[94]

As with Rousseau, Godwin pinpointed the economic forces behind despotism: "A perpetual struggle with the evils of poverty" will induce the "poor man . . . to regard the state of society as a state of war."[95] In light of this gap between the rich and the poor, society was "not for protecting every man in his rights and securing him to the means of his existence" but rather for "engrossing all its advantages to a few favored individuals, and reserving for the portion of the rest want, dependence and misery."[96] It was precisely this total and demoralizing dependence of the poor on the rich, even as they lived in misery, that made nine-tenths of the world's governments despotic in Godwin's estimation. The endurance of such systematic oppression made the rise of the poor's "destructive passions" against the rich almost inevitable, even if typically ineffective.[97]

For Godwin, the cycle of bad government persisted because despotism fed upon itself. Economic oppression led to conflict and the use of state power to subdue the poor. Although government had proven to be bad for people and their experience of society, it was nonetheless necessary for their security from injustice and conflict. Quoting his friend Thomas Paine, Godwin concurred, "'Government even in its best state was a necessary evil.'"[98] He concluded that an ultra-minimalistic state, focused upon "two legitimate purposes" of (1) "suppression of injustice against individuals within the community" and (2) "the common defence against external invasion" was the best of all the bad forms of government.[99]

In the opening line of *Emile*, Rousseau famously proclaimed that "everything is good as it leaves the hands of the Author of things; everything degenerates in the hands of man."[100] A few lines later, he employed a metaphor that captivated the imaginations of Shelley and her parents: "[Man] disfigures everything; he loves deformity, monsters. He wants nothing as nature made it, not even man."[101] We have seen how Wollstonecraft used this metaphor of monstrosity to decry the deformation of girls by bad education. Looking at economic and political injustice on the broadest scale, Godwin described the feudal system as a "ferocious monster" whose skin has been "stuffed" and "exhibited" by the rich with "the hope still to terrify mankind into patience and pusillanimity."[102] Reversing Hobbes's positive representation of the absolute state as a kind of salvific monster or benevolent Leviathan (made of the human subjects it ruled), Rousseau, Wollstonecraft, and Godwin each used the metaphor of the monster to capture the ways that the educational, economic, and political systems of their time were not only made by (or of) bad or monstrous people but also made people bad or monstrous.[103]

By applying Rousseau's distinction between good and bad education to politics, Godwin developed an ingenious political theory of education. Godwin followed Rousseau and Wollstonecraft in understanding the present system of education as pernicious for children and in need of drastic reform. Yet he took this argument a step further by showing how the vicious cycle of bad education was at root a political problem—specifically, a problem with the form of government itself. For Godwin, the solution to bad education could not merely be the reform of private education, as Rousseau prescribed in the *Emile*. Nor could the solution be Wollstonecraft's 1792 proposal for education to become a "grand national concern" under the current regimes of France and Britain.[104] Neither Rousseau's nor Wollstonecraft's proposals for educational reform addressed the root problem: that the current structures and functions of government were corrosive of human character and therefore antithetical to good education.

Although Wollstonecraft's vision of free, public, coeducational, equal, and mandatory primary education was unprecedented, in philosophy and policy, it did not go far enough for Godwin in terms of its politics. In her political theory, Wollstonecraft supported a republican form of government, but she did not insist that such a government be in place before true educational reform could transpire. Godwin, by contrast, believed that only once government was reformed along his minimalistic lines would true educational reform be possible. In the opening chapter of *Political Justice*, he reflected, "As long as parents and teachers in general shall fall under the established rule, it is clear that politics and modes of government will educate and infect us all."[105] Godwin identified bad government as the underlying cause behind the infection of bad education. The underlying cause needed to be treated, or political corruption would continue to infect the mind-sets of parents and teachers and, in turn, each and every generation of people. Even the very best tutors and pupils, such as Rousseau imagined in *Emile*, could not escape corruption due to internal, virtuous resistance to it or physical distance from it. There was no quarantine for political corruption as long as the political system itself was diseased.

In addition to making some radical political inferences from their educational theories, Godwin took Locke and Rousseau's theories of child development to a new extreme. As we have seen, Locke's epistemology did not deny the possibility that prenatal sensory impressions shaped "faint ideas" in the unborn baby's mind. Taking this argument a step further, Godwin argued that a baby's mind and "character" were shaped by "impressions" of sensory experiences even in the womb.[106] He went so far as to conclude, "At the moment of birth man has really a certain character, and each man a character different than his fellows."[107] Countering the view popularized by Rousseau that "the education of man begins at his birth," Godwin put forth the provocative rejoinder that the education of children in fact began in the womb.[108] Many parents today might agree, especially those who abide by the contemporary, commonplace injunction to play Mozart for their babies during pregnancy for the sake of good fetal mental and physical development.[109]

Godwin then considered "education under three heads": (1) the "education of accident," or the involuntary education imbibed from one's circumstances, as in the prenatal stage of life; (2) "education of design," or the intentional education of children by parents and other adults; and, most important, (3) the "political education" caused by the deep influence of the prevailing system of government upon people's characters.[110] Taking Locke's epistemology to its logical extreme, Godwin argued that people were products of their broader "circumstances" from the very beginning of their lives, even before they had a separate physical identity from their mother's bodies.[111] Yet the mother's womb was ultimately a product of broader circumstances beyond her immediate control, too (today, we might think of the negative impact of secondhand smoke on the fetus).[112] Godwin identified the "political institution" of society as the ultimate force behind the shaping of its people's circumstances. With a "comprehensive" power to educate human character within its bounds, a government "for the most part" exerted "absolute control" over its people's "actions and dispositions" as well as "opinions."[113] Thus, Godwin suggested that government was ultimately responsible for the circumstances surrounding child development. If the government was bad, then the social circumstances for child development would be bad. Only by stripping government down to its two legitimate purposes—justice and security—would those social circumstances become favorable for the virtuous education of individuals who could grow up to be good citizens of a minimalistic and therefore legitimate state.

The problem with Godwin's political theory of education was that it required a long and complex process of reform for both government and education. As he readily admitted, this process of reform would have to be slow, not revolutionary, in order to avoid fueling the economic conflicts and political injustices that only his proposed system of minimalistic government could eliminate.[114] Ironically for a radical, an anarchist, and a follower of Paine, Godwin found himself agreeing with much of his contemporary Edmund Burke's antirevolutionary theory of political reform. At the same time, Godwin knew that a slow and organic process of reform could either hinder or outright prevent the development of the social circumstances necessary for good government and good education. By following a Burkean model of reform, he risked the replication of bad cultural and political traditions for the sake of reducing the conflict that prevented good political change over time. An undesired consequence of this trade-off, he knew, might be to indefinitely stall good political change rather than gradually realize it.[115]

Wollstonecraft's Wild Girls and Godwin's Clay Babies

Wollstonecraft and Godwin were both deeply influenced by Locke's theory of the mind and Rousseau's theory of education. While they each rejected the use of the concepts of the state of nature and the social contract to justify government, they shared Locke and Rousseau's assumption of the difference between the blank slate of the child's mind and the broader social forces that threatened to pollute it. This binary opposition between the original purity of the mind and the danger of social influences inspired their distinctive resurrections of the image of the stateless orphan in their respective political theories. However, neither theorist considered how their uses of the image of the stateless orphan stood in tension with both their moral principles and their principled criticisms of the social contract tradition.

Wollstonecraft invoked the image of the wild, or feral, child in an argument for the right of girls to greater physical and mental freedom. Perhaps alluding to the eighteenth-century European fascination with Native American Marie-Angélique Memmie Le Blanc, the so-called Wild Girl of Champagne who lived alone in the woods in France during her adolescence, Wollstonecraft observed in her *Rights of Woman* that girls who "have accidentally been allowed to run wild" have grown up to "act like rational creatures."[116] She contrasted the moral and physical corruption of the typical upper-class women of her time with a few recent examples of wild girls who primarily grew up in a free, outdoor environment.[117] Formulating a forward-looking conditional, she wondered if girls were generally raised with freedom akin to feral children, would they then develop the strength of mind and body necessary to develop the full range and degree of human virtues previously associated only with men.

Wollstonecraft's thought experiment on the potentially beneficial effects of abandoning girls to the wilderness is considerably less problematic than the thought experiments on children conducted by the social contract thinkers. For one, she was not using the concept of the state of nature to justify a form of government. On the surface, her thought experiment was merely testing the theory that girls would be better off with more physical freedom than they currently enjoyed. Although she uncritically employed the image of the stateless orphan, she did not callously imagine the suffering, killing, or abuse of children for the sake of justifying the rights of adults. Rather, she traded on the popular resonance of the idea of the wild girl to argue that all children, regardless of sex, have a right to physical and mental freedom while young, for the sake of the healthy development of their minds and bodies into adulthood.

On the other hand, Wollstonecraft's thought experiment envisaged the benign neglect and social isolation of girls, for the sake of making a point about the potential of women to realize the same capabilities as men if they enjoyed the same right to freedom from a young age. Even more problematically, her thought experiment implicitly relied on the Rousseauian idea of the state of nature, which she had rejected as a "false hypothesis" on human nature in the first chapter of the *Rights of Woman*.[118] In her view, humans were not capable of living alone, in perfect atomistic freedom, in a state of nature without society and government. There was therefore no political point in even entertaining such a counterfactual. In addition, she found Rousseau's binary between the goodness of the state of nature and the evils of human society to be "impious" on the grounds that it aggrandized the power of the human will to introduce evil into the world and undercut the Christian conception of the omnipotent will and omnibenevolent providence of God.[119]

Contradicting her own principled political and theological rejection of state of nature theory, her thought experiment on the wild girl proposed a possible scenario in which girls would benefit from isolation from society. In tension with her earlier claim that humans are fundamentally social creatures, she alluded to actual women with "vigor of intellect" whom she knew to have "run wild" as girls in order to support the plausibility of the results of her thought experiment.[120] Troublingly out of tune with her broader feminist principles, her thought experiment reinforced the more-than-a-century-old, gender-biased, contractarian imaginary that situated girls and women in nature beyond the protective auspices of the masculine and patriarchal political community.

Putting a disturbing twist on the storyline of *Emile*, Godwin's *Political Justice* conducted several thought experiments in which infants were isolated or taken from their families, then manipulated or even intentionally hurt by adults, in order to draw a contrast between the immaturity and malleability of children and the autonomy of adults qualified to be citizens.[121] On the face of it, Godwin's most perverse thought experiment featuring an infant refutes the idea that babies are born with an instinct to protect themselves from pain: "If a baby's hand is stroked in a certain way, it will provoke the gesture of grasping. Present to the child, thus far instructed, a lighted candle. The sight of it will produce a pleasurable state of the organs of perception. He will probably stretch out his hand to the flame, and will have no apprehension of the pain of burning, till he has felt the sensation."[122] This thought experiment elucidates how the infant mind must process sensory data and form complex ideas about its environment before it can fear pain. What is strange and even sinister about the thought experiment is its detached treatment of the vulnerable infant as a suitable subject for psychological manipulation and physical torture. He coldly imagines an infant isolated from family and lured into pain for the sake of making a fine point about Lockean epistemology.

In other thought experiments, Godwin orphaned babies or switched them in the cradle in order to show that children were like clay in the hands of the adults who raised and educated them. He concluded, "Children are a sort of raw material put into our hands, a ductile and yielding substance, which, if we do not ultimately mould in conformity to our wishes, it is because we throw away the power committed to us."[123] Fortunately, Godwin's disturbing experiments on children transpired entirely in his mind. Whether he construed them as hypothetical or real, however, Godwin's babies were utterly malleable, for even in the womb, the contents of their minds were a product of the circumstances of their mother's bodies as well as the body politic. This conception of the child as putty in the hands of adults led Godwin to ally himself with the social contract tradition more than he ever admitted.

Following Hume, Godwin had rejected the idea of the social contract on the grounds that it unrealistically presumed the possibility and desirability of popular consent as the basis for legitimate government.[124] Rather than derive justice from consent, he derived justice from morality. From his utilitarian view of morality as the increase of happiness and pleasure and the reduction of misery and pain for the greatest number of "intelligent beings," Godwin deduced a universal moral "principle of virtue."[125] This principle obligated "one man" to relieve "the wants" of another "man" when he had the "ability" to relieve them. This obligation, he insisted, "arises out of no compact, direct or understood."[126] Any promise to fulfill it would be redundant because the obligation obtained independently of any expectation of its fulfillment. When derived from popular consent, rules of justice were circumscribed within a particular political community. No one was obliged to follow the rules beyond the bounds of that political community. As a corrective to this moral relativism engendered by contractarian thought, Godwin held that his utilitarian principle of virtue "ought to be observed indifferently by a native or a stranger."[127]

Godwin understood his conception of justice as cosmopolitan, applying to all men irrespective of national membership. Yet Godwin often seemed to literally mean men.[128] Despite his critique of social contract theory, Godwin ended up in a position much like Kant when it came to the liminal relationship of children and women to the state. The ductile quality of children meant that they were dependent on adults to carefully sculpt their minds and characters to understand and enact the principle of virtue required for good citizenship. Worse, Godwin insinuated through the consistent use of masculine nouns and pronouns that such virtuous and independent citizenship was ideally for adult men, not children and women. However, like Locke, he never explicitly and formally excluded women from rights. He rather reserved such political banishment for children. Children alone belonged to his conception of a true state of anarchy. Without the capability to perform perfect and universal duties of assistance, children would always lack those rights to justice and security that his model minimal state was designed to provide.

The Specter Transfigured: The Creature's Plea for the Rights of the Child

Immersed in the ideas of Locke, Rousseau, Wollstonecraft, and Godwin, Shelley had a hothouse education at the hands of her philosopher father like her contemporary, John Stuart Mill. Although he claimed to not believe in "overloading the faculties of children," Godwin seemed not to follow this advice (given to a friend in 1802) in the case of the then five-year-old Shelley.[129] As Mellor points out, he encouraged his young daughter to write for his press for children's literature and published a work she helped to write, "Mounseer

Nongtongpaw," when she was only eleven. Shelley also wrote "weekly lectures" for her younger brother to deliver to guests on topics such as the core thesis of *Political Justice*: "The Influence of Government on the Character of the People."[130]

The high expectations of her homeschooling did not cause her a nervous breakdown like Mill, but she probably suffered psychologically for it as much as she benefited intellectually. Similarly to Mill's growing up to reject his father's views in favor of his own liberty-centered version of utilitarianism, Shelley's immersion in the social contract tradition and its critics gave her the tools to enact a transformational critique of the most radical political/educational theories of her time. In bringing the tragic story of an abandoned child to the narrative heart of her first novel, she transfigured the specter of the stateless orphan begat by Hobbes and adopted by Locke, Rousseau, Kant, Wollstonecraft, and Godwin. No longer was the specter haunting the margins of the social contract tradition and the radical political and educational theories it inspired. In the figure of the Creature, the stateless orphan gained a hulking frame and looming presence. Still alone but no longer silent, the specter's demands for the rights of the child could finally be heard through the telling of the Creature's unforgettable story of survival of exposure at birth.

Following in her mother's footsteps, Shelley adopted the image of the stateless orphan not to exclude children from rights but rather to engage the idea of rights for children. Unlike Wollstonecraft, she did not advance a systematic theory of children's rights. Shelley instead gave the specter of the stateless orphan an important story to tell with his own unique, first-person voice. This story-within-a-story-within-a-story, as told by the Creature to Victor and then by Victor to Captain Walton, is the narrative core of *Frankenstein*. Hearing this astounding story makes Victor (and the reader) pause to contemplate a profound moral question: Do children have rights even when they are denied enjoyment of them by parents and other adults? If so, why? And what are these basic rights that apply to children at least from birth, if not from the womb, or even before their creation?

Shelley's inclusion of the Creature's story was innovative not only for its engagement of the question of children's rights but also for giving a "monster" a highly educated voice. In his otherwise positive review of the novel, Sir Walter Scott complained about the author's unprecedented decision to make a monster not just speak in imitation of his oppressors, like Shakespeare's Caliban, but also speak intelligently and critically about his circumstances. He thought the Creature would have retained "mysterious sublimity" if he was kept silent and infrequently seen, like the supernatural beings that typically haunted the closets and castles of Gothic literature of the era.[131]

Otherwise an astute reader of *Frankenstein*, Scott missed the point of giving the Creature a highly educated voice. Just as her mother put the story of the poor servant woman Jemima at the center of *Maria*'s many-layered tale of female oppression, Shelley took the voice of a victim of extreme injustice and made it the narrative core of her novel. Mellor has recognized *Maria* as a groundbreaking text for feminist literature because it gives a poor woman a chance to tell her story of oppression in the first-person voice.[132] Shelley modeled her Creature's story partly after Jemima's, yet, in so doing, made her own radical innovation to the modern novel. Shelley gave an apparent "monster" a highly—indeed, preposterously—educated voice to undermine the very idea of a natural, or born, monster. Illustrating the thesis of *Political Justice*, the Creature was as much a product of education or circumstances as anyone else. Extraordinary circumstances made for an extraordinary creature.

Shelley elicited a new kind of domestic horror in the nascent Gothic imagination by making her "monster" a survivor of infanticide. In her classic feminist reading of the novel, Ellen Moers explained the genius of Shelley's melding of Gothic and domestic themes: "What Mary Shelley actually did in *Frankenstein* was to transform the standard Romantic matter of incest, infanticide, and patricide into a phantasmagoria of the nursery. Nothing quite like it was done in English literature until that Victorian novel by a woman which we also place uneasily in the Gothic tradition: *Wuthering Heights*."[133] In exposing the Creature to the most extreme forms of child abandonment, abuse, and isolation, Shelley heightened reader awareness of the special vulnerability of children to harm by parents and other adults. By giving the highly literate Creature the opportunity to critically recount the impact of his abandonment, she gave readers (and even Victor) a twofold opportunity: to feel the emotional vulnerability of an abandoned child and to understand his monstrous behavior as a product of his unjust circumstances.

The Creature's voice is arresting because of what it pleas to his maker: "Remember that I am thy creature . . . I was benevolent and good: misery made me a fiend. Make me happy, and I shall again be virtuous."[134] Stopping to listen, Victor "for the first time . . . felt what the duties of a creator toward his creature ought to be."[135] After recalling his traumatic search for warmth, food, water, clothing, shelter, family, care, education, and community—all basic needs denied him at birth—the Creature asks his father to finally fulfill a deeper need for love. Pathetically, the Creature accepts that he cannot expect his delinquent father to love him. At the same time, he raises the stakes for his father's choice to abrogate the most fundamental of parental duties. The Creature beseeches his father to make him a female companion "as deformed and horrible as myself . . . with whom I can live in the interchange of those sympathies necessary for my being."[136] This he demands "as a right." Moreover, it is a right that his father "must not refuse" because he is obligated as a parent to give it.[137]

The Creature's plea to his father articulates a "right" to share love—or, in his more poetic words, to live in the interchange of sympathy. This interchange of sympathy is "necessary" not only for happiness but also for the sustenance and beneficial development of one's very "being." This interchange of sympathy ideally begins with the parent-child relationship, but it should teach the child to feel affection and show concern for others: family, friends, nonhuman animals, neighbors, and eventually romantic partners and fellow citizens. Tragically, in the case of the Creature, there must be a substitute for his lack of parental love: his derelict father's dutiful making of a female companion for him. In voicing this demand for love to his father, the Creature claimed an expansive right for children that corresponded to an equally substantial parental duty. To use Isaiah Berlin's words, this plea is part of "the heart of the great cry for recognition" that characterizes both individuals and groups in the modern age.[138] The Creature wants the fulfillment of a right to be recognized as part of something bigger than himself—most fundamentally, a right to be part of a family tied together by love. As we shall see in Chapter 2, Wollstonecraft's otherwise visionary theory of children's rights stopped at the justification of the right of children to parental care, without considering the question of a more robust entitlement to share love with parents or fitting substitutes. Shelley's most ingenious philosophical and literary innovation was to raise precisely this question in the voice of the Creature.

CHAPTER 2

Wollstonecraft's Philosophy of Children's Rights

To the present day, many people confuse Mary Wollstonecraft Godwin (1759–97) with her youngest daughter, Mary Wollstonecraft Godwin Shelley (1797–1851). The overlap in the mother's married name and her daughter's given name alone explains this common mistake. Yet this mistake is ironic for two reasons. First, it usually elides the philosophical contribution of the mother in favor of celebrating the literary achievement of the daughter. As we have seen in Chapter 1, the mother's political theory was in fact influential on the daughter's crafting of her first and most important speculative fiction, *Frankenstein* (1818). Second, the elision of the mother in public remembrance of the daughter suggests that the two women are one and the same. Although they shared a number of moral and political concerns, especially surrounding the ethics of parent-child relationships, Wollstonecraft and Shelley in fact each made distinct contributions to addressing the radical question of children's rights.

Do children have rights? It was an uncommon question in the postrevolutionary European cultural and political landscape. Hence, it was a radical question to raise, whether we are thinking of Wollstonecraft publishing her first political treatises in the early 1790s or Shelley commencing her literary career just after the end of the Napoleonic Wars. Indeed, it is still an uncommon and radical question to ask today.

How each of these writers responded to the question of children's rights was radical as well. We shall see how Wollstonecraft advanced a systematic theory of children's rights—the very first of its kind in the history of Western political thought. This chapter sets forth an exposition and analysis of Wollstonecraft's groundbreaking philosophy of children's rights for two reasons: (1)

it allows for a deeper appreciation of her special philosophical genius, separate from her daughter's work, and (2) it surveys the most immediate and important philosophical background for Shelley's unique literary approach to engaging the radical question of children's rights.

Wollstonecraft and the Idea of Human Rights for Children

Over the course of her oeuvre, Wollstonecraft developed a theory of the human rights of children that had no philosophical precedent. It was a theory of children's human rights in the sense of "moral rights."[1] Moral rights obtained solely on the basis of children's humanity, regardless of whether such rights were formally institutionalized in law or politics.

Although she responded in part to broader cultural trends in the modern Western European reconceptualization of childhood during the eighteenth century, Wollstonecraft arranged these precirculating ideas into a coherent and distinctive political theory. According to David Archard, some of the most important of these precirculating ideas were (1) children's moral desert of a different, more playful and innocent lifestyle than adults; (2) children's gradual or stadial development into adulthood and its distinctive responsibilities; and (3) children's potential for reason and a rational education under the tutelage of adults. Wollstonecraft synthesized and systematized these ideas with others, such that she generated an altogether new kind of political theory: a theory of children's rights and, specifically, a theory of children's human rights.[2] It was original not only in the content and scope of rights she imagined for children but also in the justification she provided for understanding children as rights-bearing subjects alongside adults.

As for the content and scope of children's rights, Wollstonecraft theorized children's possession of the same rights as adult humans, minus the right to full citizenship. Full citizenship included fair and equal access to formal political rights such as voting and office holding, as well as to economic rights to other public goods such as property and careers. We saw in Chapter 1 that the social contract thinkers either implicitly (like John Locke) or explicitly (like Immanuel Kant) excluded girls and women from their residually patriarchal conceptions of subjecthood or citizenship.

In a radical move that distinguished her from the social contract tradition, Wollstonecraft explicitly included girls and women in her truly egalitarian conception of citizenship. While she thought that formal political rights should only be granted at the age of majority (or legally recognized adulthood) to either sex, children ought to gradually come to enjoy rights to property and careers after the age of nine and before they gained complete access to these economic rights in adulthood. Most important for this process of children *growing into* their full and equal rights as citizens was the state's provision of the right to free primary and secondary education, including the options of vocational training courses or a liberal arts curriculum after the age of nine.[3] Such a coeducational system of "national" education would enable girls' and boys' development into full citizens who were capable of authentic and virtuous participation in a modern representative republic.[4] Before becoming full citizens, children would still exercise a formal and formative civil right in attending state schools. Public education would thus function as a kind of school for citizenship.[5]

In yet another radical move that distanced her from even the most progressive theorists of family life in the seventeenth and eighteenth centuries, Wollstonecraft also specified the fundamental right of children to be free from physical or psychological abuse by their parents or elders, which derived from the perfect (or complete), universal, and fundamental obligation of adults to not abuse minors.[6] The experience of such abuse, on her account, nullified the perfect yet special or relationship-specific duty of adult children to care for their parents in their old age.[7]

Wollstonecraft paired this *negative* right, to be free from abuse by adults, with a *positive* right, to receive care and a rational education from parents and parental figures. If children were given care and a rational education at home rather than abuse, they might also experience the family as a school for citizenship like the local schools they attended during the day.[8] In addition, they would freely and reciprocally care for their parents in their old age. If the state failed to guarantee their negative right to be free from domestic abuse, children could still find at school an expansive space for the free and full development of their capabilities as human beings through the exercise of their positive rights to physical, moral, and intellectual education.[9] If both the state and the family failed them, adult children at least had the right to extricate themselves from any further obligation toward their abusive parents.[10]

The Theological Background for Wollstonecraft's Theory of Children's Human Rights

Wollstonecraft's justification for these children's rights was rooted in her metaphysical/ethical conception of the human being. Inspired by her mentor, the

Reverend Richard Price, Wollstonecraft had a Dissenting Christian theological view of humans as creatures of God made in His rational image.[11] She wryly rejected the creation myth of Eve as made from Adam's rib as a "poetical story" with a patriarchal bias.[12] Wollstonecraft rather began from an abstract and universalistic, metaphysical, and theologically informed view of all humans—independent of any physical trait or social status—as moral equals due to their God-given potential for reason. Her most famous and feminist formulation of this metaphysical perspective on the human being was to claim there was no "sex in souls."[13]

Wollstonecraft did not assume, however, that all children or adults could or would exercise reason, whether partly or fully. This distinguished her from Kant, who—as we saw in Chapter 1—viewed children as incapable of reason and excluded anyone, child or adult, from citizenship rights if they lacked the use of reason. Although Wollstonecraft saw such development of rationality as generally good for individuals and society, she drew a distinction between the *potential* for reason—written, as it were, on the human soul by God—and the *presence or practice* of reason.

From Wollstonecraft's capacious metaphysical perspective, all humans—including children—have a God-given potential for reason whether or not they ever actualize it. In her 1788 *Original Stories* for the moral education of children, the governess Mrs. Mason makes a distinction between children's reason "in its infancy" and the mature, actualized reason of an adult. Beyond this developmental difference between children's and adults' rational capabilities, Mrs. Mason also highlighted the difference between the God-given reason, which universally "exalts a man over a brute," and the "cultivation" of such reason in any particular person.[14] On this account, a child was still a rational being made in the image of God, even if she was born without the physical faculties or social opportunities to develop or cultivate this metaphysical potentiality.

Like Price, Wollstonecraft drew a sharp line between humans and "brutes" (or nonhuman animals): the former were rational and sentient, and the latter were merely sentient.[15] Unlike nonhuman animals, children could and should develop their rational capabilities in order to fully realize their potential as moral beings. According to her deontological and correlative theory of human rights, all rights derived from duties, but not all duties entailed rights: "every right includes a duty."[16] While humans had a duty to respect sentient life, animals did not have a corresponding right to be free from abuse by humans. On the other hand, human children had a right to be free from abuse because humans in general had a duty to respect each other as "moral beings" capable of rational self-governance.[17]

Although Wollstonecraft's theory of children's rights does not apply to nonhuman animals, she developed a related account of animal ethics. A perfect (complete), universal, and fundamental duty to refrain from cruelty to nonhuman animals arises from the obligation to respect sentient life in general. Performance of this duty can be reinforced through education, especially in the primary school years. Following Locke's *Some Thoughts Concerning Education*, Wollstonecraft advocated that children be taught from an early age to at least respect, if not actively care for, animals and insects—not abuse or torture them.[18] Going far beyond Locke, she even envisioned a state-mandated policy of animal ethics as part of the core curriculum of her ideal public coeducational day school system: "Humanity to animals should be particularly inculcated as a part of national education, for it is not at present one of our national virtues."[19]

For Wollstonecraft, the ethical treatment of animals was a duty of humans at each stage of their lives, beginning in childhood, not a right of animals. Although children and "brutes" shared sentience and a vulnerability to abuse by adult humans, the human capability for reason made children rights-bearing subjects rather than mere objects of dutiful care. Wollstonecraft's theory of children's rights insisted upon the basic respect and even active care of nonhuman animals but ultimately valued all human life more highly than other forms of sentient life due to its rational nature.

Wollstonecraft's Radical Account of the Fundamental and Universal Human Rights of Children

Wollstonecraft, like many eighteenth-century Western European philosophers, used the language of natural rights. She did not use the language of natural rights as commonly as other terms for rights, however. She preferred the revolutionary-era language of the "rights of man," "rights of woman," "rights of humanity," and, most simply, "rights" to the older concept of "natural rights" that arose in late medieval Catholic theology and became prominent in seventeenth- and early eighteenth-century Protestant, neo-Stoic, neo-republican, and social contract thought.[20]

One reason why Wollstonecraft did not like the concept of "natural rights" as much as other formulations of rights is that the former was predicated upon what she took to be a false binary between the natural and the social in human life. As we have seen in Chapter 1, social contract thinkers such as Thomas Hobbes, Locke, and Rousseau construed natural rights—especially the primordial right to self-preservation— as obtaining even in a "state of nature" outside of society and government because these rights were grounded upon human nature, not the artifice of society and law. From Wollstonecraft's skeptical perspective, there was no such thing as a "state of nature" beyond society and government. Humans needed to live in society in order to realize their improvable faculties such as reason.

In addition, Wollstonecraft deemed such a fanciful concept as a "state of nature" as unnecessary for the rational justification of the rights of humans. Rather, the "rights of humanity" could be justified via a metaphysical/ethical conception of humans as rational, equal, and social creatures of God.[21] Even if one did not believe in God or share Wollstonecraft's particular theological commitments, one could appreciate her empirically grounded view of human beings as typically social and rational beings. One could even detach her view of humans (including children) as moral equals from its theological and metaphysical assumptions, just as she had detached the concept of equal rights from earlier conceptions of natural rights.

Beyond theories of natural rights, Wollstonecraft also read deeply in seventeenth- and eighteenth-century philosophy of education, particularly Locke, Rousseau, James Burgh, Catharine Macaulay, and Charles Maurice Talleyrand-Périgord, but ultimately moved far beyond these thinkers on the question of children's rights. Other than Locke and, even more briefly, Rousseau, none of these writers had applied the concept of rights to children. As shown in Chapter 1, Locke and Rousseau's applications of the concept of rights to children were minimal and ultimately self-contradictory. Burgh, Rousseau, Macaulay, and Talleyrand-Périgord followed Locke's *Some Thoughts on Education* (1693) in advocating for children's physical, intellectual, and moral freedom from parental and especially paternal tyranny. Wollstonecraft built on but moved beyond all of these theorists in developing her extended philosophical argument for the fundamental human rights of children: from Locke, Burgh, and Rousseau, she took a general interest in the physical education, health care, physical freedom, and outdoor exercise of children; from Rousseau, a special concern with the physical and moral benefits of maternal breastfeeding for infants and families; and from Macaulay and Talleyrand-Périgord, the inspiration to apply Lockean and Rousseauian arguments on the best form of early education equally to girls and boys.

The immediate context of Wollstonecraft's concern for children's human rights was the radical politics of late eighteenth-century England, especially amid its Dissenting Christian community. Under the theological tutelage of Price at the Newington Green church in London in the late 1780s, she learned the theory and rhetoric of the abolitionist cause. According to Price, a country that tolerated slavery in any form was "a spot where he enjoys no right, and is disposed of by owners as if he was a beast."[22] The logic of abolition was simple and elegant: chattel slaves—or people bought and sold into forced labor—were human (not beasts) and therefore deserved the same rights as other humans, including the fundamental right not to be enslaved. Humans had a right not to be enslaved because under slavery, they were denied the conditions of freedom necessary for rational agency and self-development. In short, slavery denied humans the capacity to develop their humanity because it denied their very humanity. Slavery was thus the ultimate form of domination—extinguishing the very possibility of freedom through the totalizing and oppressive use of force—as Rousseau had powerfully argued in the opening lines of his *Social Contract* (1762).

Many late eighteenth-century thinkers had followed Rousseau in applying the abolitionist argument against chattel slavery to other domains of human social and political life. For example, Thomas Paine, in his *Rights of Man, Part the Second* (1792), contended that the "hereditary system" of aristocratic and monarchical politics was a kind of "slavery" and violation of "human rights" because it suppressed the freedom of most people.[23] Wollstonecraft has been most renowned for applying the abolitionist argument to women. In *A Vindication of the Rights of Woman* (1792), she wrote that girls and women, as humans, deserve not to be raised to submit to the "the slavery of marriage."[24] This analogy between patriarchal marriage and slavery was an old one, however, as Mary Astell, Macaulay, and other early feminists had regularly appealed to it.[25] Wollstonecraft's philosophical innovation was to apply the abolitionist argument to children, including girls, in order to contend for their rights as humans. Those rights of children included the right to be educated in a way that was compatible with freedom from domination, in marriage or in any other social or political institution.

As early as her 1788 collection of children's tales, *Original Stories*, Wollstonecraft compared children to chattel slaves: "why then do we suffer children to be bound with fetters, which their half-formed faculties cannot break?"[26] While she certainly echoed Book I of Rousseau's *Emile* in this passage from the preface, the rationalist pedagogy of *Original Stories* pushed beyond Rousseau's primary concern with the physical freedom of children. Outdoing Rousseau by extending his own educational principles far beyond his own application of them, Wollstonecraft focused on the need to liberate children from irrational modes of education that were both intellectually and morally damaging.

Wollstonecraft went still further in *A Vindication of the Rights of Men*

(1790). Here, in her first political treatise and the first published response to Burke's *Reflections on the Revolution in France* (1790), she argued that "there are rights which men inherit at their birth, as rational creatures."[27] These rights were not received, as Burke would have it, from their "forefathers" but rather from "God."[28] God made humans different from "the brute creation" in that humans had "improvable faculties."[29] In order to improve their human faculties, such as reason, children had to exercise certain fundamental rights. Wollstonecraft thus established that rights are grounded in the moral status of humans as rational creatures of God, who raised them above the brute creation through their improvable faculties. This implied that humans have rights but not nonhuman animals, and reason (and, antecedently, God's endowment of humans with reason) accounts for this difference in moral status.

In the *Rights of Men*, Wollstonecraft specified two fundamental children's rights and strongly implied their correlative parental duties:

> It is necessary emphatically to repeat, that there are rights which men inherit at their birth, as rational creatures, who were raised above the brute creation by their improvable faculties; and that, in receiving these, not from their forefathers but, from God, prescription can never undermine natural rights. A father may dissipate his property without his child having any right to complain; — but should he attempt to sell him for a slave, or fetter him with laws contrary to reason; nature, in enabling him to discern good from evil, teaches him to break the ignoble chain, and not to believe that bread becomes flesh, and wine blood, because his parents swallowed the Eucharist with this blind persuasion.[30]

According to this initial formulation of Wollstonecraft's theory of children's rights, children have a "right to complain" when their "fathers" (1) try to sell them into "slavery" or (2) "fetter" them with irrational laws, such as religious rules or beliefs that are rationally unjustifiable.[31] She strongly implied that these two rights are derived from a fundamental set of parental/adult obligations: Duty 1 is to not abuse children in general, and Duty 2 is to provide basic care and education to their own children that allows for their rational development as humans. By "own children," I mean children under the direct parental supervision and care of a particular adult or a particular set of adults. In contemporary terms, this could mean biological, adoptive, foster, step, or institutional (e.g., orphanage-based) parenting. Although the terms were in some cases different, Wollstonecraft was familiar with these various forms of parenting and indeed was a foster parent to her ward, Ann, before she parented her biological daughters, Fanny and Mary. [32]

In Chapters 10 and 11 of the *Rights of Woman*, Wollstonecraft more fully developed her definition and justification of the adult duties that corresponded to children's rights to (1) freedom from abuse and (2) freedom from irrational education. Chapter 10 ("Parental Affection") set forth a scathing critique of child abuse as a prelude to arguing for the adult duty to refrain from abuse of children (Duty 1). Chapter 11 ("Duty to Parents") defended the duty of parents to care for and rationally educate their own children (Duty 2) as a prelude to explicating the reciprocal duty of adult children to care for their parents in their old age and a related parental right to friendship with their adult children.

Comparing Wollstonecraft with Onora O'Neill's Kantian Theory of Children's Rights

It is illuminating to apply Onora O'Neill's contemporary Kantian typology of obligations that correspond to children's rights to Wollstonecraft's schema. According to O'Neill's now-classic typology, a *universal* duty is an obligation that is owed to each and every person. Universal obligations are *perfect* or "complete" in the sense that they specify not only who owes the obligation but also to whom the obligation is owed. A *fundamental* duty is an obligation that is neither derived from any more basic moral claim nor contingent upon broader circumstances or prior commitments. In O'Neill's strict Kantian moral view, only perfect, universal, and fundamental obligations to children beget universal and fundamental rights for children.[33]

Looking at Wollstonecraft's schema of adult duties and children's rights through the lens of O'Neill's typology of obligations, Duty 1 is clearly perfect, universal, and fundamental in the sense that adults must refrain from abuse of children in general, not solely their own children. Duty 1 therefore begets a universal and fundamental right to be free from abuse for each and every child, which obtains independently of the particular social situation of any child. On the other hand, O'Neill would categorize Duty 2 as perfect but not universal and fundamental in the sense that only parents have the duty to provide a rational education to their own children. Duty 2 would thus seem to beget a *special*—not universal and fundamental—children's right to parental care and rational education, which is dependent upon a particular set of family relationships.[34]

In contrast to O'Neill's narrow, Kantian interpretation of Duty 2 as begetting a special but not universal and fundamental right of children, Wollstonecraft theorized Duty 2 as begetting a universal and fundamental right to parental care and rational education. It is universal in the sense that all children are entitled to care and rational education from their parents or parental figures, even though not all adults are responsible for providing these rights to children in any given context. It is fundamental in the sense that this right obtains independently of children's particular social contexts. Because of the differences in development between children and adults, as well as the fundamental dependency of children on parental figures (biological, adoptive, step, foster, or institutional), there cannot be a neat symmetry between the scope of parental duties and children's rights in the way we typically conceptualize the correlative rights and duties of adults. Parental duties to their own children are by definition narrower and deeper than the universal adult duty to refrain from abuse of children, whereas children's rights to parental care and rational education have the same universal reach and fundamental basis as children's rights to be free from abuse. However, the asymmetrical scope of parental duties and children's rights does not mean that children's rights to parental care and rational education are not fundamental in theory with respect to their humanity, even as they are specific in practice to particular parent-child relationship(s).

Hence Wollstonecraft established in her *Rights of Men* and elaborated in her *Rights of Woman* two categories of universal and fundamental rights for children—the *generic right* to be free from abuse (begot from perfect Duty 1) and the *specific right* to be cared for and rationally educated by parents or parental figures (begot from perfect Duty 2)—because she had justified children's absolute possession of these rights on the basis of their moral status as rational creatures of God. Wollstonecraft's metaphysical/ethical conception of the human being thus emerges as an essential feature of her expansive theory of children's rights. Although O'Neill shares Wollstonecraft's deontological, duty-based approach to justifying rights for children, the former is not able to defend as broad a scope of rights for children as the latter as a result of taking a nonmetaphysical approach to ethics. Children's right to parental care and rational education cannot be fundamental for O'Neill because it derives from the duty of specific parents to specific children, understood as constructed within their relationship in a particular social context.

For Wollstonecraft, children's right to parental care and rational education is fundamental because it is justified by her metaphysical conception of the human being first and foremost and, secondarily, in relation to particular relationships of dependency. Because all adults were once children dependent upon adults' benevolence and care for their rational development as humans, children's rights—whether the generic right to be free from abuse or the specific right to parental care and rational education—are for Wollstonecraft the most fundamental type of human rights. Despite its supplementary role in her broader metaphysical theory of rights, this empirical view of children—that is, as dependent on adult care for their very development into adults—furnishes a nontheological and nonmetaphysical reason for accepting her inclusion of children within her broader theory of human rights.

In Chapter 11 of the *Rights of Woman*, Wollstonecraft built on the *Rights of Men*'s commitment to defending the universal human rights of the poor, oppressed, and enslaved but placed even greater emphasis on the human rights of girls and women as a group oppressed by patriarchy. She again compared children to slaves, claiming, "A slavish bondage to parents cramps every faculty of the mind," but underscored that "females, it is true, in all countries, are too much under the dominion of their parents."[35] She also elaborated her earlier theory of the fundamental and universal rights of children that derived from the specific duty of parents to care for and rationally educate them (Duty 2). From observation of her own family's misfortunes alone, Wollstonecraft was poignantly aware of the problem of sexual discrimination within families when primogeniture governed the passage of property to the eldest son at the expense of the other children.

Chapter 4 of the *Rights of Woman* proposed an alternative, egalitarian model of the rights of children with respect to siblings. In contrast to Locke's privileging of the favorite son, as we saw in Chapter 1, Wollstonecraft insisted that children in the same family have an "equal right to" (1) a rational education that enables them to become independent adults and (2) their parents' provision of their material needs during the time of their dependency on them.[36] Parents have a specific and perfect obligation to supply these rights equally to their children because their children are humans, made in God's rational image, who each need their educational and material needs met for their development as humans. Boys are not more deserving of education or development than girls because their rational capabilities are roughly the same. Eldest sons, by the same argument, do not deserve preferential treatment but rather ought to be treated the same as their siblings with respect to these two family-related yet fundamental and universal rights to equal parental provision of education (Duty 2a) and material needs for development (Duty 2b).[37]

In an extended case study unveiled in Chapter 4 of the *Rights of Woman*,

Wollstonecraft dramatized the injustices that arose from the differential parental treatment of girls and boys with regard to these fundamental and universal rights to education and material means of development.[38] Girls who are denied a rational education do not grow up to be independent and often find themselves dependent upon both the reason and the property of their older brothers. When the brother married, the wife often forced her sister-in-law out of the house due to jealousy—a scenario also explored in Jane Austen's novel *Sense and Sensibility* (1811). Wollstonecraft made the insightful point that these two women were more similar than different in terms of their moral psychology. Neither woman had learned to respect herself or others through the exercise of reason. If the wife had done so, she would have had the moral capability to love her husband for his virtues, including his generosity toward his sister. If the sister had done so, she would have had the moral capability to be independent, thus rendering unnecessary either expulsion or support.

Such consequentialist arguments in favor of extending equal rights to siblings of the same families do not override Wollstonecraft's deontological justification for equal human rights. Rather, these consequentialist arguments supplement and reinforce, as well as enhance, the rhetorical persuasiveness of her basic deontological and metaphysical argument for human rights as derived from duties grounded in the rational moral law of God. If parents do not fulfill their duties by providing equal rights to their children, she warns us, there will be bad consequences for society. But those bad consequences are not the reason why children have rights in the first place. Children have rights because they are rational creatures of God. Wollstonecraft's metaphysical/ethical conception of the human being is the normative standard or orientation point by which children's rights are justified in an absolute sense. From this moral standpoint, the bad consequences of children's lack of provision of basic and equal rights within the family are merely symptoms of the deeper problem of parental failure to fulfill their perfect obligations.

Parsing Children's Rights and Adult Duties: Wollstonecraft Versus O'Neill on Perfect and Imperfect Obligations

In her typology of obligations, O'Neill went on to distinguish between perfect and imperfect obligations. "Perfect" obligations are those like the *Rights of Men*'s definition of Duty 1 (to not enslave or otherwise abuse children) and Duty 2 (to provide care and rational education to one's own children): they specify "completely or perfectly not merely who is bound by the obligation but to whom the obligation is owed."[39] Conversely, O'Neill defined "imperfect" obligations as those that do not specify to whom they ought to be fulfilled, even though the obligation is fundamental. Her example was the duty of adults to care for children in general, regardless of family relationship. This nonparental duty to care for children is generic without being universal; while one person in practice cannot possibly owe it to all children, the obligation is nonetheless binding to each and every adult. Because it is generic, it cannot be owed merely to particular children either. In the abstract, the question of how to perform such a duty is ambiguous at best. Because the imperfect obligation cannot be discharged outside of the directives of a particular social context, it cannot beget a right without the aid of positive law or institutions that specify the right's content and help to enforce its provision. In other words, it is difficult if not impossible to know how to fulfill successfully one's obligation to care for children in general without the prescription of law or other institutions.

O'Neill goes still further in provocatively concluding that children do not have a universal and fundamental right to care from adults in general. This conclusion poses a moral dilemma: if adults have an imperfect duty to care for children in general, without children having a corresponding right to such care, then why should adults discharge this duty without some internal or external compulsion? This imperfect obligation appears to be so weak as to be contingent on either one's personality or prescribed norms. It seems unlikely that it would ever be discharged without the artifice of society and law imposing it upon us. In this light, the ambiguity and contingency of the imperfect obligation of nonparental care for children seems to undermine the project of theorizing children's rights as universal moral absolutes.

Wollstonecraft's philosophy of children's rights is instructive for resolving this dilemma born of O'Neill's distinction between perfect and imperfect obligations toward children. According to both O'Neill and Wollstonecraft's deontological ethics, all rights derive from duties, but not all duties entail rights. Chapter 11 of the *Rights of Woman* puts forward a simple and clear formulation of the first part of this moral principle: "a right always includes a duty." She then "inferred" the second part of the principle: "they forfeit the rights, who do not fulfill the duty."[40] Her example was parents who failed in the performance of their perfect duty to rationally educate their children: they consequently forfeited their right to direct the education of their children. Implied was the converse point: all parents had a duty to care for and rationally educate their own children, but this duty did not entail a right or "privilege" to warp the minds of their children as a result of their "indolence" as parents.[41] In terms of their understanding of the deontological basis of rights, O'Neill and Wollstonecraft are in complete agreement.

Due to her metaphysical approach to ethics, however, Wollstonecraft diverges from O'Neill in her view of imperfect obligations. Wollstonecraft does not conceive of imperfect obligations as practically infeasible or as infertile ground for corresponding rights. From Wollstonecraft's metaphysical/ethical standpoint, the imperfect obligation of adults to care for children applies to all children in the abstract, even if in practice it is difficult, if not impossible, for the duty to have this sort of reach. This imperfect adult duty to care for children in general might be conceived as a positive corollary of Duty 1, to refrain from the abuse of children in general—as such, we might call it Duty 1a.

In the *Rights of Woman*, Wollstonecraft gave an example of how this imperfect duty to care for children in general should play out in practice. Because "women" and their "husbands" in her time had not been trained to "take that reasonable care of a child's body, which is necessary to lay the foundation for a good constitution," it was necessary for "public schools" to teach girls "the elements of anatomy and medicine" so that if they became mothers ("the first instructor(s)" to children), they would be "rational nurses to their infants."[42] Here, Duty 1a is held by society as a whole: it is the obligation of the people to support the education of women in medicine, so that mothers as the "first instructor(s)" of infants are prepared to give children the bodily care they need to grow and develop well. Because Wollstonecraft argued that schools ought to be coeducational, this argument ultimately applies as much to the ideal medical education of boys and men as to girls and women. All men and women ought to be educated in a way that enables them to take "reasonable care" of any child's basic physical and medical needs, should they be posed with fulfilling that imperfect duty. Even if they never have children of their own, such medically trained women and men would provide children in general a kind of social safety net: children would be surrounded by adults who had the capability to take "reasonable care" of them, if for any reason their parents were unavailable or unfit to do so.

As conceived from the God's-eye point of view, such an imperfect duty to care for children applies universally and may eventually be applied in law in a general way (say, through the establishment of public coeducational education, including but not restricted to medicine). This is the key difference between Wollstonecraft and O'Neill, as well as between Wollstonecraft and Kant: Wollstonecraft conceived of imperfect duties to children as universally applicable to adults (and therefore generating fundamental and universal human rights for children) when such imperfect duties are considered from the God's-eye point of view. Neither Kant nor O'Neill assume this theologically informed metaphysical/ethical perspective due to their commitments to different forms of constructivism. Because of his constructivist account of how the human mind shapes its rational understanding of reality and morality without reference to the noumenal realm (which includes the fundamentally incomprehensible God's-eye point of view), Kant's strong distinction between perfect duties (those that must be performed and admit of no exception) and imperfect duties (those that admit of exception and whose performance must be judged case-by-case) is actually far closer to O'Neill than to Wollstonecraft, despite his other similarities with his philosophical contemporary.[43]

Because her capacious metaphysical perspective accommodates it, Wollstonecraft conceptualizes the imperfect duties of adults as begetting fundamental and universal rights for children. In addition, all children's rights—even if imperfectly specified or implemented—have a fundamental (not secondary or contingent) moral status. Despite being derived from duties, children's rights are moral absolutes that are ultimately rooted in a metaphysical/ethical conception of the human being. In other words, the foundation of her conception of children's rights is her conception of the moral status of children as human creatures made in the image of their rational God.

The Wollstonecraftian Cascade of Duties and Rights Concerning Children

The process of parsing the duties of adults and parents toward children led Wollstonecraft to construct a multilevel philosophical cascade of duties and rights concerning various forms of adult-child and parent-child relationships. We have seen how Wollstonecraft teased out the meanings of Duty 1 (not to abuse children) and Duty 2 (parental care and education) and their correlative rights for children over the course of the *Rights of Woman*. In Chapter 11 of the *Rights of Woman*, Wollstonecraft further elaborated her conception of Duty 2 (parental care and rational education) by looking at its long-term implications for the parent-child relationship.

Wollstonecraft argued that there is a "reciprocal duty" of parents and children to care for one another in their respective stages of dependency.[44] Like Locke, she claimed that minors have an obligation to respect and honor their parents if and only if their parents have cared for them and educated them in their dependency. Like Locke, she believed that adults forfeited their status as parents and the legitimate authority associated with it when they failed to provide such care and education for their children.

Unlike Locke, Wollstonecraft absolved adult children of the obligation to respect and honor their parents merely because they gave life-sustaining care and education to them, for "to subjugate a rational being to the mere will of another, after he is of age to answer to society for his own conduct, is a most undue stretch of power."[45] Moving far beyond Locke, she called attention to the problem of parental abuse of children and subsequently absolved victims of any residual duty to respect, honor, obey, or care for the perpetrators even if they had once received care or education from them.[46] Yet Wollstonecraft did not go so far to suggest that abused and neglected children retained a right to the experience of love that they were denied by their parents—a point that Shelley's Creature would make with force to his own derelict father.

Reiterating a claim made in the *Rights of Men*, Chapters 10 and 11 of the *Rights of Woman* contended it was both cruel and unjust to subject a child to irrational rules (such as unjustifiable religious teachings) as a means for establishing parental authority. Such exercise of parental tyranny is "injurious to morality as those religious systems which do not allow right and wrong to have any existence, but in the Divine will."[47] For Wollstonecraft, reason was the basis for morality, not human or divine will. Against voluntarists who posited God's will as the basis of morality, she understood God as following His rational nature in dictating the content of morality and obeying those moral rules Himself. By analogy, the mere will of parents to be served by their children was not a justification for their parental authority or their use of irrational religious ideas to garner such authority. Authoritarian parents of this sort used "parental affection" as a "pretext to tyrannize."[48] For Wollstonecraft, such oppressive parental relationships with children are by definition "brutal" and abusive and therefore as illegitimate as chattel slavery.[49] By contrast, a justified parental authority—one that is benevolent, limited, and temporary—can only be achieved by following the rational moral law in fulfilling their children's rights.

Wollstonecraft challenged Locke's (residually absolutist) notion of a persistent duty of children to give "respect, honour, gratitude, assistance, and support" to their parents even into adulthood.[50] She instead posited an egalitarian "reciprocal duty" for mutual care, shared to different degrees between parents and children over the course of their overlapping life cycles.[51] Initially, children have no responsibility for care because they are incapable of it in their "helpless infancy," but once they have grown up and their parents are needy of care in the "feebleness of age," then the adult child has an obligation to provide "the same attention." Moreover, Wollstonecraft conceptualized this obligation as begetting a parental "right" to elder care by the children they had nurtured.[52]

Thus, Wollstonecraft elucidated an intergenerational cascade of duties as producing a correspondent series of rights. First, Duty 1 begets the correlative right of children to not be abused. Duty 1 is the primary condition for the practice of other duties toward children (such as imperfect Duty 1a, to care for children in general) and children's corresponding rights (such as to public education). Second, Duty 2 begets the correlative right of children for parental care and rational education. Third, the fulfillment of Duty 2 entails the second-generation duty of adult children to care for their elderly parents (Duty 3). Fourth, Duty 3 begets the correlative right of parents for elder care by their adult children (see Table 1).

Later in Chapter 11 of the *Rights of Woman*, Wollstonecraft distinguished between "the natural and the accidental duty due to parents."[53] On one hand, she acknowledged that children's "instinctive natural affection" for parents can generate a sense of obligation toward them in their old age. On the other hand, this obligation is far stronger if the bond between parent and child is due to the rational education provided by the parent. Wollstonecraft calls such an education an expression of "the parental affection of humanity," which "leaves instinctive natural affection far behind."[54] Thus, she counterintuitively reframed "natural" affection as weak and merely instinctive and "accidental" affection as strong, deliberate, and truly humane.

Similarly to the generation of the right of parents to elder care, the "accidental duty due to parents" (Duty 3) begets the right of parents to friendship with their adult children. Duty 3 is the duty to care for one's elderly parents (if and only if they had cared for one in one's dependency). This duty, in turn, begets "all the rights of the most sacred friendship" for parents with their adult children.[55] Unlike Locke, who would have adult children "respect" and "honour" their parents simply on the basis of their antecedent provision of "life and education" by them, Wollstonecraft drops the adult duty to *honor* parents and instead gives the enduring duty of *respect* for parents both a narrower construction and a deeper foundation.[56] On her model, an adult child has a duty to take "advice" from a parent under "serious consideration" only when a "sacred friendship" born of "the parental affection of humanity" abides between them.[57] We might call this Duty 3a.

Again, a cascade of duties toward children generates a series of parental rights: the provision of rational care and education for one's children (Duties 2, 2a, and 2b) ultimately begets "all the rights of the most sacred friendship," which include having one's parental advice taken seriously even in one's old age and dependency (see Table 1). Interestingly, Wollstonecraft's theory of children's rights to care, education, and provision of basic means for development leads her to theorize a new set of parents' rights. Rather than irrationally and immorally asserting a right to tyrannize their offspring, parents rationally earn a right to be genuine friends with their grown children.

Table 1. The Wollstonecraftian Cascade of Duties and Rights Concerning Children

Wollstonecraft's Rank-Ordered Derivation of Duties and Rights	*Fundamental Duty*	*Correlative Right*
Duty 1	Not to abuse children in general	Not to be abused by adults
Duty 1a	To care for children in general	To receive care from adults (including public education)
Duty 2	To care for and rationally educate your own children	To receive care and rational education from parents
Duty 2a	To equally care for and rationally educate your own children, without discrimination among siblings	To receive equal care and rational education from your parents as do your siblings
Duty 2b	To equally provide the material means of development among your own children, without discrimination among siblings	To receive equal means of development from your parents as do your siblings
Duty 3	To care for your elderly parents if and only if they cared for you when you were dependent on them	To enjoy friendship with your adult children and be freely cared for by them in your old age
Duty 3a	To listen to your parents' advice as you would a friend	To give advice to your adult children as you would a friend

Wollstonecraft's Transformation of Natural Rights Language and Its Implications for the Parent-Child Relationship

Wollstonecraft transformed the meaning of the language of natural rights by underscoring how the "rights of humanity" had to be defined in relation to other humans and their shared social contexts.[58] At first glance, her account of rights as defined in terms of relationships and social contexts might not seem too distant from the "social construction" of rights that O'Neill advocates.[59] However, Wollstonecraft differs from such constructivists in that she grounds all of her arguments for rights upon a metaphysical-ethical view of the human being. Hence, while even "natural rights" are defined according to relationships and in social contexts for Wollstonecraft, they are justified by way of her theological conception of the human being as a rational, improvable, and social creature.

A letter to her common-law husband, Gilbert Imlay, in January 1794 provides a fascinating and deeply personal case of Wollstonecraft's philosophical transformation of natural rights language. To Gilbert, she confided her feelings about her pregnancy with their soon-to-be-born daughter, Fanny: "Considering the care and anxiety a woman must have about a child before it comes into the world, it seems to me, by a *natural right*, to belong to her. When men get immersed in the world, they seem to lose all sensations, excepting those necessary to continue or produce life! — Are these the privileges of reason? Amongst the feathered race, whilst the hen keeps the young warm, her mate stays by to cheer her; but it is sufficient for man to condescend to get a child, in order to claim it. — A man is a tyrant!"[60] As Virginia Sapiro perceptively noted, this passage stands out in Wollstonecraft's corpus because it claims a mother's "natural right" to a relationship with her biological children.[61] By contrast, in her *Rights of Woman*, she had followed Locke in establishing parental care, not the biological acts of begetting, gestating, or birthing a child, as the basis for legitimate parental authority.[62]

In this light, it might seem that Wollstonecraft's 1794 letter to Imlay contradicted her earlier view that parental rights are "accidental" (based on rational and deliberate practices of care and affection toward children), not "natural" (based on biological relationships with children). However, it is more accurate to understand Wollstonecraft as applying her broader concept of "accidental" parental care and affection to the specific case of women in pregnancy. If the mother shows "care and anxiety" for the unborn child, then she develops through the application of her reason an "accidental" and therefore stronger set of duties and rights with regard to the child. Showing care for the child in pregnancy is the rational performance of a duty to provide for the dependent child. But this relationship is not merely biological or instinctual. Many women do not show care and anxiety for their unborn children.

Those pregnant women who deliberately apply their reason to deduce this obligation to care for the unborn begin at the earliest opportunity to fulfill Duty 2. They establish an early foundation for the correspondent right to become friends with their adult children. Thus, this letter's transformative use of the language of natural rights actually reinforces her earlier view of the "accidental" or rational, deliberate, and relational basis for legitimate parental authority. Wollstonecraft was consistent in conceptualizing a mother's "natural right" to feel a sense of belonging toward a baby as an accident of the caring relationship of the mother toward the child in pregnancy. In so doing, she effectively downplayed the moral significance of the biological aspects of mother-child relationships and instead underscored the moral importance of their relational, deliberate, and rational aspects.

Wollstonecraft's January 1794 letter to Imlay reflected her own anxiety about her absent husband's lack of involvement in her pregnancy. Indeed, he was unfaithful to her and abandoned her soon after their child was born. This personal subtext pushed her to develop a corollary to her conception of the "natural right" of biological mothers by applying her reasoning to the case of biological fathers. If the father does not fulfill his duty to care for the pregnant mother as well as their unborn child, he has no "natural right" to the child. His rights are merely the arbitrary product of patriarchal law, which unfortunately was the governing law of the time.

Wollstonecraft used a satirical contrast between chickens and humans to reinforce her point that "natural" human rights are ultimately relational or social rights. Roosters care for hens while they are warming their eggs and therefore establish a relationship with the chicks even before they are hatched. By contrast, men often tyrannically assert a right to control a child that they fathered without caring for the pregnant mother or their unborn offspring. Wollstonecraft curtly implied that Imlay should follow the example of the rooster if he expected to have a relationship with their unborn child. Unfortunately, he did not seem to want such a relationship and effectively gave up any right to conduct the care and education of the child by abandoning both her and her mother. As a result, Wollstonecraft was left to raise Fanny alone but with the moral certainty that her parental authority was legitimate because it arose from the "care and anxiety" she had shown the baby since her earliest months of growth in the womb.

Wollstonecraft made a similar point about the deliberate, rational, and relational basis for parental duties and children's rights in her posthumously published novel, *Maria: or, the Wrongs of Woman* (1798). The character of Jemima is a poor servant who works as a jailor in an asylum where Maria is kept against her will by her abusive husband. The two women bond by telling each other their personal stories of oppression at the hands of men. Jemima reveals that her mother died soon after her birth, but the loss of her biological mother was nowhere near as devastating as the lack of a caring nurse: "The chicken has a wing to shelter under, but I had no bosom to nestle in, no kindred warmth to foster me. Left in dirt, to cry with cold and hunger til I was weary, and sleep without ever being prepared for exercise, or lulled by kindness to rest; could I be expected to become any thing but a weak and rickety babe?" So neglected by "the cheapest nurse my father could find," Jemima grew up "to learn to curse existence."[63] Had the nurse enacted her duty to care for and educate Jemima, she would have fulfilled the duties of a mother. Jemima's story implies that children have a right not be to neglected and abused (derived from Duty 1) as well as a right to parental care and rational education (derived from Duty 2 and its corollaries 2a and 2b). What matters most for the child's development and positive sense of self is the actual provision of this parental care and rational education, not whether the relationship of the caregiver to the child is biological or not.

The Indivisibility of (Children's) Human Rights and Its Implications for Their Legal Institutionalization as Civil and Political Rights

Contemporary international children's human rights law conceptualizes children's rights in particular and human rights in general as indivisible. The 1989 United Nations' Convention on the Rights of the Child (CRC) is the immediate political source for this concept of indivisibility. By "indivisible," it meant the overlapping, interdependent, and mutually reinforcing relationships between the numerous rights of children it legislated for member nations.[64] Because of these relationships, any particular rights of children cannot be effectively guaranteed unless they are protected and encouraged as a set. Moreover, children's rights must be treated as a subset of universal human rights. Because all adults were once children, the failure to secure their rights as children has pernicious effects upon the protection and realization of human rights over the whole life cycle and across generations.

As Tristan McCowan has argued, education is a paradigmatic illustration of the indivisible nature of children's (and other human) rights. If children are denied education at any stage of youth, then they may fail to develop their basic human capabilities (or what Wollstonecraft called "improvable faculties"). This lack of education can lead to other deprivations: lack of skills for either personal independence or familial support, lack of economic opportunity, lack of access to necessary health care and medical knowledge for sustaining oneself and one's family, and lack of political participation and influence.

In his *Development as Freedom* (1999), Amartya Sen gave a powerful empirical example of how the denial of the right to education even to a single group can have exponentially negative effects on broader populations. When girls in his native India were denied education, they were more likely to marry at a young age and have increased fertility, thereby causing population pressure; exacerbating poverty, disease, and premature death; and reinforcing dangerous gender norms that discriminated against girls' right to education in the first place.[65] The indivisibility of children's (human) rights thus requires that their implementation in law and policy be as even and as interconnected as possible.

About two centuries earlier than the CRC, Wollstonecraft's theory of the legal implementation of children's rights began with this premise of indivisibility. She also highlighted the central place of education in securing other human rights. Similarly to McCowan and other contemporary philosophers of education, she conceptualized education not only as a fundamental and universal right of children but also as a "conduit" for other rights.[66] In particular, she theorized that if the moral or human right to education was institutionalized as a civil right for all children, then it would more effectively serve as a "conduit" for the realization of other vital citizenship rights.

Most important, education would enable adult citizens to develop their "improvable faculties" such that they were capable of exercising civil and political rights to public speech, civic association, voting, and office holding in modern republican (representative democratic) governments. Moreover, the formative experience of receiving an equal right to education not only in the family but also in free, public, coeducational schools would acculturate people to respect the equal rights of citizens in other spheres of society and politics. These egalitarian conditions within familial and formal education enabled egalitarian citizenship, in the broadest sense, both in and beyond families and schools.

Some contemporary democratic theorists of children's rights, such as

Andrew Rehfeld, have argued that children ought to have a legal right to vote as early as it is practical for them to formally participate in politics. Rehfeld's proposal is to gradually and fractionally increase the voting power of children from the age of twelve through the legal age of majority. This gradual progression to full voting influence would teach adolescents the rules of formal participation in politics, instill in them a sense of the value of participation even when one's say in any given vote is small, and, most crucially, make the political system more democratic overall.[67]

Wollstonecraft, by contrast, never advocated for children's (even adolescents') inclusion in formal political rights, fractional or otherwise. She rather advocated an alternative gradualist model for provision of children's civil and political rights, whereby children *grew into* the exercise of citizenship rights with the guidance of parents and teachers. She conceived children's exercise of the civil right to education, in public schools for ages five to eighteen, as a conduit for the later yet complete enjoyment of the full slate of civil and political rights as full citizens in a modern representative democracy.

A striking philosophical predecessor to Amy Gutmann, Wollstonecraft envisioned public schools as sites for sustained democratic and egalitarian value formation.[68] In her ideal classroom, the Socratic method would be used to encourage children to participate in vigorous discussion with their teachers and peers on civic-oriented subjects, such as history and politics. While children could not vote, they could rationally deliberate on political issues in school and gain valuable skills for formal political participation, broadly understood. The coeducational, free, mandatory format of her ideal day school also meant that children would be raised to appreciate the equal capabilities of the different sexes, races, and classes at least in school if not at home.[69]

The moral and social comprehensiveness of Wollstonecraft's schooling for citizenship would authorize children's complete adoption of citizenship rights at the age of majority (eighteen), without any formal introduction to such rights as adolescents. From Rehfeld's perspective, Wollstonecraft's gradualist model for the inclusion of children in citizenship would be less formally democratic than one with his fractional voting scheme for adolescents. However, it could potentially be more informally democratic in the sense that children and adolescents would be encouraged to actively practice the deeper values of egalitarian citizenship and to understand the right to public schooling as the most fundamental of their civil rights.

While Wollstonecraft theorized the causal relationship between children's civil right to public education and their later practice of full and equal citizenship rights as adults, she conversely theorized the causal relationship between adults' equal access to civil rights (especially child custody, property ownership, and divorce) and the realization of the full slate of children's rights in law and policy. In her last major work, the unfinished novel *Maria*, she depicted the heroine as fleeing her abusive husband. Her husband's attorney threatens to seize her property, which she had inherited from an uncle and, worse, assert paternal custody over their infant child.[70] Under coverture, married women were "reduced to a mere cypher" in the eyes of the law because they had no independent legal identity from their husbands.[71] In the case of a marital separation like Maria's, the wife found herself in an absurdly powerless position: she could not effectively defend her rights or those of her children because the court assumed her husband represented both her interests and those of the whole family.

When Maria goes to court, she claims before the judge that an equal right to divorce is necessary for women to fulfill their duties toward their children. Maria's courtroom speech was unrealistic in terms of late eighteenth-century British legal protocols, but it underscored Wollstonecraft's political reason for writing one of the first feminist novels. In the case of a bad marriage like Maria's, a wife often had to abandon her property (losing her material means of caring for her children) as well as forfeit custody over her children (losing at least her role as caregiver and, in extreme cases of paternal neglect, losing the assurance of care for her children altogether). Maria dramatically pleads for a right to divorce from a violent and adulterous drunk for the sake of ensuring her provision of her child's fundamental rights to parental care and rational education: "If I am unfortunately united to an unprincipled man, am I for ever to be shut out from fulfilling the duties of a wife and mother?"[72] The indivisibility of women's rights and children's rights becomes clear through Maria's tragically realistic story of estrangement from her child, which sadly reflected the actual lives of many of the women Wollstonecraft knew. The trials of these women and children teach us that human rights must be treated as an interdependent and intergenerational set in order for the moral rights of vulnerable or disadvantaged groups to be fully realized as legal rights.

The story of Maria brings full circle Wollstonecraft's philosophy of children's rights, reminding us of its original principles. All children have fundamental rights to parental care and rational (not tyrannical) education because all adults have the duty not to abuse or otherwise tyrannize children (Duty 1), and all parents and parental figures have the duty to care for and rationally educate their own children (Duty 2). If society and law do not support the rights of women, then women may not be able to fulfill their duties to their children. Parental provision of children's most fundamental rights may be thwarted due to the broader political system's inequitable treatment of adults under the law. The latter point is also true with regard to children's inequitable treatment under the law. As we have seen with the story of Jemima, if children are born into conditions of poverty and other forms of social and economic discrimination, then they may never have parents or parental figures who provide them the basic care and education they need and deserve.

Chapter 12 of the *Rights of Woman* expanded this thesis to address the failure of states to equitably provide children's right to education. Even in cases when parents do not fail to fulfill their duties to their own children, a legitimate state had an obligation to provide education as an equal civil right to each and every child, regardless of gender, class, or other social status, between the ages of five and eighteen. In Wollstonecraft's vision of the ideal republic outlined in the dedication of the *Rights of Woman*, a representative democracy would only be truly legitimate if it used law and other formal political institutions to protect the rights of its whole people, including children and women.[73]

If Jemima had been born into such a legitimate state, then she would have at least found a safety net in school, which might have spared her from the tragedies that befell her while living in and working for abusive families. As she grew up, she might have grown into the exercise of her civil rights to freely work and hold property while attending school rather than resort to prostitution and theft due to poverty. Even if she were nonetheless born to abusive parents who failed to fulfill their fundamental duties to her, the state would have an obligation to nullify the parental rights of those abusers and remove her to the care of a new set of dutiful parental figures. From the age of five, she would have exercised a civil right to a public education that taught her and her peers the meaning of equal citizenship. By the time she was eighteen, Jemima would have been ready to accept the full slate of civil and political rights (and related duties) of an equal citizen of a modern democracy.

Wollstonecraft's theory of children's rights as indivisible from human rights is the most radical dimension of her political theory. No one prior to her had made such a systematic and comprehensive argument for universal human rights or the rights of children. It is her most dramatic and insightful yet unsung contribution to the history of political thought. Rather than marginalize children in her political theory, as the social contract thinkers had done, Wollstonecraft actively and overtly brought children from the margins to the center of politics. This may have been the most important lesson that Shelley took from reading her mother's work: children and their rights belong at the heart of any good political story.

Chapter 3 explains how Shelley took inspiration from her mother to author a new kind of novel—a speculative fiction, built around a series of five thought experiments, which approached the question of children's rights from a different angle. This different angle was the estranged perspective of Frankenstein's Creature. His tragic story of abandonment from birth has the power to provoke readers to wonder whether children have a basic right to not only parental care (as Wollstonecraft had argued) but also a deeper, even more fundamental, right to share love. By running *Frankenstein*'s five thought experiments on the rights of the child, the reader perceives that this right to share love would be ideally fulfilled with parents or, even more demandingly, with an intensively caring mother or, at the very minimum, a fitting substitute.

CHAPTER 3

Shelley's Thought Experiments on the Rights of the Child

In the Introduction, I made a preliminary case for understanding the narrative core of *Frankenstein* as a cascade of five thought experiments on the rights of the child. The very structure of the novel puts the reader in the position of an armchair philosopher.[1] Leaning back in the proverbial chair—mesmerized by the astounding tale of a male (and perhaps mad) scientist who artificially creates life with the parts of human and other animal corpses but without a biological mother—the reader runs the following set of thought experiments in her mind:

1. What if a man had sole parental responsibility for a child due to using science to create him without a biological mother?
2. What if the child was totally abandoned because the lone parent (and other people) did not love him due to fear and disgust of his hideous form?
3. What if the newborn child had the ability to survive on his own due to his eight-foot frame, extraordinary strength, and incredible capability for language acquisition and independent learning?
4. What if the child was not only abandoned and neglected by his parent but also hurt or abused by every human he encountered due to his monstrous appearance?
5. What if the neglected child claimed a fundamental right to share love with a sympathetic and equal female companion, thereby forcing his father-scientist to choose to either (a) make

> a female companion for his child (risking the development of a new species that could destroy the human race) or (b) suffer the angry revenge of his child who had become truly monstrous in behavior?

Despite its seemingly preposterous premise of a truly motherless child, this cascade of counterfactual scenarios yields some ideas with real-world relevance. Running the five thought experiments in sequence leads the reader to grapple with a series of moral and political questions: Do children have rights? If so, what are they? In what sense can children be said to have rights if they are denied provision or enjoyment of them? What is the relationship of children's rights, if any, to parental duties? Do all children have a right to love, to be provided in the first place by their parents? If so, are there any limits to this right to love?

Shelley's thought experiments do not always yield firm answers to these questions. This is partly because she did not write a treatise with a discrete thesis on children's and other human rights, as Chapter 2 has shown her mother's 1792 book, *A Vindication of the Rights of Woman*, to be (even the first of its kind). Shelley rather wrote a speculative fiction that could open the reader's mind to a range of ethical and political possibilities concerning the rights of the child.

Yet, like any well-designed thought experiment, each of the five counterfactual scenarios that constitute the core narrative of *Frankenstein* is structured to generate an illuminating conceptual distinction in the mind of the reader. When run in sequence, *Frankenstein*'s five thought experiments on the rights of the child form a cascade of concepts essential for thinking clearly and philosophically about the basis, scope, and content of children's rights. These conceptual distinctions highlight the differences between (1) *biological parenthood* and *mothering* (or the social practice of intensively caring and loving parenting), (2) the robust *parental duty to love one's own children* and the minimal *parental duty to care for one's own children* even in the absence of love, (3) children's *mere survival* without love and children's *thriving development* with it, (4) the *injustice of child abuse* and the *justice of extrafamilial care for children*, and (5) children's passive and consumptive *right to be loved* by parents or substitutes and children's active and relational *right to share love* with parents or substitutes. Born of *Frankenstein*'s five thought experiments, these conceptual distinctions encourage the reader to develop her own moral and political perspectives on the complex philosophical issues surrounding the idea of children's rights.

Negative Capability: Shelley's Literary Approach to the Question of Children's Rights

The reader will not find in *Frankenstein* a theory of children's rights in the sense that it is found in Mary Wollstonecraft's work or in contemporary philosophical thought on rights. First of all, the novel only furnishes one explicit demand for and definition of a right of the child: the Creature's plea to his father for the fulfillment of a "right" to "live in the interchange of those sympathies necessary for my being" or, as he rephrases it soon after, to experience "love of another" with someone to whom he is closely "attached."[2] To some degree, Shelley's novel implicitly relies upon distinctions concerning rights that her mother had made in her writings. But rather than simply accept her mother's terms, definitions, and arguments, she employed the Romantic-era poetic principle of "negative capability" to explore what these particular arguments—and arguments about rights in general—lacked.

It is an uncanny coincidence in British Romanticism that John Keats, the poet and friend of the Shelleys, had coined the term "negative capability" when *Frankenstein* was in press. In a private letter to his brothers in December 1817, Keats defined the term amid a reflection on the genius of Shakespeare and other great literary writers: "I mean *Negative Capability*, that is, when a man is capable of being in uncertainties, Mysteries, doubts, without any irritable reaching after fact & reason."[3] Shelley was likely not aware of Keats's formulation of this concept at the very time she was awaiting the publication of *Frankenstein*. She nonetheless shared his view that there was an intellectual, affective, and artistic virtue to dwelling upon what was dubious, missing, or strange because of the mental chaos it wrought and the creative thought it could spark. Shelley preferred the uncertainties of fiction to the certainties of philosophy. Strongly feeling the pull of the counterarguments against her political views, she could not commit to writing a treatise in straightforward defense of any one position.[4]

In the spirit of negative capability, Shelley dared to use literature to apprehend issues in their complexity, rather than seeking comfort in the certainties of logic, abstract argumentation, or dogmatism. As with great dramatists and novelists from William Shakespeare to Jane Austen, negative capability also allowed her to "negate" herself and create a story with characters so vivid that readers could sympathetically connect with their thoughts and feelings as if they were living their lives.[5] Applying this poetic principle of negative capability to the core narrative of *Frankenstein*, Shelley explored the question of children's rights from the strange and counterfactual case of the Creature—dwelling on the disturbing details of what he lacked, missed, and desired the most—to elicit sympathy from readers for this child's terrible experience of deprivation.

From reading the *Rights of Woman* at the time she wrote *Frankenstein*, Shelley learned of the distinction between the moral rights of humans (what Wollstonecraft called "the rights of humanity") and the legal rights of humans (what Wollstonecraft called "civil and political rights").[6] For Wollstonecraft, moral rights were justifiably demanded and held by people independently of what the law or the state prescribed on the matter. As with other republicans and abolitionists of the era, her paradigmatic example of a moral right was the right to be free from slavery: people legitimately demanded and exercised it even if the law or the state prescribed slavery as a norm, because slavery absolutely deprived people of the conditions for freedom necessary for a truly good and happy life.[7] Ultimately, Wollstonecraft's theory of rights focused on the prescription of familial, educational, cultural, and political reforms to bridge the gap between the moral and legal rights of humans, such that legal rights would eventually institutionalize only morally justified rights for each and every member of the (ideally republican) political community.

Paradoxically emboldened yet chastened by her sense of negative capability, Shelley took a different—not positive, direct, and didactic but negative, indirect, and unnerving—tack than her mother in addressing the question of children's rights. *Frankenstein*'s five thought experiments on the rights of the child push the reader to peer into the gap between moral and legal rights, not simply to bridge them but to gain a deeper, even vertiginous, perspective into what is most painfully missing as a result of this chasm. The Creature's counterfactual predicament—to be a motherless, loveless, stateless orphan who lacks even a niche in the ecosystem—trains the mind's eye on the seemingly insuperable divide between his complete, de facto lack of rights and his own profound sense of morally deserving—and therefore "having"—the fundamental right to love. By daring to peer into this abyss, the reader steals insight into what children most need and deserve from what they most lack and desire.

Following the Cascade: The Philosophical Framework for *Frankenstein*'s Five Thought Experiments

Before we enter Shelley's fictional laboratory to run her five thought experiments in depth, we need to equip ourselves with a toolkit of philosophical concepts and questions that informed her design of the cascade. As we have seen in Chapters 1 and 2, the architectural framework of *Frankenstein* is broader and deeper than the cascade of thought experiments that constitute its core narrative. When read against the background of its philosophical and literary sources, *Frankenstein* functions even more forcefully as a kind of mental incubator for radical moral and political ideas on children's rights and parental duties. By examining the contending influences of John Milton's *Paradise Lost* (1667) and Wollstonecraft's *Rights of Woman* on *Frankenstein*, we better understand the questions and concepts concerning love, friendship, and family that drive Shelley's five thought experiments on the rights of the child.

The work of Shelley's mother was particularly informative for writing a novel that provoked the questions of whether and, if so, in what sense children have rights. However, *Frankenstein*'s five thought experiments on the rights of the child push readers to consider questions that Wollstonecraft never explicitly entertained. Most strikingly, the twenty-one-month-old Creature's plea to his maker for the fulfillment of a "right" to "live in the interchange of those sympathies necessary for my being" suggests that something important is missing from the Wollstonecraftian typology of rights and duties concerning children (see Chapter 2, Table 1).[8] While Wollstonecraft emphasized the fundamental right of all children to parental care and rational (nontyrannical) education, Shelley suggested through the story and voice of the Creature that care and education are not sufficient, but in addition, *love* is necessary to generate the conditions for children's well-being. As part of his plea to his maker, the Creature argues that "love of another" is what he needs the most to overcome the "vices" of hatred and violence born of his lack of "ties" and "affection" and to instead practice the "virtues" of sympathy and peace.[9]

It is the Creature's demand of his father for the provision of the right to love that makes *Frankenstein* a vital and visionary text for philosophical thinking on children's rights. Children's *right to be loved*—or to passively receive and consume love from parents and parental figures—has been defended by the political philosopher S. Matthew Liao.[10] By contrast, children's *right to love*—or to actively share a loving relationship with parents or fitting substitutes—has been relatively undertheorized.

Although written in novel form, *Frankenstein* sheds philosophical insight into the value of conceptualizing children's right to love in active and relational, not merely passive and receptive, terms. Indeed, the Creature's claim for a parental duty to fulfill his "right" to share love with a sympathetic companion provides a plausible (and poetic) working definition of such relational "love":

to experience "love of another" is to live in the interchange of sympathy with someone else.[11] For a child, such a sympathetic companion is ideally a parent, whether biological or social, but if a parent is not available or fit to give and receive such love, then the parent (like Victor) still holds an obligation toward the child to arrange for a fitting and loving substitute.

By entertaining the question of who ought to be such a loving substitute for an unloving parent, *Frankenstein* spawns some subversive yet fertile ideas on how children should enjoy the right to love. The Creature requests his father to make such a substitute in the form of an "equal," a "female," and a "companion . . . of the same species" who is as "deformed and horrible" as he is in appearance.[12] The Creature projects that this equal female's similar deformity and resultant ostracization by humankind will make her capable of "living in the interchange" of "sympathies," "kindness," "affections," and "love" with him.[13]

Pushing his argument in an explicitly moral and political direction, the Creature argues that only the experience of "the love of another" will "destroy the cause of my crimes."[14] In a poignant allusion to his own plight as a motherless creature abandoned by his father-scientist, the Creature metaphorically construes his past "vices" as "children of a forced solitude." He hopefully contends that his future "virtues" will "necessarily arise" from living "in communion with an equal."[15] The purpose of the union of the Creature and the female, it seems, would not be actual children but rather a metaphorical and moral kind of children: the generation of the virtues of sympathy and love, mirrored between equals. The Creature insists that they would leave Europe for the "vast wilds of South America," where no "other human being would ever see us again."[16] There they would live in a truly "peaceful and human" manner as nonviolent, vegetarian gatherers of "acorns and berries," without even a hovel, hut, garden, or farm, leaving little imprint upon the natural state of the wilderness around them.[17]

At first glance, the Creature's proposal for an equal female companion might suggest that his right to love, in the absence of a loving parent, could only be fulfilled in a romantic or sexual relationship. This assumption invites the criticism that such a romantic relationship would have an incestuous quality either in terms of the child's projection of his desire for parental love upon a sexual partner or in terms of the partner's emotional exploitation of the child's desire for a parent. Yet a close analysis of the text clarifies that the Creature foresees this relationship as a nonparental equal and sympathetic friendship, not an incestuous relationship between a child and a parental substitute.

Running counter to Victor's later assumption that his child's relationship with the female would be sexual and reproductive, the Creature only suggests that it would be equal, sympathetic, peaceful, and loving and therefore virtuous. Although the Creature learns of "the difference of sexes; of the birth and growth of children," he never explicitly entertains the thought that he and the female would have sex or become parents.[18] Indeed, the Creature seems to want a friendship between equals of different sexes, not a marriage or sexual relationship of any sort. If it were a marriage, it would be a marriage designed to rid him of the vices born of his "forced solitude."

Between nine and twelve months of age, the Creature had read Milton's *Paradise Lost* while living alone and observing the DeLacey family from his hovel.[19] His conception of "communion with an equal" builds upon Milton's portrait of Adam, who felt lonely and thus asked God to make him a woman. The Creature anticipates his relationship with the female to be more like Adam and Eve's innocent companionship before the Fall rather than their sinful, sexual, and reproductive relationship after the dawn of sin.

But there are important differences between the Creature's and Milton's ideas of what an innocent companionship between man and woman could be. The Creature's vision of "communion with an equal" lacks the explicitly romantic (and implicitly sexual) aspect of the poet's representation of Adam and Eve's "nuptial bed." While "With flowers, garlands, and sweet-smelling herbs, / Espoused Eve decked first her nuptial bed," the Creature more simply imagines him and his equal female companion making "our bed of dried leaves."[20] The creatures' primitive bed would not be decked with flowers, symbols of fertility, but rather made with dead leaves, symbols of infertility. While Milton made Eve so sexually alluring that her own reflection enchanted her, the Creature imagined the making of a female partner so ugly that she could be a moral and virtue-inspiring companion to a "monster."

When she set up Thought Experiment 5—in which Victor deliberates upon the possible consequences of making or not making his Creature an equal female companion—Shelley likely had her mother's philosophy of friendship, marriage, and the family in mind as much as Milton's Adam and Eve. The *Rights of Woman* set forth extended defenses of the moral and political equality of siblings, spouses, and friends, regardless of sex.[21] Wollstonecraft had also argued for marriage as a kind of virtuous friendship between equals, distinguished by lifelong mutual "dignified affection" rather than merely sexual attraction or sexual reproduction.[22] For Wollstonecraft, spouses could and should be affectionate and sympathetic friends who were respectful of each other's moral equality, even when they ceased to have a sexual attraction or if they never had children.[23] She even used a feminist critique of Milton's emphasis upon Eve's sexual allure for Adam to support her alternative conception of marriage as ideally and primarily a friendship between moral equals.[24]

The Creature's claim for a "right" to live in the interchange of sympathy with an equal female companion may well be understood as a Wollstonecraftian demand for new and virtuous form of marriage in which women and men are equal, but sex and reproduction are not essential to their primarily moral relationship. In the voice of the Creature, however, Shelley put two distinctive twists on the Wollstonecraftian formulation of a "right" to an equal (fe)male companion—both of which underscore its moral ties to the prior parent-child relationship. First, the Creature's father-scientist must satisfy this "right" because he forsook his sole responsibility to provide intensive care and love to his own child. Second, this equal companionship serves as an emotional and moral substitute for the Creature's total lack of love from a parent-child relationship as a result of a worst-case scenario of child abandonment, neglect, and abuse.

In the impassioned, pathetic, yet powerful voice of the abandoned and lonely Creature, the novel ultimately raises two sets of broad yet profound moral questions concerning the basic ethics of parent-child relationships:

1. *Does one as a parent have a fundamental and universal duty to share love with one's own children? If one is or expects to become unavailable or unfit to give and receive such love, then should one arrange for one's own children to share love with another parent or other substitute?*
2. *Conversely, do children have a fundamental and universal right to share love with a parent? If a parent (of any sort) is neither available nor fit to give and receive such love, then do children have a right to share love with a substitute?*

These questions are fundamentally moral ones—as in, they concern the duties and rights of individuals with respect to one another—but they also have political implications:

1. *If parents and parental substitutes have a duty to love their own children, then should a political body have a role in the assignment of parental substitutes when parents fail to share love adequately with their own children?*

2. *If children's fundamental right to share love ought to be satisfied with a nonparental substitute if and only if a parent (or parental substitute) cannot fulfill this role, then should a political body have a role in the assignment of both parental and, if necessary, nonparental substitutes?*

Reading the story of the abandoned Creature provokes these sets of broad moral questions and their political corollaries. To nuance the questions and find answers to them, it is helpful to reverse the process. By conducting Shelley's five thought experiments on the rights of the child with these basic moral and political questions in mind, the reader can perceive more clearly the political background of the plight of the Creature or any child who is abandoned, neglected, or abused. The Creature's tragic political predicament as a stateless orphan is not solely due to his lack of a loving parent or substitute of any kind, his monstrous appearance, or his liminal relationship to the human species but also due to his lack of a state that recognizes him as a rights-bearing member of its community.

In considering Shelley's cascade of thought experiments in light of these basic moral and political questions, the reader uncovers even more specific and difficult questions to ask concerning the ethics of parent-child relationships. For instance, one can frame the seemingly preposterous premise of the whole novel—*making a motherless child through science*—with the second set of moral questions: Do children have a right to share love with a parent? Or at least a substitute? This pairing prompts an even more provocative thought: Do children have a right to love not simply with a parent but, more specifically, with a mother? If so, what defines a mother—a physiological or a social relationship to a child or perhaps some combination of the two? Does gender or sex determine motherhood, or is motherhood best understood independently of sex or gender? To concretize these questions by putting them in the terms of the plot of the novel: Could have and should have Victor Frankenstein been not merely a parent but, more important, a loving mother to the Creature he made without a woman?

Thought Experiment 1 sets up a counterfactual scenario in which Victor has total responsibility for his Creature due to using science to make him without a biological mother. In terms of contemporary medicine and biotechnology, this still has not been achieved: one cannot yet make a human life (or a close human relative) without an egg and a womb of at least one female plus sperm from a male. By removing any mother—genetic, biological, surrogate, social, or any combination thereof—from the process of bringing the Creature to life, the novel's first counterfactual scenario trains the mind's eye on the meaning of parental responsibility for *one's own* children. Given that Victor is the sole maker of the Creature, he would seem to have sole parental responsibility for him, at least initially. Victor cannot pass the buck, so to speak, by blaming another parent or, more specifically, a mother for the unexpected and undesired outcome of his experiment in creating human life. The Creature is his *own child* and his alone.

Over the course of the novel, the reader learns that Victor must take responsibility for his own child or suffer the moral and legal consequences of his initial failure to do so in Thought Experiment 2. In real life, of course, this would not hold true: both scientific knowledge of human biology and the current state of biotechnology entail that there is never solely one parent involved in the making of a human child.[25] Hence, parental responsibility must be initially understood in the plural, in terms of *their own* children. Even in the real-world case of a single mother who uses anonymous gamete donors, in vitro fertilization, and a surrogate for gestation, the question of parental responsibility must be sorted out through legal contracts and, sometimes, informal personal agreements before officially assigning the single mother sole parental responsibility for the child.[26]

By reducing the number of parents to one, Thought Experiment 1 simplifies the question of parental responsibility and thereby clarifies the meaning of the concept of *one's own* children, both in the counterfactual scenario of Victor Frankenstein as well as in real-world scenarios of initially plural parenthood. In either case, *one's own* children are those children for whom one has a primary responsibility. In the case of Victor Frankenstein, his sole responsibility for the Creature arises from using science to bring him to life without a biological mother.

Following the duty-based arguments for children's rights found in Wollstonecraft's *Rights of Woman*, Thought Experiments 1 through 4 explore the moral basis of children's right to love through the question of parental responsibility for one's own children. Like other children, the Creature did not ask to be made. As Milton's Adam pointedly—and poignantly—reminds God after the Fall, "Did I request thee, Maker, from my clay/ To mould me man? Did I solicit thee/ From darkness to promote me?" Shelley used this evocative verse from Book X of *Paradise Lost* as the epigraph on the title page of the first edition of *Frankenstein*.[27] Since they are products of circumstances beyond their control, the Creature and other children, like Adam, have no responsibility for their lives in the first place. Moreover, the youngest children in the real world are completely dependent on adults—especially parents—for the basic means of surviving and thriving. The most fundamental of these means is the experience of love. In the late twentieth and early twenty-first centuries, psychiatrists, psychologists, and anthropologists have documented that babies will often fail to thrive and even die without love—especially the intensive, life-affirming, life-protecting love of a parent or parents and, even more, a mother or maternal substitute.[28] Even if babies somehow muster the strength to survive without their parent(s), like the Creature does, children have neither responsibility for being brought to life nor even a duty to preserve their lives without the means to do so.[29]

Thought Experiments 3 and 4 vividly illustrate these reasons for children's right to share love with a parent or substitute by counterfactually separating the issue of *surviving* from the issue of *thriving*. Unlike newborns, infants, toddlers, and other young children, the Creature's "superhuman" size, strength, and intelligence allow him to physically survive his early years without a parent or parental figure.[30] Yet because his "hideous" appearance frightens off his father and everyone else, he has no one to intensively care for him, let alone love him.[31] Unlike young children in real life, the Creature has the physical and intellectual abilities to take care of himself, even in infancy. Despite this "superhuman" capability for self-care, the Creature nonetheless fails to thrive emotionally due to his utter lack of love and total abuse from his parent and other people.

By having the approximately five- to six-year-old Creature intend to commit suicide in the wake of his father's death, Thought Experiment 5 culminates with an exploration of the emotional need of children for feeling (or at least remembering) parental love in order to sustain interest in life itself.[32] As this overview has revealed, Shelley's cascade of thought experiments on the rights of the child suggests that parental love is the primary means not only for the preservation of a child's very being but also, even more crucially, for the full realization and sustenance of a child's well-being. Now, as we turn to running each of the five thought experiments in sequence and in depth, we readers are philosophically equipped to clarify and deepen our understanding of the moral and political issues surrounding a child's—still controversial and contested—right to love.

Thought Experiment 1: Motherlessness

What if a man had sole parental responsibility for a child due to using science to create him without a biological mother?

The first thought experiment at the core of *Frankenstein*—the making of a motherless child through science—gets at a deep psychological question: what would be the impact of lacking a mother *at all*? This is a difficult question for a human being to consider because it overturns one of the most basic preconditions of being human (at least so far). "All human life on the planet is born of woman," as Adrienne Rich wrote.[33] It does not matter if one never knew one's genetic mother and/or gestational mother due to death or desertion, anonymous gamete donation or anonymous surrogacy, or adoption, foster care, or institutional care. All humans have at least one mother, and many have two or more, depending on the varied circumstances of conception, gestation, and rearing. *Frankenstein*'s first thought experiment on the rights of the child presents a counterfactual scenario that spurs readers to imagine something that the human species has not yet achieved, even two centuries later—namely, to make a child without any mother.

If a reader looks at Thought Experiment 1 solely through the lens of science, it might appear like a kind of prognostication of a form of assisted reproductive technology, wherein organ donation could be used to create human life differently than sexual reproduction through intercourse, intrauterine insemination, or in vitro fertilization. From a broader moral and political perspective, however, the foundational thought experiment of the novel proves to have a more immediate and pressing psychological and social concern. If a man could make a child without any mother, what would such utter *motherlessness* mean for the child—and for society at large?

Beyond the Creature himself, *Frankenstein* is filled with motherless creatures.[34] Almost the whole Frankenstein clan is rendered motherless due to the death of a mother. The wife of Alphonse Frankenstein, Caroline, was motherless before she died and left her children, Victor and his brothers Ernest and William, motherless, as well as their cousin and adoptive sister, Elizabeth, motherless twice over (for Elizabeth's biological mother had died before she was adopted by Caroline and Alphonse). Even the trusted servant of the family, Justine, suffers the death of her mother—a personal tragedy that propels her back into service for the Frankensteins at the rather inopportune time to be framed by the Creature for William's murder. Like Elizabeth, Justine is made motherless twice over because Caroline was in many ways more of a mother to her than her own.

In the innermost layer of the novel, the often "unhappy" DeLacey clan—whom the "orphan" Creature observes unnoticed from his hovel and considers his only family—also lost a mother to death.[35] In the outermost layer of the novel, Captain Wallace sends letters to his sister, revealing that the death of their mother has made the bachelor explorer all the more emotionally attached to his married sibling. Anne K. Mellor pointed out that the sister's initials (M.W.S.) are the ones "coveted" by the unmarried author of *Frankenstein*, who was motherless, too, due to Wollstonecraft's death soon after her birth and Godwin's failure to provide a stable maternal substitute during her early childhood.[36] The impact of such maternal loss and lack was enduring. Even at age thirty-eight (the same age her mother had died), Shelley saw herself as a "dependent thing—wanting fosterage & support"—as she wrote in an 1835 letter to her mother's friend, Maria Gisborne. Although Gisborne had become a kind of mother figure to her, it was not enough to fill the void left by the absence of a stable mother figure in her earliest years: "Loneliness has made a wreck of me." This inner sense of isolation persisted through her adulthood: "I am left to myself—crushed by fortune—And I am nothing."[37]

In Shelley's first and greatest novel, the protagonist's experience of maternal loss is the most immediate source of his impulse to create a motherless child. The adolescent Victor's loss of his mother to a sudden illness leads him to seek scientific knowledge of the mysterious relationship between life and death. In asking "Whence . . . did the principle of life proceed?" Victor determined that "to examine causes of life, we must first have recourse to death."[38] He then studied the parts of human corpses in order to understand how life once animated them. By making a new life from the parts of human and other animal corpses and not by reviving a corpse (say, of his dead mother), Victor successfully substituted science for woman's reproductive power to gestate life. On the night that he brings the Creature to life, Victor confuses in his dreams the images of his fiancée, Elizabeth, and the dead Caroline, kissing them both before he recoils in disgust of his mother's rotting face. This nightmare suggests that Victor's darkest and most repressed desire was to have a woman's or, more specifically, his fiancée's and mother's power to gestate life even in the face of death.[39] Several feminist psychoanalytic readings of the novel have proposed that Victor—by making his Creature in the wake of his mother's death and in avoidance of his nuptials—provides the most vivid illustration of "womb envy" in Western literature.[40]

Despite his latent envy toward his mother's and his fiancée's generative powers, Victor fails to become a mother himself. Not only does he make the Creature motherless, but he also lovelessly abandons him. Resisting the irreversible fact of his mother's death, Victor appears to want to have the generative powers of a mother but uses them for a cruel and vindictive, not nurturing, purpose: to visit an immeasurably greater loss and sense of grief upon his own child than he had felt when Caroline died. His playing God is a crude power play, with his child as victim of his tyranny. As stated to Captain Walton, Victor's plainly selfish motive was to make a "new species" that would "bless" him as "its creator and source" such that "no father could claim the gratitude of his child so completely as I should deserve."[41] In his quest to become an omnipotent father through making the motherless Creature, Victor ensures that he is not the most solitary and lonely of the motherless. He outdoes his dead mother twice over by making a child without a woman and by making that child's abandonment and consequent suffering the worst conceivable due to the lack of any mother or maternal substitute. As the infant Creature wonders with regard to his own isolated and miserable condition, "Was I then a monster, a blot upon the earth, from which all men fled, and whom all men disowned?"[42] What Victor had not anticipated is that the "spectre" of his "monster" would haunt him unto his own death, giving him an inescapably eerie sense of being watched from the shadows by the child he had abandoned.[43]

Although Victor could have acted as a mother to the Creature by feeding, sheltering, otherwise caring for, and, most important, loving him, he fails to do so. Moreover, he outright rejects the possibility of doing so because he is "unable to endure the aspect of the being I had created." In the copy of the 1818 edition that she annotated and gave to her friend Mrs. Thomas in 1823, Shelley specified the Creature's "un-human features" as the cause of what she had earlier described as Victor's "emotions" of "horror and disgust."[44] Like Elizabeth and Justine, the Creature is made motherless twice over but in a distinctively horrifying way. Lacking a mother in the first place, he is also lacking typical conditions for being mothered—not only by his father-scientist but also by every prospective parent he encounters—due to his alien and frightening form. Only a few hours after bringing the Creature to life, Victor severely and rashly concludes that "no mortal could support the horror of that countenance."[45] The Creature thus becomes absolutely motherless. Eventually he even assumes that he cannot possibly find a mother of any sort (whether female or male, biological or social) to fill the psychological void left by his father's making of him without a woman: "Cursed Creator! Why did you form a monster so hideous that even you turned from me in disgust?"[46]

Unlike the Creature, Victor and the other motherless creatures of *Frankenstein* are merely lacking a mother in the present. They all had mothers once and have found, or have the potential to find, maternal substitutes. The Creature has no such past and holds no such hope: "No father had watched my infant days, no mother had blessed me with smiles and caresses."[47] He feels more "solitary and detested" than even Milton's Satan after the Fall.[48] In the aforementioned 1835 letter to Maria Gisborne, Shelley echoed her Creature's sense of desolation in the wake of maternal (de)privation and paternal desertion: "I have been so barbarously handled both by fortune & my fellow creatures . . . I have no hope."[49]

Perhaps her own experience of maternal loss and paternal neglect led Shelley to see the importance of a mother's intensive care and love for a child's healthy and happy development. She did not romanticize or prescribe the benefits of a particular kind of mother-child relationship in her writing, however, as Wollstonecraft had often done.[50] Shelley rather used the literary technique of negative capability to dwell on the uncertainty, instability, and discomfort brought by the lack or even the very idea of lacking a mother. Following this poetic principle, Thought Experiment 1 draws the reader's attention to the discomforting idea of maternal privation by presenting a counterfactual scenario in which a child is totally without any mother or intensively loving and caring parental figure.

It is hard to contemplate the counterfactual idea of total maternal privation of the sort the Creature experiences. By challenging at the deepest level our received ideas of what it means to be motherless, this worst-case scenario allows the reader to think with greater precision about what one misses the most when one lacks a mother. In the extreme case of the Creature, the total lack of a mother meant that he had only a father-scientist as a parent who was unfit and unavailable to intensively care for and love him. The total lack of a mother thus begets an even deeper privation for the Creature: the absence of *any* intensively caring and loving parental figure.

Both in the novel and in most human cultures, women are associated with the type of intensive parental care and love for children that, as an institution, is called motherhood and, as a practice, is called mothering.[51] The feminist poet Rich argued that the institution was patriarchal, for it entailed female self-sacrifice for the benefit of men. At the same time, she held that mothering could be empowering for women if they did not practice it according to patriarchal norms that exploit women for the benefit of men in power. In addition, mothering was not necessarily rooted in women's biological nature or reproductive roles.[52]

Shelley's radical imagining of a man making a child without a woman likewise suggests that mothering need not be seen as a simple function of female biology. The work of Rich and anthropologist Sarah Hrdy shares this insight: across cultures and epochs, mothering is a moral and social practice adopted by humans with regard to their children, not a role solely determined by female biology and genetics.[53] Hrdy has devoted much of her work to studying how primates, including humans, rely on allomothers—or nonmaternal caregivers, such as men, grandmothers, aunts, and older children—to carry out the successful rearing of young. In some cultures, such as the Aka pygmies of central Africa, men are leading contributors to allomothering. Aka men spend more than half the day carrying their newborns and nurse them when the mother is not available.[54] In the context of late twentieth-century Western culture, the feminist political theorist Susan Okin made the related point that "nothing in our nature dictates that men should not be equal participants in the rearing of children."[55]

Frankenstein illustrates this distinction between the social practice of mothering and the biological basis of women's reproductive capabilities by giving several examples of nonbiological mothers who step in to intensively care for and love children who had lost their biological mothers to death. Caroline formally adopted Elizabeth as her daughter, and Elizabeth and Justine both acted as mother figures to William after Caroline died. Blind Mr. DeLacey inhabits the role of a mother for his humble household, with the lives of his children revolving around him in his perch in the kitchen.

On one hand, the literary examples of Caroline, Elizabeth, and Justine support the historical fact that women have typically taken on the maternal practice of intensive care and love of children, even if they are not the children's biological mothers or relatives. On the other hand, Thought Experiment 1 prods the reader to ask a sexually subversive and gender-bending question: Was Victor's greatest mistake (a) to make the Creature motherless or (b) to not act as the Creature's mother? If (a) was his worst mistake, then the novel might have concluded with its first thought experiment by showing how the creation of a motherless being immediately brought about the destruction of the father-scientist or his Creature. One could imagine a clever short story that ended with the giant Creature killing his maker as soon as he was brought to life. Another plot twist could have been to make the Creature a stillborn, incapable of living without a woman to gestate and nurture him.[56] The moral of the story would have been clear in either case: men shouldn't mess with the powers of a mother. Tellingly, Shelley did not take these narrative routes. Rather, she used Thought Experiments 2 through 5 to deduce the bad consequences of Victor's making the Creature motherless twice over by not intensively caring for and loving him.

Following the poetic principle of negative capability, the reader may reasonably infer what the most salient features of a mother *are* from what they *are not* in the novel. On a descriptive level, a mother is not necessarily a woman. Victor usurps the gestational powers of a mother and has sole responsibility for his Creature as a result of using science to create him without a woman. The kind old man DeLacey acts as a mother to his children and even to the Creature in their brief but affectionate meeting. Furthermore, a mother is not necessarily a biological parent, as the cases of Victor, DeLacey, Caroline, Elizabeth, and Justine illustrate in different ways. On a moral level, a good mother is not an absentee or unfit parent like Victor. A good mother does not deny care and love to his or her own child like Victor. A good mother is not irresponsible toward his or her own child like Victor.

We may piece together a positive yet broad, descriptive, and moral definition of a mother from these elements of what a mother is not. Such obverse reasoning leads us to see that a good mother is a parent of any gender or sex who intensively cares for and loves his or her own child out of a sense of fundamental responsibility for that child, without necessarily having any biological relationship to that child. Interestingly, from his observations of the DeLacey family, the Creature himself arrives at a similar definition of the mother's social role, without using gendered language: "all the life and cares of the mother were wrapt up in the precious charge."[57] He does not specify the mother's sex, leaving it open for consideration that a man could fulfill this social role as well as a woman.

If we run Thought Experiment 1 over again with this negative reconstruction of motherhood in mind, then we see that Victor's greatest mistake was in fact (b), to not act as the Creature's mother. But given his extreme fear of and disgust for his creation's "unearthly ugliness," Victor finds himself in a tragic predicament.[58] Without the affective basis for the intensive provision of parental care and love, Victor is unfit to follow through on the duty that he must perform in order to be a good mother to the child for whom he is solely responsible.

In the abstract, Victor comes to recognize this parental duty to his "creature of fine sensations": "I had no right to withhold from him the small portion of happiness which was yet in my power to bestow."[59] Ironically, he lacks those "fine sensations" necessary for performing this duty toward his own particular child. After he hears his child's demand for an equal female companion, Victor "compassionated him, and sometimes felt a wish to console him."[60] Nonetheless, he confesses to Walton, "When I looked upon him, when I saw the filthy mass that moved and talked, my heart sickened, and my feelings were altered to those of horror and hatred."[61]

Beyond Victor's affective obstacles to loving his child, the broader circumstances of Victor and his Creature are equally tragic. There appears to be no human who is motivated to intensively care for, let alone love, the Creature due to his fearsome form. While DeLacey greeted him with warmth because he could not see him, the kind old blind man abandoned him once the sighted members of the family returned to expel the "monster" from their cottage. Even the Creature concludes that among people not made like him, "I cannot inspire love."[62] To his father, he pointedly raises a rhetorical question to which he knows the answer all too well: "am I not shunned and hated by all mankind?"[63]

Thought Experiment 1 thus leads the reader to an uncomfortable question about the scope of parental responsibility, even in the face of utter motherlessness. As I framed it at the beginning of this chapter, it is the first of the two sets of moral questions that animate the core narrative of *Frankenstein*: *Does one as a parent have a fundamental and universal duty to share love with one's own children? If one is or expects to become unavailable or unfit to give and receive such love, then should one arrange for one's own children to share love with another parent or other substitute?* Looking at Victor's tragic predicament through the lens of these moral questions, the reader might wonder if he, as the sole parent, should have at least met a minimum standard for caring for his own child. Couldn't Victor have met such a basic threshold for parental care by arranging for a suitable, stable, intensively caring and loving maternal substitute? In this light, Victor's extreme fear of and disgust for his Creature explains his failure to act as a mother to him, but it does not justify his failure to arrange for a fitting substitute to take on this crucial role for a child's well-being.

As we learned in Chapter 2, Shelley's mother had argued in a letter to her first, common-law husband, Gilbert Imlay, that she had a "natural right" to the child in her womb because she felt "care and anxiety" for it during pregnancy.[64] Wollstonecraft grounded her right to mother the unborn child upon her intensive, even anxious, feeling and practice of care for it. In short, her maternal right to raise the child derived from her performance of the duty to care for the child in her womb. While it was a natural right in the sense that it pertained to a biological process (pregnancy), Wollstonecraft ultimately construed it as a relational or social right because it was a mother's habit of "care and anxiety" for the child during pregnancy, not the pregnancy itself, that generated her fundamental right to determine the best conditions for the child's rearing. A biological mother who never showed care for a child, in or out of her womb, would not have had such an entitlement. Wollstonecraft was thus concerned with the questions of whether and, if so, why mothers have a right to rear their own children.

In Thought Experiment 1, Shelley raised the converse question: do children have a right to a mother? From a twenty-first century standpoint, this question may seem problematic—especially for a feminist, who might even feel allergic to its invocation of an (implicitly female) mother as an object of a right for a child. Following Wollstonecraft, Westerners have come to view parenting—at least in the abstract—in gender-neutral and egalitarian terms.[65] On this normative model, men and women ideally should take turns in childcare, sharing equally the burdens and benefits of the office of parenthood. Thought Experiment 1 derails the Wollstonecraftian model of parenthood before it can even begin to be implemented by making it difficult, if not impossible, to practice in the context of Victor's tragic predicament. Victor's affective obstacles to intensively caring for and loving his Creature make him unfit to be a parent, let alone to share parental responsibility with another person. From the Creature's standpoint, the utter lack of a mother, not the lack of a perfectly balanced parental unit, is the ultimate privation. By focusing on the special danger of maternal (de)privation, not the broader issues of parental deprivation or parental equality, Thought Experiment 1 might seem to reinforce traditional gender norms and the sexual division of labor with regard to parenting.

On the other hand, it was visionary for Shelley to put a male protagonist at the heart of a story about who should provide intensive care and love to a child. While Victor fails to act as a mother, his failure can be read as an indictment of men's broader failure to contribute to the intensive loving practice of caring for children, especially infants dependent on such loving care for their health and well-being. The fundamental question of Thought Experiment 1 is thus a fundamental feminist question. It returns us to the second of the two sets of moral questions that animate the core narrative of *Frankenstein*: *Do children have a fundamental and universal right to share love with a parent? If a parent (of any sort) is neither available nor fit to give and receive such love, then do children have a right to share love with a substitute?* Giving even greater specificity to this initially broad formulation of the question of children's right to love, the first thought experiment pushes the reader to ask not only why mothers matter to children but also why men are not expected to be mothers as much as women. Even in Shelley's late eighteenth-century infancy, the maintenance of a single devoted wet nurse and loving caregiver would have enabled her widowed father to satisfy his obligation to provide a stable maternal substitute while continuing in his other parental duties. It is little discussed that men, in all times and places, can nurse babies in their care if they induce lactation by nipple stimulation and a related hormone surge. Male nursing is even more practicable in the twenty-first century due to the use of electric breast pumps to induce lactation or the assistance of artificial breasts, pumped breastmilk, and supplemental nursing systems.[66] The availability of formula and, more important, paid maternal and paternal leaves are also potential equalizers for men and women's contributions to the mothering of infants.[67]

Still, like Victor Frankenstein, not all men may be fit or available to be mothers to their own children or to even provide a loving substitute. The tragic predicament of Victor—a parent who is solely responsible for a child whose hideous form scares people from intensively caring for or loving him—raises a provocative political question for the reader to consider: who or what should provide a loving maternal substitute if a parent is unable to even arrange for a replacement? The Creature's tragic predicament as a "human being" made unlovable by his "un-human features" renders him a motherless and a stateless person beyond the reach of both family and politics.[68] This discomforting double privation presses the reader to contemplate a related political question: *If parents and parental substitutes have a duty to love their own children, then should a political body have a role in the assignment of parental substitutes when parents fail to share love adequately with their own children?* Thought Experiment 1 does not yield a firm answer to this political question. It rather prods the reader to begin to consider the challenging, real-world political implications of maternal deprivation for both children and society in general.

Thought Experiment 2: Lovelessness

What if the child was totally abandoned because the lone parent (and other people) did not love him due to fear and disgust of his hideous form?

Frankenstein's second thought experiment picks up right where the first one left off. Thought Experiment 1 rendered the Creature motherless twice over—due to being made (a) by a father-scientist without a woman and (b) with "un-human features" so horrifying and disgusting that all people, including his lone parent, appear to lack sufficient affective motivation to intensively care for, let alone love, him. As a result, the Creature suffers immediate abandonment by his father only to endure living alone without much human contact for the remainder of his documented five to six years. Thought Experiment 2 begins with this worst-case scenario of child abandonment but trains the reader's eye on the variables of infant features and parental emotions in order to focus attention on an aspect of the novel's first set of moral questions: to what extent must the feeling of love attend the proper and complete performance of the duty of parental care?

Adoration of the beauty—indeed, perfection—of newborns and infants is typically expected of Western parents, as well as their relatives and friends and even strangers who pass them on the street. Going one step further, it is often said that parents will think their own baby beautiful even if the child seems ugly to others. In this modern Western familial ideal, a powerful parental affection arises from parental reverence for the infant's beauty, regardless of the child's appearance to others.

Ethologists and psychiatrists have tested these folk ideas about the affective impact of infant cuteness on potential parents or caregivers. The ethologist Konrad Lorenz proposed the concept of a "baby schema" or set of cross-species animal infant features ("large head, round face, and big eyes") that is "perceived as cute" and "motivates caretaking behavior in other individuals."[69] Psychiatrists have since shown that human babies who are rated highly for their cute features are more likely to elicit the affective motivation for caretaking than those who are rated lower on a scale of cuteness.[70]

Psychologists have furthermore demonstrated that human caretaking motivation toward cute babies does not depend upon the baby sharing the same species or ethnicity as the potential caregiver.[71] The sex of the potential caregiver does not matter much either, except that women expressed greater caretaking motivation in response to pictures of cute babies than men. From an evolutionary perspective, women may have developed a stronger caregiving motivation in response to infant cuteness as an adaptation to their expectation of a far greater share of caregiving for children. Since women—across cultures and epochs—have been more likely to act as mothers of infants, they have needed more affective motivation than men to carry out this intensive practice of mothering.[72] Nevertheless, men and women share a similar affective response to infant cuteness, which supplies a cross-cultural motivation to act as parents to those infants who are dependent on their care and love for surviving and thriving.

But let's say, for the sake of counterargument, there is no such caretaking motivation because there is no such infant cuteness. This is the conceptual point of Thought Experiment 2. By tweaking the variables of infant features and parental emotions, it generates a worst-case scenario for any child: total abandonment at birth due to lack of any affective bond with parents and even potential parental figures. In his reading of *Frankenstein*, Stephen Jay Gould argued from the perspective of evolutionary theory that "all humans reject and even loathe the monster for a visceral reason of literal superficiality: his truly terrifying ugliness."[73] While Gould indicated that such an "instinctive aversion to serious malformation" is a genetic inheritance of the human species, he quickly reminded his readers, "Nature can only supply a predisposition, while culture shapes specific results."[74] On this evolutionary interpretation of the novel, it was not biologically or genetically determined that Victor and others would abhor and reject the Creature due to his "deformity." Rather, an unfeeling culture fostered the environmental conditions under which it was permissible for even his parent to abandon him due to his supposed monstrosity.

Despite its focus upon the exposure of the Creature due to his deformity, the primary aim of Thought Experiment 2 is not to explain the phenomenon of abandonment of babies due to physical disability. Rather, the thought experiment constructs an extreme counterfactual scenario—a child is born so hideous that no one, not even his sole parent, can love him—in order to prod the reader to wonder whether and, if so, why any parental obligations persist in the absence of parental love. More precisely, do parents have a duty to arrange for some sort of love and care for their own children when they don't love and cannot care for them?

Cleverly, Shelley places Victor himself in the position of conducting this thought experiment at the same time as the reader. After listening to the Creature's account of the bad consequences of his abandonment and his demand for an equal female companion to ease his loneliness, Victor "shuddered" when he "thought of the possible consequences" of making the female but nonetheless "felt there was some justice in his argument."[75] Torn by conflicting feelings of "compassion" and "horror and hatred," Victor nevertheless reached the conclusion that he, "as his maker," must "owe him all the portion of happiness that it was in my power to bestow."[76]

Despite his complete lack of love for the Creature, Victor deduces an enduring parental obligation toward his child. This obligation is to arrange for someone else to love his child. In Victor's case, this is a difficult obligation to fulfill because the extreme ugliness of the Creature means that nobody appears to have the affective motivation to lovingly care for him (except DeLacey, whose blindness allowed him to show sympathy and concern for the Creature for a few minutes before his sighted family returned home). Hence, Victor accepts the Creature's reasoning that only a creature "as hideous as myself" could possibly love him.[77]

It would appear that only by making this equal companion for his child could Victor satisfactorily perform his parental duty to arrange for someone else to love the child he cannot. This would constitute Victor's one and only act of parental care toward the Creature. Although it would be done without love, it would generate conditions of love for the child. This act of parental care would not fully heal the "injury" caused by the Creature's abandonment.[78] However, it would at least partly redeem Victor as a parent in the eyes of the Creature: "Oh! My creator, make me happy; let me feel gratitude toward you for one benefit!"[79] The Creature feels his demand is "reasonable and moderate" because he only asks his father to "have a care."[80] He does not expect what he cannot get from him: love.

By playing with the variables of parental emotions and infant features, Thought Experiment 2 accomplishes two important philosophical tasks. First, by replacing parental adoration of a baby with "horror and hatred," it allows readers (as well as Victor) to separate the issue of parental care from parental love. Parental care is relatively simple to define in moral terms. To care for one's own child is to provide for that child's needs. It is more difficult to provide a moral definition of love because it involves a set of emotions, as well as a related set of practices.

To love one's own child is to feel a strong set of emotions toward that child that govern one's behavior in relationship to that child: a sympathetic affection for the child that can be intense and pleasant, a psychological sense of attachment that persists in the child's absence, and a related feeling of deep personal responsibility toward that child and its well-being. This set of strong emotions motivates a parent to engage in a set of loving caregiving practices, which enable the child to fall deeply in love with the parent (usually between three and six months of age).[81] Borrowing from the words of the Creature, parental love allows a child to "live in the interchange of those sympathies" necessary not only for "being" but also for being "happy." In Thought Experiment 2, the mental separation of care from love allows us to see that even in a worst-case scenario of loveless child abandonment, the parental duty to care for one's own child can and should be satisfied by arranging for someone else to lovingly care for that child.

Challenging some Kantian views of love and duty, Thought Experiment 2 leads the reader to wonder if there is a duty to arrange for one's child to share love even if one feels no love toward that child. According to Kant, love was a feeling and thus could not be willed. One was either in love or not; one could not choose to love someone if the feeling wasn't there in the first place. Kant also held that the performance of a moral action must be the product of a free and rational (autonomous) will, motivated by a sense of duty. While (heteronomous) desires and feelings such as love could accompany the dutiful performance of a moral action, they could not serve as the grounding for its moral worth. For Kant, love had no real moral worth—it was simply a feeling that might supplement one's dutiful motives for doing the right thing. Kant severely concluded that there could be no duty to love anyone, not even a vulnerable child for whose care and contentment one was solely responsible.[82]

Moving beyond the Kantian binary between duty as the source of moral worth and love as lacking moral worth, Thought Experiment 2 pushes readers to explore two alternative conceptions of the relationship between duty and love with respect to the parent-child relationship: ideal and nonideal. Ideally, the feeling of love happens to coincide with the parental sense of duty to lovingly care for one's own child. In these happy cases, love is the way or manner in which the duty to lovingly care for one's own child ought to be performed: the feeling and the duty are fused in their delivery. This parental sense of duty to share love with one's own child typically arises, at least in part, from firsthand response to the child's need for parental love to survive and thrive. Through this process of responding to the child's needs, caring for one's own child becomes a practical and a moral condition for developing not only a profound feeling of love toward one's own child but also a deep sense of one's duty to love that child. Nonideally, a minimal duty to arrange for the loving care of one's own child persists even in the absence of feeling any love for that child. In this initially sad but hopeful case, the arranged-for substitute becomes the parent by performing the parental duty to share love with the child in a loving way.

Second, Thought Experiment 2 accomplishes another important philosophical task: by changing the baby's features from cute to "un-human," it explores the contested definition of the human. Unlike her mother, Shelley in *Frankenstein* did not invoke theological, metaphysical, or universalistic ideas concerning the nature of the human being. Nor did she use such questionable concepts to justify the idea of children's rights.

Shelley designed Thought Experiment 2 in a way that fundamentally challenges the idea of a static or universal definition of the human. Initially, Victor tasks himself with the project of "the creation of a human being."[83] To speed up the complex and difficult process of working with the "minuteness of the parts" of a typical human being, Victor decides to "make the being of a gigantic stature . . . about eight feet in height, and proportionally large."[84] By identifying both the "dissecting room" and "the slaughter-house" as the sources of "many" of his "materials," he leaves open the possibility that he used the parts of humans as well as other animals in making the Creature's body.[85] Immediately after bringing this new and likely chimeric or hybrid "being" to life, however, Victor describes the Creature's "horrid" features in a way that suggests he is either "un-human" (as Shelley wrote in the margins of the 1818 edition that she gave to Mrs. Thomas), subhuman (a "wretch"), inhuman (a "monster"), suprahuman (a "demoniacal corpse"), or posthuman ("a thing such as even Dante could not have conceived").[86]

The Creature shares his maker's confusion about his identity and relationship to humanity. During his early years of abandonment, the Creature comes to see himself as "an unfortunate and deserted creature" with "no relation or friend upon earth."[87] He contends that he and his proposed female companion must be of the "same species," implying that he is not of the human species.[88] Although they "shall be monsters" together, the Creature and the female will have a "peaceful and human" life in the wilderness.[89] Even the Creature cannot settle on whether or not he or any projected member of his kind is human.

The novel's refusal to settle the questions of the Creature's humanity or the broader definition of the human makes the ethical and political implications of Thought Experiment 2 all the more provocative. Although made by a human from (at least some, if not mostly) human parts, the features of the Creature are not seen as human. Consequently, he is made to feel inhuman, subhuman, and nonhuman. Ironically, it is the Creature's outsized capacity for feeling outside humanity that gives him his most human feature: the longing for love and the sense of security and belonging that comes with sharing love with another.[90]

Ultimately, Thought Experiment 2 overturns the genetic view of the human being as defined in terms of its origins: "Who was I? What was I? Whence did I come?"[91] As we saw in Chapter 2, Wollstonecraft set forth a religious version of a genetic argument about the nature of humanity: God made the souls or minds of human beings in His rational image. She used this genetic argument about human nature to argue that each and every human had equal rights and duties based on their rational capability to grasp and implement God's universal, rational, moral law. In contemporary political philosophy, Liao has recently advanced a scientific version of a genetic argument about human nature. Liao contends that it is the human genome that is the source of the nature of humanity, including its capacity for moral agency. He uses this (literally) genetic argument about human nature to argue that human children hold fundamental human rights, as do human adults, because their shared genetic heritage accords them the same human status as persons with the capacity for moral agency and thus for being rights-holders in the first place.[92]

In *Frankenstein*, Shelley rejected such genetic approaches to the conceptualization of the human being, whether religious or scientific. Thought Experiment 2 opens the door to a new, open-ended, and poetic approach to understanding humanity in terms of negative capability or what it lacks and yet desires. From this literary and psychological perspective, what defines one's humanity is not how one was made with certain features or how one looks but rather how one feels—especially how one feels about the lack of love, whether in ourselves or others. Viewed from the vertiginous perspective of negative capability, humanity is neither a biological nor a metaphysical concept but rather a moral category for those persons who have felt in themselves or, in sympathy with others, the longing for love.

Thought Experiment 3: Mere Survival

What if the newborn child had the ability to survive on his own due to his eight-foot frame, extraordinary strength, and incredible capability for language acquisition and independent learning?

Thought Experiment 3 tests the limits of the reader's suspension of disbelief. Shelley gives the newborn Creature an eight-foot frame; the strength, balance, and coordination to walk and "wander on with liberty" (albeit with some tendency to fall at first); the ability to clothe, feed, and hydrate himself in response to his first sensations of cold, hunger, and thirst; and sufficient practical reason to infer and avoid the causes of pain, learn to use fire for cooking nuts and berries, and find various shelters for safe repose from the elements and the villagers who react violently to his fearsome form.[93] If the newborn Creature is a child, he is a highly advanced one. At first glance, he appears to have more in common with an older child, adolescent, or adult in terms of his motor and cognitive skills, even during his first few days of life. A skeptic of the view that the Creature is a child might reasonably ask, "At what stage of life is the Creature when he is brought to life?" Is he an infant, a toddler, an older child, an adult, or something else—perhaps an altogether new kind of being with "superhuman" powers, such as astonishing "speed," as Victor describes him at twenty-one months of age?[94]

The first obstacle to seeing the Creature as a child is his eight-foot frame. True to the counterfactual form, Shelley makes her newborn Creature the opposite of a baby in terms of his size. Yet this feature of the Creature is not as wildly imaginative as the premise that grounds Thought Experiment 1: motherlessness. While science has not yet achieved the making of a human without a mother, a human can grow to be eight feet tall. In fact, in late eighteenth- and nineteenth-century Europe, there were two well-known "giants" recorded around this height, including the "Irish Giant" Patrick Cotter O'Brien (1760–1806), the first person to be measured at just over eight feet tall.[95] The skeleton of a sixteenth-century German man with the name Anton de Franckenpoint was later measured at eight feet and displayed in the Museum Anatomicum at Marburg in 1810.[96] There is no evidence that Shelley knew of either case directly—although the showman O'Brien was well known in London, and she came quite close to Marburg during her honeymoon in 1814—but awareness of such giants was part of public discourse of the era. In European literature of the period, the seven-foot-tall "sympathetic criminal hero" of Schiller's *Der Verbrecher* (1786) may have also inspired Shelley's decision to give the Creature a "gigantic stature."[97]

Given that the Creature is not of woman born, there is no limit for his size due to the constraints of the womb. As Peter Swirski has argued, a coherent thought experiment may begin with a far-fetched or even implausible premise, but the conclusions deduced from such a premise must be internally consistent and logical.[98] In this light, the absolute motherlessness of the Creature allows for his gigantic size and proportional strength, which is consistent with Victor's scientific claim that working with larger body parts was a faster and more effective method for making a "human being" without sexual reproduction.

For humans and other animals, a new life is a baby. Although the Creature is a new life, he is the opposite of a baby in terms of size, strength, and ability to survive on his own. Human babies are small and relatively weak, as well as vulnerable to illness, poor development, and death due to their tiny, immobile bodies. Unlike some animal species, human babies are totally dependent upon parental care and love for surviving and thriving.[99] By manipulating a number of these infant features in the person of the newborn Creature, Thought Experiment 3 invites the reader to consider what makes the youngest children vulnerable and which kinds of vulnerability are worst for the youngest children.

The most vulnerable of people are newborn babies due to their smallness, weakness, inability to move independently, lack of language, and emotional and physical dependency on adults for care and love. By reversing this and making the Creature a giant person at birth with the strength to walk, care for himself, and survive on his own, Shelley encourages the reader to distinguish between the different forms of newborn vulnerability. In eliminating *physical vulnerability* due to smallness, weakness, and immobility from the Creature's postnatal predicament, Thought Experiment 3 highlights the dangers of *emotional and social vulnerability* due to other factors, such as motherlessness (as introduced in Thought Experiment 1) and lovelessness (the focus of Thought Experiment 2). Shelley's gradual revelation of the growing Creature's "superhuman" cognitive features—especially his incredible capability for language acquisition and independent learning—ultimately allows Thought Experiment 3 to sever the concept of children's vulnerability from both *physical* and *cognitive* factors and instead focus the reader's attention upon the *emotional* and *social* dimensions of very young children's vulnerability.

In contemporary legal and political philosophy, Martha Nussbaum and Rosalind Dixon have developed a similar typology of children's vulnerabilities as a starting point for justifying children's human rights. They distinguish between physical, cognitive, emotional, and economic/legal forms of children's vulnerability.[100] In addition, they make a distinction between particular vulnerabilities that children face due to their special relationship to parents or other caregivers on whom they are dependent, as well as general vulnerabilities that children share with other members of their society. For example, a child may be particularly vulnerable to sexual violence within her family but share a general vulnerability to poverty with the rest of her society.

Armed with these distinctions, Dixon and Nussbaum address the question of whether it is justifiable for children to have "special priority" in the provision of certain human rights.[101] If human rights are meant to be universal and thus available to each and every human, how can children stand first in line, so to speak, for the provision of certain rights, such as to be free from sexual abuse? Their answer is that if a child's vulnerability is a result of her particular relationship to a parent or parent figure on whom she is dependent and not solely a general vulnerability shared by other people in society, then the child has a right to stand first in line for provision of a right or rights that will reduce or eliminate this vulnerability.[102]

Dixon and Nussbaum's particular-general distinction can be modified and applied in a way that illuminates the conceptual purpose of Thought Experiment 3. There is a difference between the vulnerabilities of the youngest children due to their particular dependencies upon parents or other caregivers and the vulnerabilities of the youngest children in general. In the counterfactual case of the Creature, Thought Experiment 3 directs us to distinguish between his particular (and extreme) emotional and social vulnerabilities (due to being made motherless twice over by his father-scientist) and more general vulnerabilities that he shares with infants and other very young children. Despite his "superhuman" physical and cognitive features, the Creature is still very much like other very young children in terms of his emotional and social vulnerabilities and, initially, in his physical and cognitive vulnerabilities.

To better distinguish his particular vulnerabilities from those generally shared by the youngest children, Shelley emphasizes how the Creature is both like and unlike a human baby in the first few months after he is brought to life. Although like Adam, he is brought to life fully grown in body, the Creature shares some physical vulnerabilities of human babies. Like a newborn human, he begins life with a "confused and indistinct" sensory awareness of his surroundings.[103] He "saw, felt, heard, and smelt, at the same time" and "it was, indeed, a long time" before he "learned to distinguish between the operations of [the] various senses."[104] He does not see very well or far at first and finds high heat and bright light "oppressive."[105] Like a human baby, hunger commands the Creature's sensory attention when it hits. Unlike human infants, who usually taste mother's milk or formula given to them by a parent or nurse soon after birth, the Creature does not eat until he is overcome with hunger and then feeds himself berries and nuts (and even some roasted "offals" left behind at a campfire) that he finds in the woods.[106] Unlike a human baby, he "walked" within hours of birth, but like a human baby, he fumbled and "descended" in the process of learning to move independently.[107]

Cognitively, the Creature shares some vulnerabilities with human babies as well. Like human infants, the Creature's cognitive development is swift, vast, and oriented toward communication (nonverbal and verbal), problem solving, and logical thought, but it is also dependent upon learning from the example and tutelage of adults.[108] By observing the DeLacey family talk and read, he learns to pronounce his first words at approximately six months, around the same time many human infants begin to babble and say simple words, such as "mama" and "dada."[109] Between six and twelve months—when human babies start to enjoy story time with their parents and often pick up more vocabulary—the Creature learns to speak and read by listening to and imitating the DeLacey family, especially their teaching of French to the Turkish Safie through reading books aloud such as Volney's *Ruin of Empires*.[110] Although his process of language acquisition is accelerated far beyond that of a human infant, the Creature remains reliant upon human adults for becoming literate. He is not born with speech but rather must learn it from those who already have it. For this reason, he shares with the youngest human children a particular cognitive and social vulnerability to bad instruction in language, communication, and the ethics of relating to others.

Emotionally and socially, the Creature is most like a human baby. As the psychiatrist John Bowlby theorized through his cross-cultural, cross-epoch, and cross-species studies of mother-baby relationships, human infants need to feel the warmth and security of a psychological and physiological attachment to a mother—meaning, an intensively caring and loving parent—in order to survive and thrive.[111] A child develops a sense of psychological security by having a mother who serves as a kind of emotional "base" from which she feels safe to explore the world around her.[112] Bowlby challenged some of the main suppositions of psychoanalytic theory concerning the importance of the mother's breast for an infant's psychological development. He demonstrated that a mother's provision of warmth and security was far more significant for a baby's healthy attachment than the delivery of food or, in mammals, nursing.[113]

Bowlby's theory of attachment—what he originally called a theory of love—provides a psychological lens through which we can understand the Creature's behavior once abandoned at birth.[114] After Victor runs away from the Creature in fear and goes to sleep to seek escape, the Creature strives to reunite with his parent. As he peered through the curtain of Victor's bed, the Creature "muttered some inarticulate sounds while a grin wrinkled his cheeks"—much like a human infant might wake up his parents in the middle of the night for contact and comfort.[115] While a newborn would not have the ability to effect such a reunion on his own, beyond crying for attention, the

Creature's attempt to reconnect with his only parent is analogous to a very young child's need to develop and maintain a secure emotional attachment to a mother or maternal substitute in order to thrive. Poignantly, the Creature will later learn from observing the DeLaceys that, more typically, "the father doated on the smiles of the infant" instead of reacting with fear.[116]

After Victor flees from him once again, the Creature seeks a substitute for a mother in the blind Mr. DeLacey. A foil to Victor, DeLacey serves as a mother figure to his motherless children, acting as the emotional anchor of the family in the kitchen of the cottage, showing care and affection to everyone who enters—even the Creature, whose fearsome features he cannot see.[117] The closest the Creature ever comes to an intensively caring and loving parental figure is the blind DeLacey, and yet, he mainly observes the old man in secret from his hovel. Emerging from the "womb-like" hovel, the nameless Creature has a second chance at being named in relationship to a parent.[118] When DeLacey asks, "Who is there?" to his guest, the Creature identifies himself as "a traveller" who was "educated by a French family."[119] Afraid of the return of the sighted family members, the Creature quickly reveals the reason for his visit: it is not food but rather "warmth and rest" that he needs from DeLacey, his "best and only benefactor."[120]

Tragically, the Creature's one real chance for a secure attachment with a mother figure ends as soon as the sighted members of the family return and react violently to the Creature's monstrous appearance. Reacting in turn, the one-year-old Creature burns down their empty cottage in a rage. The loss of this potential family and community only compounds the Creature's angry sense of injury by his father's abandonment of him.[121] He proceeds to use his "superhuman" size, strength, and speed to enact revenge against his father for failing to provide for his most basic emotional and social needs.

In this way, Thought Experiment 3 plays with the physical and cognitive features of a human infant in order to hone attention on the emotional and social vulnerability of the youngest children. The Creature's counterfactual predicament as an "unfortunate and deserted creature" with "no relation or friend upon earth" is extreme and particular to his relationship to his father-scientist, but it nonetheless has an emotional parallel in real life.[122] Even after children grow up, physically and cognitively, their emotional vulnerability can persist into adulthood, especially if they have experienced an early loss of a parent or other loving caregiver.[123] The Creature suffered both kinds of early loss, most painfully with Victor and DeLacey. By making the Creature grow out of a child's typical physical and cognitive vulnerabilities extremely quickly,

Thought Experiment 3 jolts the reader to work out how the absence of such physical and cognitive vulnerabilities would not protect a child against the worst forms of emotional and social vulnerability.

Unlike a typical human infant, the Creature is able to survive on his own. Yet like a human infant, he fails to thrive emotionally without "love of another."[124] Thought Experiment 3 thus effects a mental separation between *surviving* and *thriving*. The Creature's survival is ensured by his size, strength, and rapid cognitive development. But even with such a "superhuman" ability for self-preservation, he cannot provide for himself two things essential for thriving or well-being: love and community.

In the fair draft of the manuscript completed in 1817, Shelley originally had the Creature's story begin the second volume of the book.[125] This break in the text signified the importance Shelley accorded the Creature's first-person testimony of growing up alone. Although the publisher changed the structure of the book when it was published in 1818, the Creature's incredible tale of survival of exposure at birth still stands out for its philosophical ingenuity. Not told in real time and retold by both Victor and Walton, the Creature's story retrospectively and indirectly takes a series of snapshots of his early development and education. Each snapshot focuses on a set of basic needs of the Creature (and, by analogy, all young human children) for healthy development and well-being: warmth, clothing, water, food, and shelter; education and language; and family, community, and love. The vulnerability of children to failure to thrive, illness, injury, disease, permanent disability, and even death due to deprivation of any of these basic developmental needs justifies children's fundamental rights to each of them.

Teased out of the Creature's story of deprivation, isolation, and despair, these fundamental rights of the child can be categorized as follows:

1. *Care rights.* The right to provision of basic needs for healthy child development: warmth, clothing, water, food, shelter, security, and education
2. *Identity rights.* The right to social identity: to have a name, a family, a community, and a state
3. *Love rights.* The right to share love, first and foremost with a parent or family, but also with friends and companions

Deprived of all three categories of rights, the Creature learns to care for himself, tries but fails to establish a social identity with the DeLaceys, and ultimately demands of his father a "right" to "love of another." It is the devastating loss of his "friends" in the DeLacey family that propels the Creature into antisocial behavior and crime. At the same time, this loss also stirs in him a sense of having a fundamental right to what he has never enjoyed: love.[126] In the moving voice of the Creature, Thought Experiment 3 leads the reader to see that a child might survive without care but will never thrive without family, community, and, most crucially, love.

By exploring the Creature's extreme emotional and social vulnerability due to his particular and tragic experiences of parental abandonment and loss, Thought Experiment 3 draws the reader back to contemplate the novel's second set of moral questions: *Do children have a fundamental and universal right to share love with a parent? If a parent (of any sort) is neither available nor fit to give and receive such love, then do children have a right to share love with a substitute?* To answer them, it is helpful to apply Nussbaum and Dixon's "vulnerability principle": if a child is vulnerable to a developmental deprivation due to a particular family relationship, then that child has "special priority" for the provision of a right to rectify that vulnerability over and above other people in society.[127] It is precisely with this sense of special priority that the Creature demands of his absentee father the fulfillment of a "right" to live in the interchange of sympathy with a loving substitute. The grounding for his moral claim to this "right" to love is that the particular circumstances of his creation and abandonment by his father-scientist deprived him of the "sympathies necessary for [his] being."

Children in general share the fundamental and universal right to parental love due to the necessity of such love for their thriving development. Children like the Creature who suffer grave deprivation of love by their own parents have a special priority for its provision by other, parental or even nonparental figures. Yet a political corollary of these moral questions remains unanswered: who or what should provide such a substitute for parental love when parents of any sort are unfit or unavailable even to arrange it?

Thought Experiment 4: Total Abuse

What if the child was not only abandoned and neglected
by his parent but also hurt or abused by every human
he encountered due to his monstrous appearance?

Thought Experiment 4 immerses the reader in a counterfactual scenario of total child neglect and abuse in order to address the broader political questions raised by the Creature's story. The Creature experiences three types of abuse that render him emotionally vulnerable to the extreme: (1) absolute motherlessless and repeated parental abandonment, (2) total social rejection due to his unlovable features, and (3) emotional and physical violence from nearly everyone who encounters him. Together, these three forms of external abuse lead the Creature to self-abuse through antisocial and criminal behavior, destructive of himself and others. This self-abuse fuels a pernicious feedback loop in which his emotional vulnerability is viciously reinforced.

What makes this scenario counterfactual is the total scope of the Creature's abuse. Strangers assault him when he appears in public; his own father tries to kill him; a fellow child, William Frankenstein, instantly reacts to him with horror and vituperation; and Captain Walton invites him to stay on his ship only to deliberate "destroying" him and impugn him as a "Hypocritical fiend!"[128] Due to his blindness and kindness, DeLacey is the only person who does not, upon meeting the Creature, intentionally harm him or react to him with emotional or physical violence. Yet even the benevolent old man abandons him, leaving the Creature painfully aware of his now truly absolute state of motherlessness and lovelessness.

In real life, abused children experience terrible neglect and horrific violence by family, friends, strangers, groups, and social and political institutions, but the scope and depth of the Creature's abuse goes beyond what a human child could survive. It could be countered that the Creature's abuse is not total because he does not die from it, as is tragically and unjustly the case with many abused children in actuality. However, his early abuse drives him to such a "sick impotence of despair" that he plans to commit suicide in the final scene of the novel once his father's death leaves him without a single affective tie to society.[129] Although he survives despite abuse, he fails to thrive because of his lack of family, friends, and love. He wishes that he was never born because of the "disgusting circumstances" of his creation: "Hateful day when I received life!"[130] The Creature's suffering of such psychological torture is more systematic and complete than abuse that ends in death: for it pushes the pain to the brink of the Creature's tolerance, leaving no end to the agony in sight.

By imagining a dystopian world in which a child suffers total abuse by everyone, Thought Experiment 4 might look, at first glance, like a utilitarian exercise in calculating pain in order to avoid it. By dialing up the degree of abuse to the highest level, the scenario would seem to urge the reader to adduce the maximum amount of pain that could be caused by child abuse. Although the thought experiment employs a kind of consequentialist reasoning that revolves around the feeling of pain (and the lack of pleasure), it is not classically utilitarian in the school of Jeremy Bentham. Shelley does not simply seek to avoid pain by calculating the greatest good or pleasure for the greatest number of sentient beings. She rather delves straight into an analysis of what pain means, psychologically and politically, for the most vulnerable of people: abused children. To focus on the calculation of the greatest good for the greatest number would obscure the needs of those persons on the fringe of society who need the most protection from pain.

Within the dystopian parameters of Thought Experiment 4, the reader encounters the total abuse of a child and its ripple effects upon the broader society. The first and most obvious victims are the members of the Frankenstein clan, whom the Creature targets for his vengeance against his creator. This outcome implies that the negative effects of child abuse are primarily felt in the families and friends of the victim and the perpetrator (for Victor and the Creature, they are one and the same, which may account for why their extended family is destroyed). Ultimately, Thought Experiment 4 impels the reader to move past such a narrow analysis of the most immediate social harm done by child abuse. Rather, it provokes the reader to take a wider look at how laws, courts, and states create (what Godwin called) the political "circumstances" that permit (what the Creature called) the "injustice" of child abandonment and abuse.[131]

Unlike an utilitarian thought experiment, which might seek to speculate the greatest extent of harm that could be done to sentient life as a consequence of a single child's abuse, Thought Experiment 4 uses the counterfactual idea of a child's total abuse to expose hidden yet systematic problems in laws, courts, and states with regard to the provision of children's rights. Following the poetic principle of negative capability, Shelley reveals the gaps in the legal and political systems that surround yet ignore the Creature. A stateless orphan, the Creature crosses German/Prussian, Swiss, French, Dutch, British, and Russian borders without ever being publicly recognized as a stranger or visitor, let alone a citizen. Courts in Geneva and Ireland put the wrong people on trial for the Creature's murders; their blindness to the real victims and criminals stems from their focus on swift and public punishment of the injustice of a violent crime rather than restoring justice as a result of uncovering the buried domestic sources of the violence. A Genevan magistrate curtly denies the credibility of Victor's story of the Creature's crimes and closes Elizabeth's murder case rather than suspending disbelief for the sake of uncovering the dark truth of the matter. In Ireland and Geneva, the refusal of public officials to seriously entertain the possibility that there is a serial murderer on the loose means that both the Creature's crimes and society's abuses against him remain untouched by justice.

Without a familial, legal, or political identity, the Creature cannot exercise rights or be punished for his denial of the rights of others. Thus, the Creature's predicament as a stateless orphan is akin to Hannah Arendt's claim that it is worse to be a stateless person than a criminal. Arendt argued that a criminal—unlike a refugee—is at least recognized under the law of the state that arrested him, if not afforded some legal rights while prosecuted or punished.[132] Thought Experiment 4 proposes it would be worst of all to be a truly stateless orphan, driven to crime due to total abuse—for no one, not even an officer of the law, would respond to your childish attempts to use crime to draw attention to your pain.

Having arraigned laws, courts, and states for enabling child abuse and the crimes of an abused child, Thought Experiment 4 raises the counterfactual question: is there any child-friendly role that these institutions could have played with regard to the Creature? Following Shelley's principle of negative capability, the reader may speculate what the child-friendly features of a legal and political system would be from what they are *not* in the novel. Throughout *Frankenstein*, the representatives of legal and political institutions failed to be fair and free from prejudice, as well as sympathetic to the victims and perpetrators of abuse and crime. By converse reasoning, any political or legal body that could ensure children's right to be free from abuse would have to show fairness and sympathy to both the victims and the perpetrators in order to stop the vicious cycle of violence in its tracks.

Mr. DeLacey is the only person in the novel to exhibit such fairness and sympathy in his treatment of the Creature. His blindness frees his judgment of prejudice, while his warm character makes him sympathetic to everyone. He even counts himself among the "condemned" and "criminal" because of his family's refugee status in Germany and his son Felix's trouble with the law in France.[133] His blindness makes him a fitting symbol for justice ideally conceived as fairness, as found in images and metaphors of justice as blindfolded from ancient art to the political theory of John Rawls. In dispensing compassion generously toward his "fellow creatures"—whether insiders or outsiders to his clan—he also represents true fairness as requiring an even-handed sympathy for each and all.[134] But even DeLacey fails to provide a safe space for the Creature to enjoy his moral rights to care, love, and community. This failure indicates a need for something more than the family to fairly and sympathetically provide the fundamental rights of children.

Confronted with the underlying legal and political injustice behind the Creature's total abuse and subsequent crimes, the reader might reasonably raise another counterfactual question: what could have been done legally or politically to prevent the abuse? Since the Creature's abuse is caused by the "disgusting circumstances" of his creation and abandonment by his father-scientist, the only satisfactory preventative measure would have been a loving substitute for his unloving parent. Thought Experiment 4 thus brings the reader to ponder another related political question: *If children's fundamental right to share love ought to be satisfied with a nonparental substitute if and only if a parent (or parental substitute) cannot fulfill this role, then should a political body have a role in the assignment of both parental and, if necessary, nonparental substitutes?* As we learned by running the first three thought experiments, parental love is crucial for the well-being of children. If parents (of any sort) can neither provide such love nor arrange for a parental substitute (of any sort), then children's right to love must be arranged by some other responsible body. This responsible body—perhaps initially a group of nonparental adult relatives—holds what Liao calls an "associate" duty to ensure the provision of the child's right to love. This duty is "associate" because it does not remove the parents' "primary" duty to arrange for the provision of their own child's right to love but rather supports it. Only in nonideal cases wherein the original parents are unavailable or unfit to provide or even arrange for their child's enjoyment of the right to love would this primary duty be transferred to the person who steps into the role of parent.[135]

While Liao assumes that nonparents have an associate duty only for the provision of a child's *right to be loved*, Thought Experiment 4 suggests that nonparents have an associate duty to arrange for a child's *right to share love*. The latter associate duty is more robust than Liao's formulation of it in that it requires nonparents to arrange for a child's right to share love (not merely receive love). At the same time, it is more flexible than Liao's formulation for it opens up the possibility that, in nonideal cases, the child's right to love could be fulfilled with a fitting nonparental figure.

When even nonparental family members cannot arrange for loving substitutes (parental or not), then an extrafamilial body must assume responsibility for the provision of children's right to love. In response to the Creature's original counterfactual predicament of total abuse, Thought Experiment 4 generates in the mind of the reader a second—and overtly political—counterfactual scenario. If there had been an extrafamilial legal or political body that could fulfill the associate duty to successfully assign a loving substitute for Victor, then the Creature would not have experienced abuse on a total scale.

If there had been such a national, international, or transnational child welfare organization, then Victor could have abandoned his Creature at its doorsteps, like Rousseau did to his five children at the foundling hospital in Paris. But unlike Rousseau's poor children, who likely died of neglect, the Creature would have found respite from his total abuse. In time, the organization might have located a compassionate blind person or couple, or even better, a school for the blind, to foster or adopt or at least be a primary caregiver, teacher, guardian, host, or adult companion to an orphan with severe physical birth defects.

Ideally, the organization would monitor and support the relationship to ensure it fulfilled the child's right to love, not just in the passive sense of receiving physical and emotional sustenance but in the active sense of enjoying a genuinely happy, affectionate, and caring relationship with another (or others), free from abuse, violence, or other forms of tyranny. As a result, the Creature would have shared love with another (or others), if not from the beginning of life, then at least as soon as it was practicable. Such love would have given him a sense of social identity and emotional security and thereby protected him from the worst psychological effects of abuse: isolation and despair.

Thought Experiment 5: The Scope and Limits of a Child's Right to Love

What if the neglected child claimed a fundamental right to share love with a sympathetic and equal female companion, thereby forcing his father-scientist to choose to either (a) make a female companion for his child (risking the development of a new species that could destroy the human race) or (b) suffer the angry revenge of his child who had become truly monstrous in behavior?

Shelley's extraordinary skills as an author of speculative fiction are fully on display in Thought Experiment 5. She designed it with the Chinese-box structure of the novel itself. In the outermost box, it is a counterfactual scenario to be entertained by the reader, like the previous four in the cascade of thought experiments that constitute the core narrative of *Frankenstein*. In the inner boxes, it is a pair of thought experiments conducted, in turn, by the Creature and Victor concerning the scope and limits of children's rights and parental duties. In other words, the culminating thought experiment of the novel is in fact a set of interconnected thought experiments staged within a thought experiment—a complex literary achievement imitated, although perhaps unrivalled, in speculative fiction since.[136]

In terms of the novel's narrative structure, Thought Experiment 5 transpires over a very long period of the story. It begins when the twenty-one-month-old Creature confronts his long-lost father on the *mer de glace* or sea of ice in the Alps near Victor's home in Geneva. After convincing Victor to listen to his story of abandonment and total abuse, the Creature justifies to his father his demand for a female companion by proposing a counterfactual with forward-looking ethical implications: "If any being felt emotions of benevolence toward me, I should return them an hundred and an hundred fold; for that one creature's sake, I would make peace with the whole kind!"[137] This argument initially persuades Victor that "the justice due both to him and my fellow-creatures demanded of me that I should comply with his request."[138]

Fifteen months later, Victor conducted a thought experiment on the possible consequences of bringing (or not bringing) the nearly completed female companion to life. Weighing these possibilities, he ultimately chooses to destroy the female to save the "whole human race" from the potential menace of a "race of devils" that could be "propagated" by the creatures rather than save himself from the vengeance of the Creature.[139] Within this long narrative arc, Thought Experiment 5 loops back in and through the previous counterfactual scenarios (especially Thought Experiments 2 and 4) to weave together focal elements of the novel into a coherent philosophical story about the boundaries and the frontiers of children's rights and correlative parental duties.

Frankenstein's culminating thought experiment returns the reader, as well as Victor and the Creature, to address the two sets of moral questions that attend the uncanny—or strange yet still familiar—parent-child relationship at the heart of the novel. Redacted down to their most basic elements, these questions can be most simply and clearly stated in tandem: do children have a right to love, and do parents have a duty to provide it? The twin thought experiments of the Creature and Victor allow the reader, in turn, to parse the definitions of children's right to love and the parental duty for its provision. Thought Experiment 5 initially trains the mind's eye on defining the *limits* of a child's right to love and what a parent must provide to fulfill it before it explores the moral frontiers of children's rights and parental duties. In the shadow of Shelley's principle of negative capability, the moral questions that animate the core narrative of *Frankenstein* take on a darker cast: with regard to love, what *don't* children have a right to expect from their parents, and what *don't* parents have to do for their children?

I. The Creature's Thought Experiment: "If only I had a sympathetic companion, I would be happy and virtuous!"

The Creature's thought experiment focuses on the articulation and defense of a child's right to love, to be provided or at least arranged in the first place by a parent. The Creature's demand of his father for the arrangement of his enjoyment of this right is predicated on a counterfactual conditional. If he had an equal female companion made to be as "hideous" as him, then he would share "love of another" with "a creature" who was not frightened by his deformity.[140]

The Creature's demand can be divided into two parts: (1) the appeal to the original duty-holder (the parent) and (2) the substance of the right (to share love with a nonparental substitute). As for (1), the appeal to Victor to fulfill this duty is appropriate because he, as the only parent, is solely responsible for the now twenty-one-month-old Creature and his well-being. As for (2), the substance of the rights claim—at least in its most general form—is valid because of the Creature's tragic predicament. The Creature has lost not only his father but also his only real chance at a parental substitute, DeLacey, due to his unlovable features. Hence, he has a right to a nonparental substitute with whom he can share love because a loving relationship is necessary for his (and, by implication, every child's) well-being, even if a parent or parental figure is neither available nor fit to fulfill this role.

In its most general formulation, the two parts of the Creature's demand for a right to love are morally valid or justified. When we examine the details of the Creature's proposal to satisfy this right, however, some serious problems emerge with its moral justification. First, the substance of the Creature's demand does not take into account the prospective female companion's agency or perspective. She has no say in the matter of her creation by Victor to satisfy the Creature's right to love. Moreover, the Creature never considers that her point of view might differ from his own, despite their similar appearance. As Victor later conjectures in his own chain of counterfactual reasoning, she might not love the Creature even though she was made for that purpose.

Second, the substance of the Creature's demand does not address the prospective female's rights independently of his own. She would be a child, too, brought to life by her father-scientist, with the same right to share love that the Creature holds. Sharing the same parent but not made by sexual reproduction, the two creatures would be nonbiological or social siblings to one another. To expect her to serve only as an equal and loving companion to her sibling would be to rob her of her own right to seek to share love with a parent or parental figure, even if such a search was doomed to failure. It would also place her in a potentially incestuous and immoral relationship with her older male sibling. While it would not necessarily be incestuous in the sexual sense (for the Creature never expresses sexual desire for a mate), it could easily be incestuous in the emotional sense of being used by an older friend or relative for their affective benefit. The fact that she would be made without her consent to satisfy a deep emotional need of her older sibling makes it likely, from a Wollstonecraftian perspective, that the relationship would be fraught with inequalities and even abuses of power from the start. As the Creature himself originally argued to Victor, his relationship with the female would need to be equal in order for them to mutually reinforce each other's learning and practice of the virtues of love and peace. In the specific formulation of his proposal for the satisfaction of his right to love, however, the Creature neglected to acknowledge the need for equality of rights and equality of agency in any fully egalitarian relationship capable of the virtue of love.

Without equality of rights and equality of agency, the creatures would lack the preconditions for the "interchange" of sympathy as genuine moral equals. The substance of the Creature's specific proposal to satisfy his right to love thus proves itself to be, upon reflection, morally incoherent and unjustifiable. By running the Creature's thought experiment concerning his right to share love with an equal female companion, the reader discerns that the Creature had a right to love with a nonparental substitute arranged by his father but not with the particular female companion whom he tyrannically asked his father to make for him.

While a product of his unjust circumstances and lack of parenting, the failure of the Creature to propose an ethical plan for the provision of his right to love uncovers some deeper moral questions beneath the issue of defining the rights and duties of parents and children: what is love, and what are the ethical limits of the search for and experience of it? Initially, the Creature defines love as "living in the interchange of those sympathies necessary for my being." This is a relational understanding of love or a conception of love as a two-way street. On the Creature's account, "love" must be shared with "another."

From her readings of David Hume, Edmund Burke, and especially Wollstonecraft during the mid-1810s, Shelley was aware of an emergent philosophical consensus that sympathy was a mutual communication of affect—a social and psychological capability that was of profound significance for ethics.[141] By definition, "sympathy"—or, etymologically, the sharing of pathos or feeling—required both a relationship and a two-way communication of affect within that relationship. A pair of sympathetic persons could extend their feelings to the point that they met and merged with the other, thereby psychologically uniting as one.

As Wollstonecraft argued, such "sympathy that unites hearts" is the only virtuous form of "love," whether one is thinking of a marriage, a mother-child relationship, or some other close affective bond.[142] Such sympathy, for Wollstonecraft, was in fact the genesis of all moral and political virtue because it motivated people to identify with each other and share the goods necessary for living together in a peaceful, happy, and otherwise virtuous political community. The Creature thus converges with a trend in eighteenth-century moral philosophy (particularly Wollstonecraft) in his abstract definition of love: love is a mutually and morally edifying practice of sharing or giving and receiving sympathy in relationship with another.

However, the Creature quickly diverges from Wollstonecraft's philosophy of love in two significant ways. First, as a child, he demands a right to love, which is his parent's primary duty to fulfill at least through arranging its satisfaction. Although Wollstonecraft envisioned a mutually sympathetic love as the ethical heart of any close relationship, including the parent-child bond, and even suggested that parents had an obligation to share such sympathy and affection with their children, she stopped at defending children's right to parental care and never took the step of claiming their additional right to love.[143]

Second, the Creature's demand of his father to make him a female companion veers from his original definition of love. The Creature's proposal implicitly relies upon a conception of a passive and consumptive *right to be loved* that contradicts elements of his earlier, coherent argument for an active and relational *right to share love*. Because the Creature does not take into account the potential for the female's different perspective or capability for free agency, his proposal treats her as a mere instrument for the satisfaction of his right to be loved. In other words, she would be the tool for the delivery of love, and the Creature would be the receptacle. Love would be a one-way street for the passive fulfillment of the Creature's affective needs, not a two-way process of sympathetic communication of affect between moral equals.

In contemporary political philosophy, the crucial difference between a child's right to love and a child's right to be loved is shown in the respective arguments of Shelley Burtt and Liao. Liao argues that children have a right to be loved because "being loved" is a "fundamental condition" of their flourishing or good and happy lives.[144] While this broader justification for a child's right to be loved is sound, Liao only formulates the right in passive terms that focus on the child's receipt of love, not in active terms that highlight the deeper moral value of a child's right to a two-way relationship of love with a parent. We have seen the problems with the Creature's imagining of the passive satisfaction of his right to love with the merely instrumental female companion. The same moral problems would persist in any parent-child relationship wherein the child functions as a mere receptacle for parental love. In each case, love is conceptualized in instrumental terms as a kind of sustenance provided by the lover to the beloved. In each case, the child is the receptacle, and the lover of the child is the instrument for delivery of love into the receptacle.

The Creature's initial definition of love as the interchange of sympathy holds far much more promise for a theory of love predicated on the idea of moral equality. By running the Creature's thought experiment in our own minds, we have seen why equality of rights, especially to freedom, must prevail between companions and siblings if their relationships are to be mutually loving as well as just. Despite their obvious differences in status and power, parents and children are also capable of realizing moral equality in their relationships. The most vital way that parents and children realize moral equality is by sharing love.

Initially, infants are not able to share love as fully as parents, but they show tremendous signs of benefiting from the love that their parents show them. By showing those signs of flourishing, often with physical affection, infants send cues to parents concerning what works well in their intensive and loving practice of parental care. If an infant lacks sufficient love and fails to thrive, then the infant's signs of poor growth and other developmental delays cue to the parents or other adults the need for different, more intensive and emotionally attentive caregiving practices. Although newborns do not share love the same way as parents do, they respond to and communicate love in their own way.

Between three and six months of age, infants begin to deeply "fall in love" with their parents, especially a mother or other intensively loving caregiver.[145] Learning from parental practices of love toward them, babies come to adore their parents. This mutual adoration enables a parent to become what Burtt has called the essential "soulmate" figure to the child.[146] In the "soulmate" role, the parent is the child's primary source of unconditional love, which in turn fuels the child's devotion to the parent. The child's healthy moral and physical development revolves around the sense of a secure psychological attachment to this "soulmate" parent (or what Bowlby would call the "mother" figure). Although a parent plays a primary role in the provision of love in the earliest stages of child development, the child's responses to the delivery of parental love pave the way for their mutual adoration as well as parental learning of the essential role of soulmate/mother.

With this relational model of parent-child love in mind, we can see that the Creature got at least part of the argument right about children's right to love. Certainly he had an active and robust right to share love, to be ideally fulfilled with his parent or, at a minimum, arranged by him. But he did not have the passive and consumptive right merely to be loved by the female companion who was—without consent—to be made exclusively for this purpose.

The Creature's thought experiment calls into question the ethics of his own demand for a female companion. In real life, the expectation of such nonparental relationships to fulfill a child's right to love is fraught with similar moral issues. Children's right to love is best and ideally fulfilled with a parent or parent figure. Only in nonideal and extreme cases should nonparental alternatives be considered, such as a mentor, coach, guidance counselor, host, teacher, team, or group home. A child who has suffered abuse by a series of parents and parental figures may—for good reason—not tolerate the introduction of another parental figure in her life. Such a child, in contemporary Western legal systems, is entitled to be legally emancipated from parental and other adult or institutional care and to function independently as an adult. At the point that Victor dashes his hopes of having a female companion, the Creature could be read as such an emancipated child. Even granted independence from his parent, the Creature or any such emancipated child would retain a right to share love with another.

But the Creature's tragic predicament suggests that there is an expiration date on the enjoyment of a child's right to love. Since he had neither a parent nor a female companion expressly made for him to satisfy this right, the Creature "grows out" of the right to love before it can be fulfilled. Similarly, an emancipated child may not find any substitute for parental love but might rather "grow into" other forms of love, such as adult friendships, romantic relationships, or parenting a child of her own. Running the Creature's thought experiment drives the reader to the insight that he or any child (emancipated or not) would not have a passive or consumptive right to a companion or romantic partner because it would deny the free agency of the desired partner. The same reasoning would apply to adults: there is no adult right to have a friend or romantic partner or a corresponding duty of someone to serve in those roles because love in these cases must respect the free agency and personal feelings of both parties in order to be fully egalitarian and hence morally respectful of the beloved other.

Engaging the Creature's thought experiment, the reader might reasonably conclude that a child's right to love pertains to the stage of childhood only and not beyond it. The right would remain a fundamental and universal right, despite the fact that adults would not hold it.[147] Because all adults were once children, all people would hold the right to love during the most vulnerable span of their lives for the basic reason that their lives and well-being depend on it.

II. Victor's Thought Experiment: "What would be worse: to animate the female companion or to abort her?"

Victor is initially persuaded by the Creature's counterfactual-conditional reasoning that it is his parental duty to at least arrange for his child to have a sympathetic companion. Fifteen months later, on a deserted island in the Orkneys, Victor starts to have serious doubts about the wisdom of bringing the almost completed female creature to life. He deliberates whether to follow through on his duty to fulfill the Creature's right to share love by developing a consequentialist thought experiment.

This forward-looking, two-pronged decision tree weighs the worst possible consequences of choosing to (1) animate or (2) abort the female companion. Which choice would bring the most "wretchedness" and the least "happiness"?[148] Victor runs the thought experiment to determine—on utilitarian grounds of avoiding the greatest ill for the greatest number—the choice he should *not* take. The moral purpose of Victor's thought experiment is to determine whether his special duty to satisfy his particular child's right to love is trumped by a general duty to save "the whole human race," in this case, from the reproduction of the Creature's potentially destructive "own species."[149]

In the first prong of his thought experiment, Victor surmises the worst possible consequences of animating the female creature. Initially, his chain of reasoning turns on the assumption that the female companion would be equal to the Creature in free agency. Because he cannot know her "dispositions" in advance (just as he could not know the Creature's), he speculates that she "might become ten thousand times more malignant than her mate."[150] Her independent will could set her in opposition to the Creature's plan to "quit the neighborhood of man."[151] Since it was "likely" she would become a "thinking and reasoning animal," she might "refuse to comply with a compact made before her creation."[152] She could instead prefer to "delight, for its own sake, in murder and wretchedness."[153] Contrary to the Creature's expectation of mutual sympathy due to their similar features, the two creatures "might even hate each other" due to their deformities.[154] The female could desert the Creature for "the superior beauty of man," making him even more lonely and vengeful.[155]

After speculating the worst consequences of making a female who would be equal to the Creature in free agency, Victor broadens the scope of this argument to consider the worst consequences that would follow from their potential reproduction. Even if the creatures fled to the "deserts of the new world," to live in a kind of state of nature with one another, their "sympathies" for each other would inevitably lead to "children."[156] Because he cannot predict or control the dispositions of the creatures, Victor fears that their offspring would become similarly unmanageable and destructive. This "race of devils" might bring the "species of man" to a "condition precarious and full of terror," perhaps even to the point of extinction.[157] In this apocalyptic scenario, there would be no containment of the creatures through their self-imposed isolation from humanity: for their offspring would be "propagated upon the earth" and threaten the "existence of the whole human race."[158] In drawing these conclusions, Victor assumes that (1) a future species would evolve from his creatures, (2) future humans would fear it, and (3) it would be destructive of humans.

In the second prong of his thought experiment, Victor assumes that he would suffer the angry revenge of the Creature if he destroyed the female companion in order to save humanity from their potential spawn. With this in mind, he weighs his duty to save himself from the Creature's vengeance against his broader obligation "to future ages" of the "human race."[159] He wonders if he had "a right" to avoid the Creature's vengeance if it meant visiting the "curse" of the creatures and their descendants upon "everlasting generations."[160] He concludes not, reasoning that it would be selfish to "buy [his] own peace at the price perhaps of the existence of the whole human race."[161]

On the face of it, Victor's choice to abort the female looks supererogatory, or above and beyond the call of duty: for he proposes to sacrifice himself for the prospect of saving humanity as a whole. It is not clear, however, whether Victor's motives are entirely selfless since neither he nor the reader has any certainty that the creatures would bring about this projected apocalypse or that the Creature would kill him in vengeance. He is making some rather biased projections about the creatures' future behavior and its consequences without any evidence except what he has generalized from his own experience of the Creature he loathes and despises.

We can productively contrast Victor's moral reasoning with a twenty-first-century model of supererogation, U.S. Navy SEAL and Medal of Honor winner Michael Monsoor. In September 2006, atop a roof in Ramadi, Iraq, Monsoor deliberately threw himself upon a grenade to save the lives of his team. He knew he would die, because of his extensive training in handling explosives and demolition. He was the only person situated on the roof to escape, yet he made the choice to sacrifice his life for the sake of others. Having caught the grenade that struck his chest, Monsoor literally had evidence in hand of either his certain death or the certain deaths of others. Unlike Victor, he used this knowledge to choose a truly supererogatory path: the definite destruction of himself to ensure the safety of those around him. As many remarked on the occasion of the christening of a Navy ship in his honor, Monsoor not only acted above and beyond the call of duty but also, and even more important, acted out of love for his SEAL teammates.[162]

Unlike the modern-day hero Monsoor, Victor's choice does not prove to be above and beyond the call of duty. Nor is it motivated by love of others but rather by fear and hate of the other. While presented as self-sacrificial and humanitarian, Victor's choice is actually an abdication of a fundamental moral duty toward his child and a denial of his child's fundamental right to love. By framing his moral dilemma in terms of a stark choice between saving himself and saving humanity, Victor elides the deeper moral conflict: his particular parental duty to assist the Creature versus his general duty to assist the human species.

Victor never considers the possibility of a third way between the two prongs of his thought experiment. He could have made an attempt to reconcile the competing but not necessarily incompatible ends of promoting the well-being of his child and the well-being of the human species. By using the good of humanity as an excuse for aborting the female, Victor conveniently avoided yet again the performance of a fundamental duty to his child, as well as the appearance of having shirked this duty.

But what, precisely, was the content of Victor's enduring duty to assist the Creature? The Creature's thought experiment yielded a sound argument for Victor's minimal duty as a parent to at least arrange for a loving companion for his child. But as we have seen by running the thought experiment in our own minds, the Creature had no right to have a female companion made for the express purpose of loving him. Hence, Victor had no correlative duty to make such a companion in the first place, independent of any possible bad consequences of making her. His decision to make, then unmake, the female worsens his already deteriorating relationship with his Creature but does not change the fact that he never had a duty to make such a companion.

Indeed, Victor's violent destruction of the female in front of the Creature constitutes an act of psychological abuse because it snuffs out—with cold and gruesome detachment—his child's expectation of a companion without even trying to provide another substitute. As the Creature cries after seeing the female torn to pieces by his father, "Shall each man . . . find a wife for his bosom, and each beast have his mate, and I be alone?"[163] At the same time as he draws an implicit distinction between his desire for an equal companion and the marriage and mating practices of humans and other animals, the Creature underscores their common motives: the fear of loneliness and the longing for community. Even as the Creature foresees a life of terrible solitude without the female, he reminds his parent of his primary responsibility for his child's enjoyment of love—even if he never provides or arranges for it. Even after his father's death, the Creature insists upon Victor's ultimate responsibility for his unsatisfied desire for "love and fellowship" and, worse, the incalculable "hours and months of misery which [he] endured" because of it. To Walton, the only spectator of his grief, he asks with pathos, "Was there no injustice in this?"[164]

Despite the practical obstacles to fulfilling it, Victor's duty to arrange for the Creature to have a loving companion persists. Victor knew of the Creature's brief domestic idyll with DeLacey and might have deduced, in another thought experiment, that finding a blind person, couple, or school community to love him might be a way to reconcile his child's good with that of the human species. Better yet, Victor might have used the metaphor of blindness to construct a thought experiment that would elucidate moral reasons for figuratively blinding himself to the features of his Creature that had prevented him from loving him or at least caring enough to find someone else to love him. By metaphorically blinding himself to his Creature's monstrous appearance and behavior, Victor might have found sufficient affective and moral motivation to strategize a way to fulfill his child's need for love without animating the female companion. If all else failed, he could have become the modern Oedipus in accepting the tragedy of his situation by literally blinding himself in order to perform his duty to love his child in the absence of any practicable substitute. In some ways, this last possibility is most compatible with the 1831 edition of the novel, which Shelley revised to emphasize Victor's view of his making of the Creature and its tragic consequences as an "immutable" product of fate and "destiny," not free will.[165]

Victor's failure to arrange for the provision of his child's right to love indicates not only his grave moral wrongdoing toward his child but also the novel's political implications for children's rights. When parents fail to fulfill their duty to provide a child's right to love, either by themselves or through the arrangement of substitutes, there must be some responsible body beyond the family to arrange for the provision of that enduring right. The bleak yet realistic possibility of parental failure to provide a child's right to love opens the door to a moral justification for some extrafamilial legal or political body to step in and arrange for its provision. The fact of parental failure to love their own children means it is ultimately the collective responsibility of society to ensure children share love with parents or fitting substitutes. The poetic principle of negative capability directs the outcome of Victor's thought experiment: for it is the lack of a dutiful parent that generates the imaginative conditions for speculating a just political supplement to and support system for families.

By conducting Victor's thought experiment, the reader perceives the moral problems with the conclusions he derives from it. We have seen how he tried to shirk his parental duty by appealing, on utilitarian grounds, to his duty to save humanity. Let's grant—for the sake of argument in utilitarian terms—that the animation of the female creature would have necessarily led to the destruction of the human species. In this case, one might plausibly argue it would be clearly wrong to animate the female because human suffering and loss of life would outweigh any joy brought by giving the Creature the female companion.

Even given such a seemingly clear-cut justification for the abortion of the female creature, Victor's appeal to a duty to save humanity over and against his parental duty would remain ethically problematic and even inconsistent with two major schools of utilitarianism. Victor treats the duty to save humanity as a kind of trump card that overrides all other moral duties, including the minimal parental duty to arrange for a loving companion for one's own child if and only if a parent cannot play that role. The problem with conceptualizing the duty to save humanity as a moral trump card is that any such trump would have to be truly comprehensive in its moral scope in order to justify its override of other duties. The duty to save humanity is not comprehensive in its moral scope because it focuses on the well-being of the human species to the exclusion of other forms of life, including the Creature.

Furthermore, Victor's use of this moral trump card would not be justified under either Bentham's or John Stuart Mill's utilitarian reasoning because it does not take into consideration the well-being of "all sentient creation" in its calculation of utility.[166] Godwin's version of utilitarianism also fell short of this classical and Millian standard because he only defined happiness in terms of human pleasure and pain, like Victor.[167] While it might be tempting, initially, to see Victor's appeal to save humanity as a cosmopolitan appeal to global justice on the broadest scale, it proves to be far more limited: a mere humanitarian impulse. This humanitarian impulse seeks not to save the world but rather only human life in it.

Victor's humanitarianism falls prey to the problem of speciesism. Much like Wollstonecraft's philosophy of children's and other human rights, it elevates the human species above all other species of life and treats humanity as more (or even exclusively) deserving of fundamental rights such as the right to life itself. As we saw in Chapter 2, however, Wollstonecraft supplemented her arguments for children's human rights with arguments for making the benevolent treatment of animals a basic part of teaching children how to be humane. Extending her philosophy of animal ethics to include the nascent vegetarian cause, Percy Shelley published *A Vindication of Natural Diet* (1813), in which he modeled his vegetarian arguments after those of the *Rights of Woman*.[168] Victor stands in striking contrast to such Wollstonecraftian approaches to nonhuman animal ethics. His callous abortion of the female creature, at the verge of her becoming "a thinking and reasoning animal" and in full view of the Creature, is the most apt and disturbing example of his disrespect for other species and forms of life.[169]

In contemporary political philosophy, the problem of speciesism has usually been identified in arguments for rights that exclude nonhuman animals and the environment from consideration.[170] Philosophers are beginning to address the need for recognizing the rights of posthuman persons, or persons who (will) have been altered or made or will have evolved as a result of interventions in science and technology such that they are strikingly different from their human ancestors/creators in features and/or capacities.[171] What is truly visionary about *Frankenstein* as a work of speculative fiction is its suggestion that a creature of a new species made by a human through science would be entitled to rights equivalent to its maker's. Perhaps even more profoundly, the novel leads readers to question whether being human or humane should be equated with the human being.

After Wollstonecraft's focus on finding social justice for the marginalized and oppressed within a modern rights-based republic and Godwin's focus on defining political justice in utilitarian terms within an ideal minimal state, Shelley pushed speculation about justice beyond the bounds of the state, beyond narrow definitions of rights and utility, and even beyond the bounds of the human to the radical question of a truly cosmopolitan—nonspeciesist and posthuman—conception of justice. For the reader, the cognitive payoff of running Thought Experiment 5 is the opportunity to define a place for children's rights within such a truly cosmopolitan conception of justice. The tragic outcome of Victor's decision to deprive his Creature of his right to a loving companion suggests that his purely humanitarian motives were too narrow and speciesist to be truly universal and just. A need for a posthuman(itarian) perspective on justice is indicated by the lack of justice to be found at the end of the novel, especially for the Creature, who still protests the "injustice" done to him by his father and society at large.

Contra Victor's narrow humanitarianism, a truly cosmopolitan perspective on justice would have been open to considering the Creature's rights alongside the rights of humans, rather than treating them as mutually exclusive. It would have even considered the rights of the female creature and other new or potential forms of sentient life, not solely those of future generations of humans. It is this posthuman(itarian) approach to rights that I explore in the concluding chapter by applying the futuristic insights of *Frankenstein*'s five thought experiments on the rights of the child to some timely twenty-first-century issues surrounding the rights of disabled, stateless, and posthuman children.

CHAPTER 4

Three Applications of Shelley's Thought Experiments: The Rights of Disabled, Stateless, and Posthuman Children

We have seen how the very design of *Frankenstein* as a cascade of thought experiments gives it the power to address a series of philosophical questions surrounding the radical moral and political idea of children's rights. But is it a successful set of thought experiments? Peter Swirski has argued that the success of any thought experiment (literary or otherwise) depends on its coherence, relevance, informativeness, and projectability.[1] As we shall see, *Frankenstein* exhibits all four of these features of a successful literary thought experiment, showing exceptional projectability to issues beyond the scope of the novel, its sources, or its context.

From organ transplants to in vitro fertilization to genetically modified foods (now known as Frankenfoods), Shelley's novel has proven to be a visionary conceptual resource for thinking through the ethics of applying modern scientific ideas and theories, especially concerning the creation or modification of human and other life forms. Jon Turney chronicled the history of the public reception of *Frankenstein* within such debates, beginning with the development of artificial reproductive technology (ART) and tools for tissue culture and transplant surgery at the turn of the twentieth century and extending to the making of "test-tube babies" and recombinant DNA in the late twentieth century.[2] In just the past few years, doctors and scientists have connected the story of Victor Frankenstein and his Creature to contemporary debates on the ethics of editing the human genome (with the newly invented CRISPR-Cas9 technology) to create what the biologist Paul Knoepfler has called "GM babies" (genetically modified babies).[3] With CRISPR-Cas9, biologists have the ability to permanently modify the core, nuclear DNA of germ (egg and sperm) cells such that new features and capacities (such as freedom from genetic disease and the related benefit of a longer "health span") would be heritable for future generations.[4] Some critics of gene editing have gone so far as to call these CRISPR-Cas9–designed, genetically modified children of the not-so-distant future "Frankenbabies."[5]

Because of the novel's incredible success in producing some of the governing metaphors of the ethics of scientific research and its applications, *Frankenstein*'s projectability in matters of politics has been less appreciated in the twenty-first century than perhaps in its own time. In 1818, the very first reviews of the anonymous novel assumed its Godwinian political subtext—and even that William Godwin or one of his circle was its author—well before Mary Shelley's name appeared on the cover in France in 1821.[6] Soon after—beginning in the 1820s and gaining international traction by the 1850s—the name "Frankenstein" became a political metaphor for public fears of the enslaved, colonized, poor, marginalized, and rightless rising up against their oppressors. Elizabeth Young has powerfully chronicled how the metaphor of the monster has been used in American literature since the nineteenth century to dramatize the struggle of black Americans against the whites responsible for their appalling, centuries-old conditions of slavery and oppression.[7] Eduardo Cadava has provocatively compared the Creature with Frederick Douglass, who used metaphors of monstrosity to criticize the dehumanizing public perception and treatment of blacks in his time.[8]

Young points out that new political uses of the Frankenstein metaphor arose in the wake of 9/11, portraying U.S. foreign policy as a kind of monster that would come back to destroy its own creators, including "Dr. Cheneystein."[9] More explicitly, political usages of the name "Frankenstein" shall undoubtedly arise as the upcoming bicentennial of the novel's publication draws more public attention to the story and its ongoing adaptation to film. The 2015 film *Victor Frankenstein*—featuring the famed *Harry Potter* actor Daniel Radcliffe as the doctor's assistant "Igor"—has an interesting political bent despite its formulaic Hollywood style. This latest return of the Frankenstein story to the big screen depicts Victor and Igor's investigation by the police for their reputed involvement in the unauthorized creation of life through artificial means. Even more recently, "Frankenstein" has been deployed in a formal political context. During the 2016 U.S. presidential primary season, one blogger used the name "Frankenstein" to describe the re-creation of the Republican

Party as a grotesque assemblage of parts previously deemed incompatible with each other.[10]

To deepen appreciation of the story's political salience in the twenty-first century and beyond, I explain why *Frankenstein*'s five thought experiments on the rights of the child project insights essential for addressing three current and future political issues at the frontiers of rights theories and theories of justice. Martha Nussbaum has outlined three such "frontiers of justice" as disability, nationality, and species membership.[11] More recently, she and Rosalind Dixon have argued that children's rights are the "fourth frontier of justice."[12] Pushing this philosophical and political agenda forward, I use the speculative fiction of *Frankenstein* to map three further frontiers for rights theories and theories of justice within the issue of children's rights.

To show *Frankenstein*'s projectability to cutting-edge issues of children's rights, I build on Chapter 3's extended reading of the novel as a cascade of five thought experiments on the rights of the child. By speculating the negative psychological consequences of the Creature's abandonment due to his deformed appearance, Thought Experiments 1 through 3 shed light on the rights of infants with severe physical birth defects, such as cleft lip and palate, which sometimes frighten or frustrate parents to the point of child abandonment or abuse. By drawing out the broader social and political implications of the Creature's abandonment and survival on his own, Thought Experiments 3 and 4 illuminate the rights of stateless orphans who migrate unaccompanied by parents or adults across state borders. Finally, the whole cascade— culminating in Victor and the Creature's joint deliberations on the ethics of making a female companion in Thought Experiment 5—projects insights for the articulation of the rights of GM babies and posthuman children. The first and last of these frontiers show the enduring relevance of science, especially the ethics of medical and biotechnological interventions, for any ambitious political reading of *Frankenstein*.

Frankenstein Meets Swirski's Criteria for a Successful Thought Experiment

Swirski is the leading exponent of the view that literary thought experiments are functionally the same as other kinds of thought experiments, philosophical or scientific.[13] As such, they must meet the same criteria for success: they must be coherent, relevant, informative, and projectable. Swirski draws upon several literary examples to illustrate this point—most vividly, the work of Walker Percy.[14] Far more famous than Percy but sharing the philosophical sophistication of his book *Lost in the Cosmos* (1983), *Frankenstein* is an especially apt and visible example of how a work of literature may successfully function as a thought experiment or even as a complex series of them.

First, like any successful thought experiment, the narrative of *Frankenstein* is coherent in its assumptions about nature, society, and science and proceeds to logically deduce consequences from those assumptions—even when it occasionally violates them. Meeting Swirski's formulation of the "coherence" criterion, Shelley's occasional violation of the basic assumptions that govern the structure of her novel is "deliberate" for the sake of a "cognitive payoff."[15] The peculiar presupposition of the cascade is a case in point: the (as yet biotechnologically unachieved) making of a motherless child through science leads the reader to think through the differences between biological parenthood and the social practice of mothering or intensive loving care of one's own child.

Second, the narrative of *Frankenstein* is relevant to the real world in the sense that it meets what Swirski calls the "minimal rewrite rule." Shelley minimally rewrote her experience of reality in a way that made her speculative fiction "identifiable with a possible world closest to reality."[16] By making her fiction reflect the features of the real world to the greatest extent possible, she allowed the ideas generated by its cascade of thought experiments to be "directly transferable and applicable" to people's actual lives, moral problems, and political predicaments.[17] Shelley's novel engaged the latest currents in turn-of-the-nineteenth-century science, especially biology, anatomy, chemistry, and the study of electricity, even as it speculated the creation of a human life (or, perhaps more aptly, a posthuman life) without sexual reproduction.[18] Even the wildest scientific ideas of the story remain relevant because of their plausibility for future implementation in some form, even if Victor's tragic experiment with making life could (or should) never be replicated.

The political ideas of the story are far more grounded in reality. They find their roots in major trends in moral, political, and educational philosophy, such as the social contract tradition and its critics, which had in fact shaped political ideology and behavior during the French Revolution and the Napoleonic era.[19] To reinforce this theme, Shelley set the novel in the 1790s and mapped the dates of pivotal plot points onto seismic political events of the revolutionary period.[20]

Third, *Frankenstein* meets Swirski's criterion of informativeness. Its cascade of counterfactual scenarios is "informed by the methodological principles and state of the art findings in germane disciplines."[21] In Britain and Germany, scientists experimented with electricity to try to reanimate corpses of nonhuman animals (and perhaps even humans) in the early nineteenth century.[22] Erasmus Darwin, the grandfather of Charles Darwin, had published a proto-evolutionary theory of how new life could be formed from inanimate matter through a process of "spontaneous generation."[23] Shelley was aware of these scientific trends and informed her novel's cascade of thought experiments accordingly. Her 1831 introduction to *Frankenstein* suggests that the genesis of the story itself arose from her listening to a discussion about Darwin's reported experiments concerning the animation of a "piece of vermicelli" in a "glass case."[24]

Fourth, *Frankenstein* shows exceptional promise in its projectability. Readers and interpreters of the novel "may tease out the testable consequences of [its] thought experiments in search of contingent generalizations, latent implications, and even occasional gaps in extant theories."[25] Swirski acknowledged that in the case of literary thought experiments, "few narrative theses could be verified in a controlled setting."[26] An exception, he proposes, might be the use of artificial intelligence research to develop computer "personoids" who could "model inner lives and social intercourses" and thereby conduct such controlled "test runs" of literary thought experiments.[27] However, readers can still productively run such literary thought experiments in their own minds (as I modeled in Chapter 3) without such a controlled, scientific setting for verifying the narrative's theses. For example, the scientific implications of the narrative of *Frankenstein* have been teased out and analyzed by scientists, historians, science fiction writers, and literary critics. Many of the political implications of *Frankenstein* have been well developed too, especially by literary critics.[28]

What remains is for political philosophers to take the novel seriously as a productive intervention in their field of study. Specifically, political philosophers ought to run *Frankenstein*'s five thought experiments on the rights of the child in order to generate new ideas on children's rights that can aid them in addressing some of the most important questions at the frontiers of right theories and theories of justice today. By using *Frankenstein* as a tool for armchair theorizing on the rights of the child, we might tease out further implications of the novel for politics, as well as fill in gaps in extant theories of rights and justice. I now turn to a sketch of how these philosophical tasks might be accomplished.

Mistaking Mutation for Monstrosity: The Plight and Rights of Infants with Birth Defects

In Thought Experiments 1 and 2, Shelley set up a worst-case scenario for any child: to be made motherless—not once but twice over—and consequently loveless due to being born with a "hideous" "deformity" to his "aspect" or facial appearance.[29] In contemporary medicine, such deformities of the infant body are called congenital or birth defects. A birth defect is an "abnormality of structure, function, or bodily metabolism which often results in a mental or physical handicap."[30] Birth defects are caused by genetic and/or environmental factors during embryonic or fetal development.[31]

The most visually arresting location of the Creature's deformity is his face, especially the area around his eyes, nose, and mouth. His father-scientist is shocked by the difference between what he expected "the creature" to look like and what he actually looks like once alive.[32] Although Victor had "selected his features as beautiful," the father-scientist changes his mind upon beholding the living Creature.[33] In his accounts of his earliest encounters with his "monster," Victor uses the word "aspect" alongside the word "countenance" to pinpoint the Creature's face as the part of his animated body that scares him the most.[34] He almost immediately finds that he "cannot endure the aspect of the being [he] had created" and furthermore determines that "no mortal could support the horror of that countenance."[35] Later, he identifies the Creature in a lightning storm by the "deformity of its aspect," which is "more hideous than belongs to humanity."[36] Although "aspect" had several main meanings in the early nineteenth century, one of them was "face" or "countenance." Lord Byron used the word "aspect" in this sense in his 1817 dramatic poem "Manfred," which he composed just a few months after he hosted the ghost story competition in Geneva that inspired Shelley to write *Frankenstein*.[37] Suggesting that Shelley's use of "aspect" is also synonymous with "countenance" and "face," Captain Walton confirms the location of the Creature's "loathsome, yet appalling hideousness": "Never did I behold a vision so horrible as his face."[38]

When recalling the reasons for why he ran away from his creation, Victor dwells on the emotions of "horror and disgust" that he felt when confronted with the Creature's face.[39] It is telling which features of the Creature he singles out for their sickening and frightening impact upon him: "yellow skin" that "scarcely covered the work of muscles and arteries beneath," "watery eyes" in "dun white sockets," "shriveled complexion," and "straight black lips."[40] It is not his "gigantic" yet proportional eight-foot frame or his "lustrous" long black hair and "pearly" white teeth but rather the "unearthly ugliness" of his "countenance" and "complexion" that drives the father-scientist to abandon his child at birth.[41]

Anne K. Mellor has argued that Victor's description of the Creature's face is latently racist. His focus on the Creature's yellow skin, black lips, and long black hair draws upon late eighteenth-century European stereotypes of non-Caucasian peoples, especially Central Asians (or "Mongoloids") as categorized in "racial science" of the period.[42] Read in light of critical race theory and postcolonial theory, the Creature's face becomes a symbol of all those people who have suffered discrimination and oppression due to racial, ethnic, and cultural prejudice.[43]

Another powerful way to read the Creature's face is to view it in light of his predicament as a child newly born into the world with a "hideous" countenance.[44] Seen from a disability studies perspective, the Creature's face becomes a symbol of the 1 in 700 children born with craniofacial deformities.[45] The most common birth defects in human babies are the craniofacial deformities of cleft lip and cleft palate, which often occur together.[46] Such clefts cause holes in the upper lip and/or palate, exposing the inner areas of the mouth and sometimes the nose. The Creature's unspecified facial deformity is similar in that it draws attention to the region of the "countenance" between the eyes and mouth; it affects the color and texture of his skin or "complexion" and the shape and color of his "lips" and exposes the inside of his body, the "muscles and arteries beneath."[47] It is not solely his body's skin but a particular area of skin on his face that evokes the visual and tactile revulsion of his father and others.[48]

Yet the Creature's facial deformity does not affect his physical functioning the way a cleft lip/palate would. Clefts cause serious problems with eating, breathing, hearing, panic, and speech acquisition for a human baby, all of which have negative effects on the child's development.[49] Thought Experiment 3, by contrast, endows the newborn Creature with the extraordinary capability to eat, drink, and acquire speech on his own in order to show the stark emotional and social differences between a very young child's merely surviving without a parent versus thriving in a loving relationship with a parent.

Children with oral clefts need not only loving parents and other caregivers in order to survive and thrive during their highly dependent stage of infancy but also corrective surgeries to ensure proper functioning of their mouth, palate, nose, and ears over the course of their lifetimes. The recommended corrective surgeries for cleft lip at three months and for cleft palate at six to nine months do not necessarily eliminate facial disfigurement or asymmetry.[50] However, such surgical improvements in facial appearance are strikingly successful in enhancing the child's self-image and well-being in the long term. These surgeries are not primarily cosmetic but rather functional: the corrections to the lip and palate promote proper eating, breathing, hearing, and development of speech and thus help the child catch up in growth and other measures of healthy development. While it may not be lifesaving, such corrective surgery can give "new life" to a child.[51]

Comparing the Creature's facial deformity to cleft lip/palate might lead one to wonder: what if Victor had used his incomparable knowledge of life science to surgically correct his child's face? In entertaining such a counterfactual, the reader engages the ethical question of how to address children's craniofacial deformities through the lens of the "medical model" of disability.[52] The medical model frames craniofacial deformities in particular and disability in general in terms of curing the patient of it or at least minimizing the impairment it causes for the patient.[53]

Critical disability theorists have advanced an alternative to this medical perspective, called the "social model" of disability.[54] The social model frames craniofacial deformities in particular and disability in general as broader, socially constructed phenomena that include but cannot be reduced to disabled persons' and doctors' experience of treating disability in these medical senses.[55] Taking a critical normative perspective on disability, the social model "posits that people with disabilities are primarily oppressed by the structural barriers in society that handicap them," not by their physical or mental impairments.[56] The paradigmatic example is a person in a wheelchair whose access to a building is blocked by the lack of a ramp.[57] While the person has a serious physical impairment, her disability is not caused by the impairment but rather by society's lack of accommodation for her handicap.

Similarly, the social model of disability allows us to see that a child with a cleft lip/palate has a serious physical impairment, but her disability is caused by society's lack of accommodation for her needs, such as insurance coverage for corrective surgeries and speech therapy, education and social support for her parents and other caregivers, and sensitivity training for her teachers and fellow students at school. Crucially, the latter educational resource raises public awareness of the need to avoid discriminatory language and behavior and instead provide social and emotional support toward children with disabilities. In both the case of the child with a cleft lip/palate and the wheelchair user, society and government could rectify their experiences of unjust inequality by ensuring the equal rights of all citizens to access public goods such as buildings, health care, and education without discrimination as to appearance, impairment, or disability.

With this distinction between the medical and the social model of disability in mind, let's return to the alternative counterfactual scenario in which Victor had surgically corrected his Creature's facial deformity soon after birth. As with corrective surgeries for cleft lip/palate in real life, it may have been impossible to eliminate either the Creature's facial deformity or scarring from its surgical treatment. Even if Victor could have given his Creature a typical face or the beautiful one he had originally hoped to make, the Creature would not have thrived unless he had his right to love fulfilled with his parent or a fitting substitute.

If we run Thought Experiments 1 and 2 over again, by tweaking the variable of the Creature's appearance from hideous to beautiful, we see that even such an exceedingly successful surgery would not have guaranteed happiness, let alone the conditions for happiness. It would have taken his experience of sharing love with a parent or a fitting substitute in order to have even the conditions for happiness. Even if Victor would have been more likely to love his child in surgically corrected form, the surgery itself could not ensure the feeling and practice of love between them. If the Creature had never experienced love with a parent or fitting substitute, even after receiving a new face, then he would be just as miserable as he was in Shelley's version of the story. The removal of the physical impairment would not have addressed, on its own, the deeper and more severe problem of the deprivation of parental love. The lack of love from parents or fitting substitutes is absolutely disabling for the Creature as well as young human creatures in the sense that it destroys the conditions for their enjoyment of life itself.

Back in the real world, the case of cleft lip/palate provides another vivid example of how the medical model of disability affords a limited view of children with birth defects and their rights. Looking at "before" and "after" photos of babies who had clefts successfully corrected by surgery, one might leap to the conclusion that such surgeries remove the disability and thereby purge the child of any negative stigma associated with the birth defect.[58] However, even after successful corrective surgeries, a child born with an oral cleft remains extremely dependent upon both parents and a "team" of medical, nursing, dentistry, and social work professionals for recovery, care, further reconstructive work, and various forms of therapy well into adolescence.[59] Plus, parents require education and support in how to provide intensive loving care to their disabled child throughout this long process of adjustment.[60] Sadly, some parents of infants born with oral clefts lack this education and support. Many children with clefts are abandoned or placed in orphanages or foster care when their parents feel unable to love or even care for them due to their deformities and the social stigma attached to them.[61] Even in loving families, children with cleft lip/palate may suffer social ostracization and subsequent isolation in the home and outside of it.[62]

Like babies who are abandoned by parents due to their facial deformities, the Creature lacks the mothering and love that he so desperately needs to flourish. From the perspective of the social model of disability, the Creature's experience of disability is solely due to extreme and deep-seated social prejudice toward his physical impairment, an unspecified facial deformity. As explored in Thought Experiment 3, his "superhuman" size, strength, and cognitive powers allow him to learn to care for himself on his own, which a human infant (with or without a birth defect) cannot do.[63] While he can survive on his own, he is the same as any human infant in that he cannot thrive without the love of another, especially a parent who would mother him. For the deformed Creature or any creature with a similar birth defect, the only way to truly disable their experience of disability would be to fully enable their experience of love and the interchange of sympathy: beginning with mothering in the family and extending into a wider web of sympathetic caregiving, medical, educational, and civic relationships.

The Creature's superhuman capability for self-care cannot overcome the social prejudice dealt him due to his facial deformity. Like babies with oral clefts since antiquity, he is stigmatized as "monstrous" from birth due to a congenital mutation beyond his (or any infant's) control.[64] This process of stigmatization turns his physical deformity into a grave social disability. According to the social model of disability, people's experiences of physical disabilities such as cleft lip/palate are shaped in social contexts. Without social accommodation for such physical challenges to well-being, the disabled are forced to adapt to suboptimal circumstances for living. A child with a cleft lip/palate may not be able to grow or speak properly due to the lack of social and legal accommodation for her most basic needs (such as corrective surgery and speech therapy). Widespread prejudices toward the physically deformed only exacerbate their marginalization in society and politics. In the Creature's extreme yet illuminating case, other people's horrified reactions to his facial features present real obstacles to his acceptance and belonging in any family, society, or state. The deformity of the Creature is so disturbing, it renders him "u[n]-namable" (even to Shelley herself); thus bereft of a social identity due to a physical disability, "ugliness" becomes a matter of "survival."[65]

Moving from the Creature's situation to the real world, we can see that children with cleft lip/palate confront similarly difficult social and political problems due to deep-seated prejudice toward their craniofacial deformities. A study conducted in the late 1990s showed that Russian newborns with cleft lip/palate had been systematically removed from hospitals to "baby houses," where they were deprived of "individual attention" and "sensory stimulation" until they found a home via international adoption.[66] The reason for the children's removal from their parents was the wider cultural "revulsion" toward deformed newborns.[67] Worse, in some developing countries, a baby with a cleft lip/palate might be killed due to the social stigma attached to the deformity.[68] Despite having the resources to pay for it, the U.S. federal government does not yet guarantee insurance coverage for corrective surgery for craniofacial birth defects, despite several recent attempts to pass the Reconstructive Surgery Act in Congress.[69] Thus, in the wealthiest country in the world today, only fifteen of the fifty states have mandated insurance coverage for corrective surgery of cleft lip and palate.[70]

Looking at the Creature's plight through the lens of the medical model of disability initially pushes us to consider a surgical solution to the problems caused by other people's prejudice toward facial deformities. Looking at his predicament from the perspective of the social model of disability, however, encourages us to take a broader look at the rights that ought to attend children with such birth defects. Perhaps the right to corrective surgery should be understood as one arrow in a quiver of rights deserved by and required for each and every child with a facial deformity or disfigurement. And perhaps the quiver represents the most basic of rights deserved by and required for each and every child, regardless of disability or other social status: the right to share love with parents or fitting substitutes.

Shelley minimally rewrote her own dark and terrible experience of reality when she imagined the Creature with a birth defect. As discussed in Chapter 1, she was possessed by the idea of the deformed Creature not long after she lost her firstborn baby, Clara, to death just a few weeks after giving birth to her prematurely. We cannot know for certain, but we might speculate from the perspective of contemporary pediatric medicine that Clara was born with internal physical defects (invisible and unknown to her parents) that contributed to her early and sudden death.[71] The waking nightmare of finding her "dead baby" in her crib was likely a dark psychic inspiration for the reverse image:

Victor awakening to find the "hideous" Creature peering at him through the "curtain of the bed."[72] Her husband Percy's failure to mourn the loss of Clara was also a likely source for her portrayal of Victor's heartless abandonment of the Creature at birth.[73]

But as Shelley explored in Thought Experiments 1 and 2, a parent's unfitness or unavailability to love a child does not remove the child's right to share love with a parent or a fitting substitute. Even a child of "unearthly ugliness" has a right to love. Born with unfaceable ugliness, the Creature is effaced from family, society, and state.[74] Yet his right to love is not erased. As we speculated through running Thought Experiment 3, such children may even have "special priority" for the right's provision due to their "vulnerability" within their own families as a result of the broader stigmatization of their disability.[75] That right obtains even when the child's cry for it is not heard—as in the Creature's unanswered plea to his father to fulfill his "right" to "live in the interchange of those sympathies necessary for my being."[76] By reading the Creature's plight through the lens of critical disability theory, we come to understand why we are called as a society to hear the cries of disabled, abandoned, or abused children with birth defects. They ought to stand first in line for the provision of their basic rights: first and foremost, the right to love.

Between Criminal and Citizen: The Plight and Rights of Stateless Orphans

In Thought Experiments 3 and 4, Shelley deepened the Creature's experience of child neglect and abuse in order to show how even the most physically and cognitively gifted infant or toddler might happen to survive but would never thrive without sharing love with a parent or fitting substitute. Thought Experiment 4 teases out the legal and political implications of this worst-case scenario of child abandonment and abuse. The tragic failure of courts and states to address the injustices surrounding Victor and his Creature indicates a gap in the postrevolutionary political order that needs to be filled.

Thought Experiment 4 pushes the reader to deduce that if parents or families do not support a child during the most emotionally and socially vulnerable stage of life, then there should be an extrafamilial support system to help with fulfillment of parental duties and provision of children's rights, especially the right to love. Writing in the wake of the Congress of Vienna of 1814–15, which negotiated peace after the Napoleonic Wars, Shelley may have entertained an international response to the Creature's neglect and abuse and vengeful crimes. The failure of multiple states to provide an institutional safety net or any form of public protection for the Creature and the Frankenstein clan points to a need for some responsible political body—whether at the national, international, or transnational level—to support at-risk children and their families.

Thought Experiment 4 is prescient in that it projects a political solution to the problem of child abandonment and abuse. Such broad-scale political solutions to children's deprivation of parental care and love gradually came to be institutionalized by and between states over the course of the twentieth century: child welfare agencies and nongovernmental organizations (NGOs), domestic and international adoption and foster care systems, and public education and legislation targeted at the problems of child abandonment and abuse.[77] Although imperfect in implementation, such extrafamilial support systems have proven to be invaluable and necessary tools for monitoring and addressing the violation of children's rights inside and outside of the family. International adoption is one such imperfect policy that has been widely criticized in recent years for its latent or overt imperialism in its treatment of non-Western children and families as people who need to be "saved" from poverty and other injustices by Westerners. Even its most robust critics, however, consider international adoption to be a crucial "last-resort" option for helping orphans without a realistic prospect of adoption or foster care in their country of origin.[78]

But what should be done in the case of a stateless orphan like the Creature, who lacks both a country to protect him and a family to lovingly care for him? A quick answer might be that there ought to be an extrafamilial and transnational support system to arrange for his adoption. In this alternative counterfactual scenario, the Creature would have become part of a loving and caring family in his adoptive country. Thus transplanted and nurtured, he would have eventually "grown out" of a child's need for the provision of the rights to love and education and "grown into" the adult use of the full slate of citizenship rights, including rights to property, careers, voting, and office holding.[79] Back in the real world, such a plan of international or transnational adoption would be apt for those children who are de jure or technically orphaned and stateless—without living parents or a national identity or officially surrendered to institutional care in a refugee camp or transnational NGO due to war or other violence in their country of origin.[80]

There may be few de jure stateless orphans, technically without any family or state.[81] But there are many de facto or effective stateless orphans, living without the love and care of family or the official protection of a state.[82] Jacqueline Bhabha distinguishes between those de facto stateless children who have a nationality yet lack a state due to illegal migration and those effectively stateless children who lack a state due to their homeland's refusal to recognize their citizenship. This distinction can be usefully applied to orphans as well: de facto orphans are those who have a family but live without their love and care, and effective orphans are those who live within a family that does not love and care for them. According to this modification of Bhabha's typology of stateless children, the Creature could be read as either de jure stateless (technically lacking a state altogether) or effectively stateless (a child with an unregistered birth in the country of origin) yet a de facto orphan (a child migrant living without the love and care of his family).

Taken together, the varied political predicaments of stateless orphans merit the revision of the outdated statutes that permit them to fall through the cracks of extant national and international legal systems. As of 2015, over two million Syrian children had fled their country, many of them unaccompanied by parents or other adults, creating a displacement crisis in surrounding Middle Eastern, Mediterranean, and European regions.[83] Many of these children lack citizenship in their home country and/or their new home due to antiquated patriarchal or ethnic ("blood"-based) definitions of citizenship.[84] Thousands of North Korean children who illegally migrate across the border to China often lose their families (to death or separation) as well as citizenship. To avoid deportation and punishment back home, they live as stateless orphans out of sight of the Chinese authorities.[85] Babies who are abandoned due to a failed international surrogacy agreement may not be eligible for citizenship in their country of birth, such as Ukraine, even when the practice of surrogacy is legal.[86] Many countries that allow international surrogacy, such as Australia and Thailand, do not have adequate laws in place to deal with questions of parentage and citizenship in the aftermath of such failed agreements.[87] When a surrogacy practice is ruled illegal, such as commercial surrogacy in the United Kingdom, children born of it abroad face serious legal hurdles to acquiring both citizenship and official parentage once brought home by their parents.[88] In a 1993 Japanese court decision, a formerly "stateless foreigner" who had been adopted by missionaries was granted the right to citizenship in Japan despite the fact that the biological mother was not Japanese and both biological parents were unknown.[89] Such a case could be a helpful model for reform of child citizenship and parentage laws in light of worldwide rises in child migration, international adoption, and cross-national use of ART and surrogacy.

Although they often lack parents or other family to love and care for them, stateless children may not be de jure or technically orphaned. Like the Creature, they may have a living parent or parents, perhaps unfit or simply unavailable to lovingly care for them. They may even be "a traveller," like the Creature, in search of a reunion with a parent who has abandoned them.[90] Read from the perspective of a critical and cosmopolitan theory of citizenship, the Creature becomes a symbol of all those children who migrate due to abandonment, abuse, or other forms of violence at home.[91] They may not be so-called true orphans, but they are truly—de facto—orphaned. This de facto loss of parents and family, especially when combined with a de jure, de facto, or effective lack of a national identity, is potentially devastating for a child's ability to flourish in the long run.[92]

In the twenty-first century, there are many of these stateless children moving across states, with and without documentation of a national identity.[93] From October 2014 through June 2015, nearly fifty thousand Central American children were caught crossing the U.S. border, unaccompanied by parents or other adults. Some of those children were seeking a parent who had gone ahead of them to try to find a safer home for the family, free from the drug-related violence of their home country. Others fled families, neighborhoods, and schools so dangerous that they quite reasonably feared for their young lives. Honduras, Guatemala, and El Salvador have recently suffered an escalation of drug gangs that prey on children to work as bullies, dealers, and often, in the case of girls, sex slaves. Given this unbearable political situation at home, thousands of children from these countries have opted for the marginally less risky life of a de facto stateless orphan.[94]

In the case of the thousands of de facto stateless orphans who have recently arrived at detention camps at the U.S. border, it is not clear what should be done. Because these child migrants often have parents either in their home countries or in the United States, the legal presumption is that they belong with their families since they are usually not de jure orphans. But who ought to be designated the parent or primary caregiver when the child migrant is a de facto orphan due to a family split across countries, or domestic violence at home? Further complicating matters, Central American children's mass flight of drug-related violence and crime makes their unaccompanied migration a political refugee issue, not solely an immigration issue.[95] The Obama administration resettled many more Central American children as political refugees than had been policy in the past through programs like Deferred Action for Childhood Arrivals.[96] Despite their assistance to stateless children and their families, such piecemeal immigration and refugee policies cannot address all the problems posed by this mass exodus of youth from Central to North America.

There is often no single, clear-cut political answer to the problems faced by stateless orphans. This hard lesson can be learned from the horrifying hypothetical scenario of the Creature's total neglect and abuse by family and society, as much as the all-too-real and harrowing example of children fleeing the deathly violence of Central American drug gangs. On a moral level, what remains clear in either case is that citizens have a duty to deal with a set of problems caused by a serious lack in extant political systems, national and international: the historic failure of societies and governments to address systemic neglect, abuse, and violence toward children. This political failure is most grave in the case of stateless orphans of all types, who often remain invisible to the law on the fringes of society, without recognition of their fundamental rights to a familial and national identity as proclaimed in the 1989 Convention on the Rights of the Child.[97]

Even Hannah Arendt, who wrote the most important philosophical reflection on the fate of stateless persons in the wake of the Second World War, did not include children in her analysis of the phenomenon of mass forced internment and migration due to racism, imperialism, totalitarianism, and genocide. Despite its generic formulation by Arendt, the "stateless persons" she described in her 1951 book, *The Origins of Totalitarianism*, were adults forced to migrate for political reasons.[98] As Judith Butler has argued, Arendt's assumption of a gendered divide between the "private" or domestic realm of women, children, and the family and the "public" realm of formal political activity (historically dominated by men) drove her to largely ignore women's and children's "embodiment" of political action.[99] This was especially ironic in light of her own political status as a German Jewish woman who was, for a time, a stateless migrant due to the threat of persecution by the Nazi regime. A further irony was that the number of child migrants during and after the Second World War was the highest in modern history until the twenty-first-century displacement crises that cover the globe.[100] Arendt's ideological conviction that children did not belong to the political realm blinded her to the plight of the most vulnerable of stateless persons, child migrants running from war, genocide, and other forms of violence. As reported in 2015, there were nearly 60 million people—half of them children—displaced by war and persecution.[101]

In her extended reflection on the plight of stateless persons in *The Origins of Totalitarianism*, Arendt made the provocative argument that it was better to be a criminal than a stateless person, because at least a criminal was afforded some civil rights by the state that arraigned, prosecuted, and punished him.[102] The stateless person, by contrast, was utterly "rightless."[103] Without a state, the stateless person had no citizenship. Without citizenship, the stateless person lacked access to the gateway for the full slate of civil rights. Without national citizenship and the consequent guarantee of civil rights by the state to which he belonged, the stateless person had no way to "enjoy" rights even if he was "granted" them in universal or international declarations of "the Rights of Man" or "human rights."[104]

Both the counterfactual case of the Creature and factual cases of stateless orphans complicate Arendt's thesis that it is better to be a criminal than a stateless person. Stateless orphans may cross borders and transition into life as illegal immigrants in a new society unnoticed or go "missing" soon thereafter.[105] They might not even attract the attention of law enforcement when they commit a crime, such as pickpocketing, in order to survive on their own.[106] This was the case for the Creature to the extreme: his serial murders are either ignored or wrongly prosecuted by the law in several countries. Such invisibility to the criminal justice system is also the case for many unaccompanied child migrants, whose only unprosecuted misdemeanor may have been to cross a border without inspection.[107] Following Kant's view of children as rightless, the modern liberal-democratic state ignores children—especially children without a legitimate place in it—to the point of willful blindness to their suffering and death.[108] Children—especially migrants—remain "hidden" to the state, without recourse to formal rights, when they are conceptually and legally sequestered in what Arendt revered as the "sacred" space of the "household" or "private" realm.[109]

Paradoxically, children—especially the stateless and orphaned—can become less visible the more they violate the law. In Europe alone, there were ten thousand missing child refugees reported in 2016.[110] The fear is that many of them have been lured or sold into sexual slavery or other criminal industries of exploitative adults.[111] For these children, it is far worse to be a criminal *and* a stateless person than solely a stateless person. Even in the dystopian world of total abuse inhabited by the Creature, crime does not satisfy his desire for revenge against (and attention from) his father. Crime rather creates an even greater sense of inner desolation due to his growing emotional and physical isolation from his father and other people. To be a criminal *and* a stateless orphan is far worse than his original predicament of being a stateless orphan.

The Creature's spectral, almost invisible, position between criminal and citizen reminds us of the liminal place of children in Western legal systems. In his brief meeting with the Creature, the old blind man DeLacey discerns the ambiguity and vulnerability of his unnamed guest's situation by listening to his speech. The Creature is a "stranger" who sounds like a fellow "countryman," a "friendless" yet "sincere" person inclined to "virtue," and a reputed "monster" who cannot be "really criminal."[112] All children to some degree dwell in such a social and legal limbo, but stateless orphans like the Creature occupy its precarious edges.

The political domination of children has been hiding in plain sight due to the legal construction of children as the opposite of free and powerful adults since ancient times.[113] Widespread (and often willful) ignorance of the political domination of children is largely due to the assumptions that govern politics in modern democracies. According to Elizabeth Cohen, the legal divide between public and private is the major culprit. The public/private divide places children outside the public or formally political realm and inside the domestic or private sphere of the family. This public/private distinction in turn generates a paternalistic legal conception of children's relationship to adults. Legal paternalism treats children as mere appendages of their parents. Like wives in subordinate relation to their husbands under coverture, children are supposed to (1) lack the capacity for self-government and (2) share the same interests as their parents. Parents, on these two paternalistic grounds, serve as children's legal representatives in modern democracies. As a result, "Children in democratic polities inhabit an uncertain space between alienage and full citizenship."[114]

Cohen cogently recommends a reconceptualization of the legal and political relationships between children, parents, and the state. She speculates the need to "create a space for children that lies between the world of the parents and the world of the state."[115] Creating such new, child-friendly communal spaces might open up room for the most vulnerable of children—the stateless, the orphaned, the unaccompanied migrant—to enjoy fundamental rights with the help of extrafamilial support systems. UNICEF has begun to set up such "child-friendly spaces" for the millions of children affected by the Syrian refugee crisis. In Macedonia and Serbia, child-friendly "centres" provide toys, clean water, and educational materials to refugee children and information on child health, hygiene, and nutrition to parents. These child-oriented "centres" and "spaces" have attracted thousands of refugee children into their care.[116]

It is precisely this undefined space between the family and the state that Shelley dwells upon in *Frankenstein.* According to Colene Bentley's perceptive reading, the novel questions "sentimental" visions of the family that assume "blood ties" or "natural affection" will suffice to build tight-knit moral communities that are protective of all their members.[117] Neither can states nor their officials be counted upon to recognize and assist, let alone show sympathy or love toward, the most vulnerable of people in their bounds: orphaned, abandoned, migrant, illegitimate, disabled, and stateless children. By indicating the need for child-friendly communal spaces between the family and the state, Shelley looked beyond both the romanticization of the family and the idealization of the state that was common in eighteenth- and nineteenth-century European political thought, including the work of her parents.[118]

Arendt took a different, state-centered view of how to award rights to the rightless. In *The Origins of Totalitarianism*, she famously concluded that the "right to have rights" was the right to citizenship itself.[119] She pointed to the de facto rightlessness of stateless persons as evidence that citizenship was the gateway to the enjoyment of all other rights. Against the objection that slaves have (or have been seen as having) rights even when states do not recognize them as citizens, she countered that slaves have "belonged to some form of human community" in the sense that their labor was deemed valuable, even essential, for slave-owning societies over the course of history.[120] Unlike a slave, a stateless person had no such membership—however marginal—in any human community and therefore no rights.

Although she did not take the argument in this direction, Arendt could have said the same of stateless orphans as for stateless persons. The political exclusion of the stateless orphan places her off the grid, so to speak, from the enjoyment of any rights. Without the civil rights of either a citizen or a criminal, the stateless orphan hovers in spectral form beyond the margins of society itself. As brutally imagined in social contract theory, she has no choice but to wander into the metaphorical wilderness of the so-called state of nature beyond law and government, where she will either survive or die on her own.[121]

However, the plight of the Creature and other stateless orphans challenges Arendt's view that "the right to have rights" is citizenship itself. This formulation of citizenship as the primordial right that begets all other rights is problematic because it presumes that rights can have no social meaning outside of a state. In speculative fiction, the Creature's plea to his father for the provision of his right to love shows how the idea of a moral right has social meaning independent of its granting in law or its guarantee by state power. In recent world politics, the willingness of tens of thousands of Central American, Middle Eastern (especially Syrian), and North African children to risk their lives to migrate unaccompanied to Europe or North America suggests the incredible conceptual and moral power of rights even (or perhaps especially) in their legal and political absence.

Arendt may have been right, however, to argue that there is, in some sense, "a right to have rights." The plight of the Creature and other stateless orphans teaches us that this "right to have rights" is not citizenship but rather a deeper and more basic right: the right to love. Without love, especially parental love, children often fail to thrive and even die. Without love, infants become like Arendt's "living corpses" of the concentration camps: deprived of the most basic of rights, they lose the will to fight for their lives.[122] Even the superhuman Creature cannot thrive without enjoying the right to love with another. He too loses the will to live when his father, his only tie to society, dies. Hanging over Victor's coffin, the Creature looks like a "mummy"—a living, "loathsome" yet "appalling" corpse.[123]

Both before and because of his plan to end his life due to his father's death, the Creature teaches us that the right to share love with parents or fitting substitutes is the most basic of the fundamental rights. It applies during the stage of greatest emotional and social vulnerability: childhood. The provision of the right to love is necessary for a very young child's surviving and thriving and for all children's healthy development and well-being through adolescence. It opens the door to the child's enjoyment of other rights and related responsibilities in community with others, such as to education, work, property, and, ultimately, formal citizenship. The enjoyment of the right to love could thus be said to be the gateway to enjoyment of all other rights. While not precisely a "right to have rights" in Arendt's strictly political and statist sense, the right to share love is the main "conduit" to the enjoyment of other fundamental rights—including citizenship—when it is in fact enjoyed by a child in relationship to a parent or fitting substitute.[124]

In Arendt's own words, the "calamity of the rightless is not that they are deprived of life, liberty, and the pursuit of happiness, or of equality before the law and freedom of opinion—formulas which were designed to solve problems within given communities—but that they no longer belong to any community whatsoever."[125] Hearing the stories of the Creature and other stateless orphans, we should be moved to add that the real calamity of the rightless child is not to be loved at all and thus not to belong to any community. This calamity of a young creature's un-belonging belongs to us all: for all people were once children, all children need to experience love and belonging in relationship to another, and the future of any community depends upon new generations of children being raised to belong to it.

Looking Beyond the Human and Human Rights: Speculating the Plight and Rights of Posthuman Children

The moral and political insights we have derived from running *Frankenstein*'s five thought experiments on the rights of the child are perhaps most projectable to the possibility of making posthuman children. Due to recent advances in three-parent in vitro fertilization (IVF) and gene editing, this possibility is immanent, if not already here. Twenty-three genetically modified (or "GM") babies were born as a result of an experimental, "unsafe" version of three-parent IVF at the turn of the twenty-first century in the United States.[126] Aiming to boost fertility by injecting a mother's egg with the ooplasm of a donor egg, this technique crossed the so-called germline by permanently modifying the heritable mitochondrial DNA of the mother's "germ" (egg) cell.[127] As a result, the eggs modified for this early form of three-parent IVF had the heritable mitochondrial DNA of two women. This was an unprecedented genetic outcome, which possibly caused chromosomal or developmental disorders in several babies made from the technique.[128] Another early form of three-parent IVF—then deemed unsafe—was attempted in China in 2003. This technique transferred the nucleus of a fertilized egg into an enucleated fertilized donor egg that lacked mitochondrial disease. Sadly, this attempt led to the death of several (reportedly chromosomally normal) GM fetuses, most between 24 and 29 weeks of gestation.[129]

More GM babies will be born in greater numbers as a result of the legalization of a new, safe form of three-parent IVF (called spindle transfer) in Britain in 2015. In April 2016, the first baby made from spindle transfer three-parent IVF was born to Jordanian parents, who sought treatment in Mexico from U.S. fertility doctors seeking to avoid regulation of their innovative technique.[130] Rather than inject an egg with the ooplasm of a donor egg to simply boost fertility, the spindle transfer technique removes the nucleus of an unfertilized egg and transfers it into an enucleated donor egg with healthy mitochondrial DNA. After replacing the mother's defective mitochondrial DNA with those of a donor egg to eliminate mitochondrial disease, the doctor fertilizes the reconstituted egg with sperm.[131] The resultant lack of mitochondrial disease will dramatically improve GM children's prospective health spans. In the case of the three-parent baby born as a result of his Jordanian parents' infertility treatment in Mexico, he avoided inheriting a deadly mitochondrial disease, Leigh syndrome, which had caused the early deaths of two of his older siblings in addition to four miscarriages.[132] As the case of the Jordanian mother shows, spindle transfer three-parent IVF also has the added benefit of increasing fertility in women who have eggs with mitochondrial defects. As with the earliest (and current and future) forms of three-parent IVF, the changes to the mitochondrial DNA will be heritable through the maternal line.[133] It is because of this "tinkering with the very substances that make us human" that Knoepfler describes three-parent IVF—in any form—as making "a new kind of human being."[134]

On the horizon is the creation of GM babies through the more powerful and comprehensive technique of gene editing, which would use the new CRISPR-Cas9 technology to permanently and heritably modify "the DNA sequence of an early embryo"—the core, nuclear DNA—which serves as the very "blueprint" for development.[135] By reading *Frankenstein* in light of these medical and legal trends, we can see the "spectre" of the Creature as a precocious literary manifestation of the posthuman child made through science and biotechnology.[136] With this analogy in mind, we may set forth a preliminary definition of posthuman children as those children who (will) have been altered or made or will have eventually evolved as a result of interventions in science and technology such that they are strikingly different in features and/or capacities from their human ancestors/creators.[137]

It is as illuminating to read debates on the genetic modification of children in light of *Frankenstein* as it is to do the reverse. By reversing our approach—moving from the novel to the debates rather than from the debates to the novel—we can productively complicate our preliminary definition of the posthuman child. As we saw in Chapter 3, Shelley did not follow her mother's "genetic" approach to the definition of the human being. Rather than rigidly and essentially define a human being in terms of its origins (such as its making in the image of God), Shelley unsettled the very idea of the human being with her imagining of a motherless Creature made by a lone father-scientist from the assemblage and reanimation of human and other animal parts. "Nameless" and "u[n]namable" even to Shelley herself, the Creature is not identifiable as a member of any kind by a positive and original set of characteristics (such as a soul or a genetic code). What defines him is not what he is but what he lacks: especially his lack of a loving relationship with his parent or any substitute for him.[138] By examining contemporary debates on the ethics of making GM babies through the lens of Shelley's five thought experiments on the rights of the child, we come to see the posthuman child not as an alien, monster, or mutant to be feared but rather as a "new kind of human being" whose lack of love would be as devastating as it would be for any child. In turn, we learn to see the development of new kinds of human beings in a fresh, more forgiving, and sympathetic light rather than fear it like a kind of specter lurking in the shadows of science, society, and law.

What Is the Posthuman?

The concept of the posthuman is highly contested in definition and usage because its applications are, even now, largely speculative and forward looking. In its most general political usage, "posthuman" refers to the idea of a new being (or understanding of being) that comes to be *after* the deconstruction of an "essential figure of humanity."[139] An essential figure of humanity is a conception of humanity that is what Anne Phillips calls "characteristics-based" or based on a view of humans as defined by an essential characteristic, such as reason or moral agency, or a cluster of such traits.[140] On this characteristics-based view, people fully realize their humanity by developing the decisive characteristic(s) of humanity. The problem with such an essentialist approach to the conceptualization of the human is that it tends to exclude large swathes of humanity—including children, the disabled, the disadvantaged, the elderly—who fail to fit its rigid and narrow criteria for inclusion in humankind.

Within continental and critical theory, Michel Foucault is often cited as a source of this political conception of the posthuman. To become posthuman, in this political vein, is to move away from past triumphalist and imperialist readings of the progress of Western European civilization as the pinnacle of "human" civilization. Rather than thinking of the human being as perfecting itself through the advancement of Western civilization, Foucault and his diverse followers (such as Judith Butler) have pressed people to think critically about pseudo-universalistic usages of the concept of the human and their harmful imperial implications: racism, sexism, cis-genderism, classism, homophobia, and ableism, just to name a few.[141]

This political approach to the posthuman is sometimes called "posthumanist" because it challenges the Eurocentric notion of the humanities in particular and elite Western culture in general as humanizing or civilizing forces of progress.[142] In her posthumanist reading of *Frankenstein*, Cynthia Pon reads Shelley's creatures (especially the dismembered female) as breaking down the idea of an essential figure of humanity and opening up a passage toward a new "feminist figure of humanity."[143] Inspired by the (posthumanist) feminism of Donna Haraway, Pon sees Shelley's feminist figure of humanity as resisting development or representation "at the expense of those who were considered less human or non-human."[144]

Phillips has helpfully abbreviated this posthuman(ist) political critique of the concept of the human as "Posthumanism 1."[145] Posthumanism 1 has inspired some human rights theorists to look toward an antihumanist or, in some cases, posthuman conception of rights.[146] For Foucauldians, an antihumanist conception of rights would not rely upon past triumphalist narratives of "Western European" (or white, wealthy, male, cis-gender, heterosexual, able-bodied) progress. Spinning out of the European Enlightenment, these triumphalist narratives of so-called human progress manipulated the notion of the perfection of humankind to rationalize the accumulation of rights for the powerful over and against the powerless.[147] While Foucault did not look toward any "future realized human . . . post-human or . . . anti-human" but rather to critical analysis of the politics of the present in light of the past, his antihumanist perspective on human rights "remains open to future possibilities and reinscriptions of the human."[148] From this antihumanist vantage, one may advance a posthuman perspective on human rights.[149] Such a posthuman perspective looks beyond the idea of rights as grounded upon a static and universal conception of human nature. It also looks past the notion of an "essential figure of humanity" by showing the experience of being human to be always contested, unfinished, and in flux.[150]

There is another, scientific meaning of the "posthuman" that maps more directly onto the domains of biology, genetics, evolutionary theory, and biotechnology. In this scientific sense, the posthuman means the idea of using science or technology to make or precipitate the evolution of a new form of life that descends from humans but is strikingly different in features and/or capacities from its human ancestors/creators. GM people, including clones, would fit this definition.[151] Phillips pegs this technologically oriented definition of the posthuman as "Posthumanism 2."[152]

Posthumanism 2 is often conflated with the related, yet narrower, concept of the "transhuman." According to Nick Bostrom, the transhuman usually refers to the use of science and technology to improve or even perfect human capacities.[153] Thus improved or perfected, transhumans (sometimes called cyborgs or hybrids of humans and machines) represent a technologically enhanced stage between the human being and forms of posthuman life.[154]

To show Frankenstein's projectability to contemporary bio-techno-ethical debates on the making of GM babies, I move betwixt and between the political and the scientific meanings of the posthuman. As with many a stage and film adaptation of Shelley's novel going back to the 1823 play *Presumption*, my conception of the posthuman child is inspired by the stand-out literary example of Frankenstein's Creature.[155] Making explicit what is implicit to many of these adaptations, my interpretation of the Creature is that he is at once a child and a posthuman. Shelley represents the Creature not only as a kind of monstrous infant but also as a new kind of posthuman being.[156] With the making of this Creature at its narrative core, *Frankenstein* functions as both posthuman literature and children's literature. In a childlike way, the novel creates an alternate reality in which the animal and the human, the animate and the inanimate, the magical and the scientific, and the moral and the political are broken down and blended in a radical new social imaginary.[157]

Making Posthuman Children

My preliminary definition of a posthuman being partly derives from Bostrom's definition of a "posthuman" as "a being with at least one posthuman capacity." He goes on to define a "posthuman capacity" as a "general central capacity" that greatly exceeds the "maximum attainable by any current human without recourse to new technological means."[158] Broader than Bostrom's definition, my preliminary conception of the posthuman being considers a striking modification of a *central feature*—the genome—to be a sufficient distinction between the human being and any posthuman being. Changes in other central features might be sufficient to effect such a transition, but here I focus on the impact of human germline genetic modification on the development of posthumans. Also unlike Bostrom, I do not take the enhancement of a *central capacity*, such as the emotions, as a necessary condition for distinguishing the posthuman being from the human being.

For example, a GM baby could be made with the same (or fewer) *capacities* as a human baby but still have a strikingly distinct *feature* (a permanently altered and heritable genome). Although the probable intention of scientists would be to make a GM baby smarter, stronger, cuter, or more immune to disease than a human baby, the use of technology to permanently modify the human genome can easily go wrong. The CRISPR-Cas9 technology that conducts gene editing is already known to make several kinds of mistakes, including the unintended alteration of genes such that they become defective.[159] Similarly, the earliest, experimental three-parent IVF technique was deemed unsafe due to an unexpected outcome: several babies made from it had chromosomal or developmental disorders.[160] These cases suggest that a central human *feature* (the human genome) could be altered in a way that severely impairs the central *capacities* of the posthuman child. These very real possibilities for grave error at the inception of life challenge Bostrom's rather optimistic assumption that most posthuman capacities would likely be, overall, positive enhancements of human capacities.[161] Although scientists continue to refine these techniques so that they are reliable—as shown by the legalization of spindle transfer three-parent IVF in Britain in 2015 and the allowance of human embryonic gene editing for purely research (not reproductive) purposes in Britain in 2016—scientists themselves continue to have quite reasonable reservations about their efficacy and ethics.[162]

Ironically, Bostrom's enthusiasm for the development of posthuman capacities runs the risk of falling back into the triumphalism of perfectionistic humanism. Bostrom's transhumanist and perfectionist conception of human development seeks to enhance or even perfect the human being's features and/or capacities through technological or biochemical interventions. The moral and political danger of such a transhumanist and perfectionist vision of optimal human development is that it suggests (or runs the risk of suggesting) that imperfect human features, capacities, or persons are or would be inferior to perfected human features, capacities, or persons. Despite its open-ended and broad-minded aspirations for humanity, transhumanist perfectionism raises the specter of eugenics: especially the artificial selection or modification of the features of babies for the sake of enhancing the capacities of the species as a whole.

Michael Sandel cautions that the quest for perfection through genetic engineering is at base a dangerous enterprise for humanity. He is particularly wary of the making of "designer babies" or children whose traits are or would be artificially selected (for sex) or modified (to be free from genetic disease) as part of the biotechnological process of their creation.[163] While supporting the regulated and rigorously ethical use of biotechnology to treat infertility or genetic disease, he also insists that science and medicine can and should be regulated in a way that prevents or at least mitigates the backfiring of perfectionism on the quality of human life and happiness, especially its profound moral worth.[164] Rather than dwell on worst-case scenarios of species extinction through biotechnological interventions, Sandel worries more about the pernicious moral effects of the quixotic quest for perfection. He makes the compelling point that many of the treasured values that capture a cross-cultural sense of humanity, such as parental love for children, respond to rather than erase the vulnerability, diversity, and uniqueness born of human imperfection.[165]

From a starker bioconservative perspective, Francis Fukuyama argued at the turn of the twenty-first century that the worst catastrophe facing the human species was the "genetic engineering" of the human genome to create a "posthuman" species.[166] He speculated, much like Victor Frankenstein in Thought Experiment 5, that the creation of a new species through genetic engineering would eventually entail the destruction of the human species. For this reason, Fukuyama called for a ban on human cloning and strict regulation of all current or future scientific and technological research and applications that could cross (or lead to the crossing of) the germline. Like Victor Frankenstein, he invoked the specter of the evolution of a new species capable of destroying human beings. He went still further and imagined the end of the millennia-old morality that he saw as arising from human nature itself.[167] From this "apocalyptic" perspective, Fukuyama warned that the view of the posthuman as better than the merely human could cause the eugenics-driven extinction of the human species and its morals for the sake of a supposedly better but fundamentally unknown condition of a future species.[168] Religious fundamentalists might also add that to make posthuman children is to make an abomination and incur the wrath of God.[169]

Unlike either Bostrom's triumphalist view of the posthuman as the perfection of human capacities or Fukuyama's apocalyptic view of the posthuman as the destruction of humanity itself, my view of the posthuman is more like those biologists and geneticists who grapple firsthand with ethical and legal issues related to modifying the genetic structures of humans and other animals. This view of the posthuman being is primarily descriptive, not prescriptive. It is speculative, provisional, and open to revision, not presumptuous and rigid. It uses knowledge of genetics, evolutionary theory, and biotechnology to speculate what a (post)human being might become. This speculative yet scientific conception of the posthuman being as evolving from the human being serves as a starting point for critical reflection on the ethical and political implications of the creation of such beings.

In taking this "political-scientific" view of the posthuman, we adopt neither a triumphalist nor an apocalyptic view of GM babies and posthuman people. Rather, we construct and conduct thought experiments about the ethics of the creation of posthuman life, much like Victor and the Creature do when they contemplate the making of the equal female companion. The "political-scientific" perspective on the posthuman resists dogmatic thinking and dares to reason through the full range of probable moral, social, and legal consequences of making GM people with the aid of science and technology. Its complex reasoning process is similar to exploring the multipronged pathways of Thought Experiment 5.

But before we run Thought Experiment 5 again with this "political-scientific" view of the posthuman in mind, we need to go back in time to make a quick pit stop in recent history. In 2015, a team of Chinese scientists used the CRISPR-Cas9 technology to make permanent alterations to the genomes of human embryos. They took the precaution of using discarded embryos that were unviable for implantation in the womb. Their attempt to use CRISPR-Cas9 to eliminate a gene for a blood disease failed.[170] But in conducting this experiment against the warnings of the global scientific community, they raised for some the specter of the creation of "Frankenbabies" in the not so distant future.[171] These CRISPR-Cas9–edited GM babies would be more dramatically modified than past and future children made from the successful forms of three-parent IVF, who (will) have altered mitochondrial DNA, which is heritable through only the maternal line. CRISPR-Cas9 could be used to forever change an embryo's core, nuclear DNA sequence in a way that is heritable through both the maternal and paternal lines—fully opening the door to the development of a wholly posthuman species. This species would potentially be free from genetic disease. It would also likely have other altered features and capacities that strikingly distinguish it from its human ancestors/creators.

The analogy between CRISPR-Cas9–edited "Frankenbabies" and Frankenstein's Creature is apt, at least in the sense that Victor Frankenstein used science and technology to make a new life with some but not all human parts. As is the case with CRISPR-Cas9–edited GM babies of the future, the Creature's relationship to humanity is unsettled. Although made by a human from the parts of human and other animal corpses, the Creature does not think of himself as a member of the human species or any other extant animal species.

In evolutionary terms, he may be best understood as a "chimera" or "hybrid" that stands betwixt and between established species.[172] Such chimeras or hybrids may have the potential to be originators of new species that might evolve, down the line, from their descendants. The same goes for CRISPR-Cas9–edited GM babies. They will be made by humans with the aid of science and technology that alters the human genome in a way that sharply differentiates them from their human creators/ancestors. At once human and posthuman, they will have the potential to be originators of a fully posthuman species that could evolve from their descendants.

Like Victor Frankenstein in Thought Experiment 5, twenty-first-century bioconservatives have invoked the specter of a future species of GM people that would be destructive of humanity. Some, like Fukuyama, conceive this possibility in terms of making changes to the human genome that would ultimately wipe out humanity through the random, long-term processes of evolution. This would constitute a "new" form of eugenics, enabled by present-day governmental indifference to the consequences of genetic engineering.[173] Others have speculated the development of posthuman people so enhanced in their cognitive capacities that they could become "supervillians" or "Frankenstein's monsters" out to purposively destroy the human race.[174] Knoepfler perceptively notes the speciesist biases behind such monstrous visions of GM people and worries that they would in fact be victims of discrimination due to "intensely negative" views of their origins, features, and capacities.[175]

Scientists have also expressed concern about what crossing the germline would mean for the future of humanity. Some reach similar conclusions as bioconservatives, arguing that the germline ought not to be crossed because we do not know for certain what negative consequences it may entail for the human species as a whole. Knoepfler is realistic in acknowledging that the germline has already been and will continue to be crossed, even in the place of bans, restrictions, and professional warnings against human experimentation. GM babies have been and will be made through three-parent IVF, and others will likely be eventually made with CRISPR-Cas9. Knoepfler calls for a "moratorium" on "heritable human genetic modification."[176] At the same time, he dedicates his book to both humans and "future *GMO Sapiens* or human clones should they come to exist."[177] The inevitability of the growth of GM people in the human population seems to be accepted by him and other scientists involved in the cutting-edge work of genetic modification of life.

Once we acknowledge the presence of GM people within the human community, the question then becomes: how should the human community treat these people? The first few CRISPR-Cas9–edited GM babies will be a new kind of chimera or hybrid, created through technological intervention in the genome. At first, they will be neither technically genetically human nor genetic members of another species. They may "pass" as genetic equivalents to humans, however, as in the case of the first three-parent IVF babies, if they are treated as no different from other children and thus move into the population largely unnoticed and unstigmatized for their different reproductive origins and genetics. Beyond some follow-up and monitoring of their health by IVF doctors, GM babies have been allowed to and will likely continue to grow up like typical human children.[178] Despite all the hand-wringing of bioconservatives, GM children have already been fused into human families under the watch of the government of the United States without a blink of an eye.

This ability to "pass" as typical children will make future GM babies both like and unlike the Creature. Like the Creature, they may be invisible to the state for large portions of their lives. Unlike the Creature, this invisibility may be largely benign if they are allowed to live as typical children like three-parent IVF children have already done. Like the Creature, however, they could find themselves stateless—effectively, due to their country of origin refusing to officially recognize their births; de jure, due to their explicit legal exclusion from citizenship rights due to the circumstances of their births; or de facto, as a result of migration due to abandonment, neglect, abuse, or violence. Unlike the Creature, they will likely pass as typical children despite their altered features, as long as those features remain unstigmatized by society and law. Like the Creature, they will have the potential, once there are enough of them in the population, to interbreed and potentially develop a new species descended yet distinct from *Homo sapiens*.

As with the Creature, it is possible that this future species of GM people might seek to establish its own community distinct from humans and "human laws."[179] Diana Reese has argued that this is precisely the Kantian political predicament of the Creature: to find himself in a limbo between past human communities and a future moral community to which he claims he has a "right" to belong as a "reasoning being," not a human being.[180] Unlike Kant, however, the Creature imagines his future community as grounded in the enjoyment of a right to love or "the interchange of those sympathies necessary for my being."[181] Even as he sees himself as a rational being in need of a new kind of political community, the Creature corrects Kant in adding the enjoyment of the right to love as an essential feature of such a future legitimate political community. He is as much a "sensitive being" as a rational one, who needs a community to support both aspects of his being.[182]

The Creature's first attempt at making such a community was with a fellow child, William Frankenstein, whom he naively hoped would be free from the prejudices of adults toward his facial deformity. Stumbling upon William in the woods near Geneva, the Creature wonders, "If, therefore, I could seize him, and educate him as my companion and friend, I should not be so desolate in this peopled earth."[183] When William failed to meet this childish expectation, the eighteen-month-old Creature committed in fit of rage his first and worst crime: the murder of a fellow child, his father's little brother.[184] The loss of his dream of founding a small community of Frankenstein children drove him to become the horrendous monster that society had presumed him to be. It was then that the Creature turned to the idea of finding community with a person equal in ugliness to him, separate from human civilization. He theorized that his enjoyment of a right to love with the equal female companion would produce an ideal community—free of violence, including violence toward humans, nonhuman animals, and the environment. His posthuman utopia would be one governed by the principle of the enjoyment of the right to love, with "peaceful and human" spillover effects for both human and nonhuman life.[185]

The Creature's envisioning of a right to love as a central political feature of any future legitimate, pacific, humane, posthuman community brings us back to the question of how posthumans would experience human capacities like love. Bostrom defined the posthuman being as enhanced in at least one central capacity, such as emotions. At the same time, he acknowledged the difficulty of articulating how a posthuman would feel emotion differently than a human.[186] Perhaps this difficulty arises because the emotional dimension of being human is the ethical heart of the experience of the human. In the words of Martha Nussbaum, "Love is what gives respect for humanity its life, making it more than a shell."[187] Without emotion, we are in some sense not human—we are said to be inhuman. To try to imagine a nonhuman experience of emotion is to stand outside of our conception of humanity, of being humane. This is a tall order for even the most speculative philosopher of the posthuman condition.

Shelley got around this problem through literature. As a novelist writing in the (as yet undefined and thus free and creative) mode of speculative fiction, she was able to construct a cascade of thought experiments that empowers readers to feel the emotional dimension of a posthuman way of being. The Creature feels deeply—perhaps maximally—the emotions of love, hate, grief, and joy precisely because of his posthuman predicament. It is the predicament of being made motherless, loveless, stateless, and even species-less that makes him feel his abandonment by his father all the more painfully. The Creature's predicament is twofold: bodily and social. His bodily predicament arises from the "disgusting circumstances" of his creation as well as other people's fearful reactions to his "hideous" face.[188] His social predicament arises from the deleterious consequences of being made motherless twice over: totally abandoned, alone, and abused.

Despite this unique bodily-social predicament, the Creature feels exactly what humans and other animals feel when others hurt them: pain. Due to his superhuman capacities, the Creature is almost numbed to physical pain but not emotional pain. Even when he faints after being shot for saving a girl from drowning, he describes the pain more in emotional than physical terms: "The feelings of kindness and gentleness, which I had entertained but a few moments before, gave place to hellish rage and gnashing of teeth. Inflamed by pain, I vowed eternal hatred and vengeance to all mankind."[189] While his unique bodily-social predicament dials up the degree of his emotional pain, the cause of this psychological suffering is the same as for humans and most, if not all, other animals: exclusion, rejection, isolation, abuse, violence, and, most grievously, the lack of love and a sense of belonging to any community. It is this emotional pain that he seeks to end with death: "I shall die. I shall no longer feel the agonies which now consume me, or be the prey of feelings unsatisfied, yet unquenched."[190]

In order to picture a posthuman experience of emotion, Shelley likens the Creature's experience of feelings to both humans and other animals. When Victor encounters the Creature twenty-one months after abandoning him, he describes the Creature's face as animated by a range of complex human emotions: "his countenance bespoke bitter anguish, combined with disdain and malignity."[191] Yet the "unearthly ugliness" of the Creature's face prevents Victor from empathizing with his creation as a fellow human. Later, the Creature relates to Victor that after he was attacked "violently with a stick" by Felix DeLacey, he "escaped" and "wandered in the wood" where he "gave vent to [his] anguish in fearful howlings."[192] The Creature suffers far more pain from the loss of his community with the DeLaceys than from Felix's stick yet expresses that pain like a canine.

Shelley tellingly represents the Creature's posthuman experience of emotion as a hybridization of human and other animal feelings. In so doing, she enables the reader to imagine a posthuman experience of emotion that does not reproduce a pseudo-universal, humanistic conception of sympathy as the marker of (an implicitly Western) "human" civilization.[193] Shelley repeatedly portrays the Creature as expressing sympathy toward humans and other animals, especially when they are in pain: he quietly assists the impoverished DeLaceys in finding firewood and doing chores, he watches the cross-cultural romantic saga of Felix and Safie unfold with great concern, he saves a girl from drowning, and he rejects the human practice of killing and eating animals. The Creature's emotional capacity and longing for sympathy suggests that it ought not to be seen as the marker of the human or "human" civilization. His murderous and other criminal behavior also suggests that sympathy is not the exclusive purview of the virtuous and benevolent.

The Creature's emotional yet reasoned plea to his father for "a right to live in the interchange of those sympathies necessary for my being" makes sympathy a (post)human political issue. The Creature's radical demand for a child's right to share love is a prescient reminder that we should expect posthuman children to share the social and emotional vulnerabilities of the human youth to whom they are and will be closely related. GM children—even if made as big, strong, and smart as Frankenstein's Creature—will have a basic need for and moral desert of living in sympathetic community with another, especially a loving parent. As Bentley aptly put it, *Frankenstein* teaches us that what matters most for people—regardless of their origins—is membership in a "community," not membership in "humanity" or any particular species.[194]

Unlike the isolated and abused Creature, none of the now young adult GM people made by three-parent IVF have shown any signs of estrangement from humanity or an impulse to separate from it politically. Alana—the only one who has spoken publicly so far—appears to be very well adjusted. She sees the circumstances of her creation as simply the means necessary for her mother to gestate a child of her own genetic descent. While she looks like her mom and dad and shares many of their other traits and talents, she happens to have mitochondrial DNA from the ooplasm of a donor egg. Referring to the donor, she says, "I wouldn't consider her a third parent, I just have some of her mitochondria."[195] She and other three-parent (or, more precisely, three-person) IVF babies have DNA from three human beings but not a new way of being human. From a purely scientific perspective, Alana and other children made by three-parent IVF might be described as *human plus*, or transhuman, because of the biotechnological intervention in their genomes that added mitochondrial DNA from a donor.[196] From a "hybrid" political-scientific perspective, they might be better understood as Alana does herself: typical human children who happen to have mitochondria from a donor egg.

By interpreting public debates on GM children through the philosophical framework of Thought Experiment 5, the reader can shift focus away from the superficial and potentially dehumanizing classification of people as non-, trans-, or posthuman to the far more profound ethical and political implications of bringing them to life in the first place. From the point of view of the Creature, what matters most is not what he is made of, metaphysically or materially, but rather that he was made by another. Discovering who made him leads him to wonder what obligations his father-scientist holds toward him and which rights he holds with respect to those obligations. In turn, the reader may ask, Which obligations do parents, adults, groups, societies, and states hold toward such children? Which rights do such children hold in relation to those obligations?

Upon further reflection, these questions turn out to be applicable to all children, regardless of their genesis. The extraordinary aspects of the Creature that set him off from humanity ultimately serve to highlight what is ordinary and humane in him. Like a human child, he needs and desires to share love with another in a moral community. His claim toward his father for the provision of his right to love thus transcends his unique (and radically counterfactual) predicament as a motherless, loveless, stateless, even species-less orphan. Put in its most general form, the Creature's claim for the right to love potentially applies to all young creatures—human or not—who need love from a parent or fitting substitute to survive and thrive in the earliest stage of life. In this sense, Shelley's so-called monster makes a provocative claim for the rights of the child that is truly universal in scope. Without settling the matter, the Creature's plea for a right to love also raises the question of nonhuman animal rights to parental love, benevolent treatment, and caring interspecies relationships.

On the flip side of Thought Experiment 5, Victor contemplates an apocalyptic scenario that considers the limits of his parental obligations toward the Creature as well as the corresponding limits of his (or any) child's right to love. He counterfactually reasons, What if the Creature and the female companion reproduced and created a new species that drove humanity to extinction? At first glance, Victor's thought experiment implies that there ought to be limits on the rights of the Creature and other posthuman beings, including their right to share love, simply on the basis of their potentially destructive posthuman capacities.

Upon further scrutiny, however, Victor produces only a more general argument that there are moral limits to parental duties and the corresponding rights of the child, including the right to love. Victor has no evidence that the Creature's potential descendants would necessarily destroy the human species and thus no species-wide or species-centric grounds for limiting the right of the Creature and other posthuman people to share love. Even if he had evidence that the Creature's descendants would destroy the human species, it would not erase his duty to find his child a (nonreproductive) companion to serve as a fitting substitute for a parent. The interests or behavior of a species, present or future, do not dictate the limits to his parental duty and his child's corresponding right to share love. On a more practical moral level, it is not clear that denying his child love could help him avoid destruction of himself or others—indeed, the Creature's calculated murders of Henry and Elizabeth, as well as Victor's death near the North Pole, suggest the very opposite.

Back on the Creature's side of Thought Experiment 5, we discover the true moral limits of parental obligations and corresponding children's rights. If we accept the Creature's most general claim to the right to love as truly universal in scope, then any restrictions on this right should apply to all young creatures in need of sharing love for surviving and thriving. The moral restrictions on the enjoyment of any truly universal right should not be drawn according to species or any other grouping or social status. On the other hand, the Creature ultimately undermined the universality of his own argument for a child's right to share love by ignoring the rights of his supposedly equal, prospective female companion. By treating her as a mere means to the end of his passive enjoyment of the right to love, the Creature failed to respect the equal rights of the female creature. In this way, he fell prey to the same pseudo-universal reasoning as his father did on the other side of Thought Experiment 5. Both father and son ultimately fail to develop a truly universal conception of the rights-bearing child, without discrimination as to sex, gender, species, or other social status or scientific classification.

As a result of running both sides of Thought Experiment 5, the reader has found the philosophical tools to reach the conclusion that Victor had no obligation to make a female creature in the first place and thus the Creature had no right to be made such a companion. Nevertheless, Victor's parental obligation to provide for his child's right to love endures until a fitting substitute has been arranged. Since Victor never arranged for such a substitute before his death, the obligation persists beyond the grave—as the Creature's harrowing cry by his coffin amply testifies. As the novel plays out to its tragic finale, we discover that a child's right to love should not be limited on speciesist or other pseudo-universal humanist grounds but may be limited for other reasons—moral, practical, and temporal: (1) the ethical challenge of finding a fitting substitute for a parent, (2) the political need to establish extrafamilial support systems to aid in this cause, and (3) the passage of time, which causes a child to "grow out" of the need or grounds for the provision of the right to love. Like Milton's Adam and Shelley's Creature, none of us asked to be made. Because all people are made *by* others—regardless of *how* or *of what* we were made—we are each owed the love we need to grow up and grow well.

Following the Creature Toward a Posthuman(itarian) Justice

After navigating this cascade of thought experiments in the narrative core of *Frankenstein*, the reader arrives at a question that was futuristic in 1818 but is timely almost two centuries later: should a truly cosmopolitan justice be posthuman(itarian)? By "posthuman(itarian)," I mean a concept and practice of justice that is posthumanistic (not pseudo-universal but truly universal in scope) and post-speciesist (not exclusive to humans but extended to nonhuman and posthuman creatures). Phillips would place this within "Posthumanism 3."[197]

Following Shelley, those in the school of Posthumanism 3 propose that we should amplify our commitment to exploring and redrawing the boundaries and frontiers of (the human) being for the sake of underscoring the relational, emotional, and social dimensions of being human or humane toward other forms of life and the broader environment.[198] Donna Haraway is the most famous philosophical exponent of the school of Posthumanism 3, despite having more recently rejected the term "posthumanist" to describe her work.[199] She did not reject the term "posthumanist" because she no longer held the above objective to playfully rethink the "boundaries" between the artificial and the natural, the human and the machine, and organic and inorganic matter, nor did she abandon the term "posthumanist" because she no longer thought people held a shared "responsibility" for the "construction" of such boundaries between humans and other beings or things.[200] Haraway rejected the term "posthumanist" because she thought it had the dangerous (and largely unintended) potential to make people forget about the real problems that still face humans as humans, even as "all" humans have become, in theory and practice, "cyborgs," "chimeras," or "hybrids of machine and organism."[201]

In order to escape this moral and political problem—the potential indifference of posthumanist thought to human beings and the injustices they face as humans—my definition of posthuman(itarian) justice bridges the political bent of Posthumanism 1 with the scientific/technological orientation of Posthumanism 2. At the same time as it seeks to bring together the best aspects of these two schools of thought, my contribution to Posthumanism 3 strives to move beyond their flaws: both Posthumanism 1's dour tendency toward a pessimistic antihumanism and skepticism of the value of rights and Posthumanism 2's potentially imperial triumphalism and naive resurrection of Enlightenment ideas of human perfectability. My articulation of Posthumanism 3 shares Haraway's objective to show moral and political concern for the pernicious effects of closed-minded boundary drawings between humans and other forms of life and matter. It also shares her desire to take "pleasure" in the "confusion of boundaries" in order to playfully broaden people's perspective on what could and should constitute a person, being, life form, creature, child, or citizen. I follow Haraway, too, in taking inspiration from science fiction for rethinking these boundaries in a way that is productive for a broad audience. Finally, I strongly agree with her literary-philosophical view that "monsters have always defined the limits of community in Western imaginations."[202]

I depart from Haraway, however, in two significant ways. First, I embrace the Creature— whom she rather dismissively calls "Frankenstein's monster"— as a literary archetype of a being who defies naming or labeling and thus provokes readers to rethink narrow, divisive, and imperial conceptions of the human, transhuman, or posthuman.[203] In her early work, Haraway drew a problematic contrast between "Frankenstein's monster" and "the cyborg" (and, implicitly, all contemporary humans) because she assumed that the Creature was motivated by desire for a "heterosexual mate," whereas a cyborg (or contemporary human), according to her definition, is "post-gender" and undercuts "heterosexism."[204] Given what I have argued in Chapter 3 about the nonsexual and nonreproductive motives behind the Creature's demand for an equal female companion, Haraway's refusal to admit the Creature into even the nebulous category of the cyborg/contemporary human looks like a regression into the kind of pernicious boundary drawing she rejects in principle. By embracing the Creature for (and not despite) his ambiguous relationship to other forms (and ways) of life and matter, I am able to use Shelley's novel to sketch the outlines of a new branch of Posthumanism 3: a posthuman(itarian) conception of justice that attends to the rights of human children alongside nonhuman, transhuman, and posthuman children.

Frankenstein points to the need for a posthuman(itarian) conception of justice, beginning in the family and extending outward to other dimensions of communal and political life. As Shelley foresaw with Victor's predicament, there may be cases where a parent's duty to a child trumps solely humanitarian considerations of justice because the child is posthuman. The adoption of such a posthuman(itarian) perspective might have allowed Victor to fairly balance his Creature's rights alongside other considerations of justice, instead of construing them as mutually exclusive.

This *Frankenstein*-inspired idea of a posthuman(itarian) justice has the power to transform the political meaning of "cosmopolitanism." With "cosmos" meaning the world or universe, "cosmopolitan"—in political theory—means a kind of justice that covers all aspects of life, including those that have been historically excluded from considerations of political justice. Shelley's cascade of thought experiments underscores how the family has been historically circumscribed as a private and nonpolitical domain. The story of the stateless and orphaned Creature poignantly shows how children's right to love persists in the face of parental failure to fulfill the obligation to provide or at least arrange for its proper enjoyment. Thought Experiment 4 indicates the need for a cosmopolitan solution to this all too common problem: the establishment of extrafamilial support systems (national, international, and/or transnational) that would ensure the provision of children's right to love when parents and families were unfit or unavailable to do so. Casting away the patriarchal view that the family and its male head of household ought to handle any and all matters of justice toward children, Shelley's cosmopolitan vision of justice allows for children's right to love to be secured and reinforced by groups and institutions beyond the family.

The Creature's plea for fulfillment of his right to love reminds us that a posthuman(itarian) and truly cosmopolitan conception of justice should be wary of discarding the concept of rights along with limiting, false, or dangerous conceptions of the human. To give up on rights entirely—especially for the most vulnerable of persons—is to "literally throw the baby out with the bathwater," as Cohen warns.[205] In a similar vein, Phillips reminds us that concepts and practices of "the human"—including human rights—are "fragile," changing and often rooted in our "embodied" and emotional experience of other people in particular social and political contexts.[206] The historic fragility of children's rights gives sufficient reason for retaining the idea of rights for the sake of helping all emotionally and socially vulnerable young creatures.

Furthermore, the idea of children's rights merits further consideration under the Shelleyan rubric of a posthuman(itarian) and truly cosmopolitan justice. Much like Bostrom's twenty-first-century transhumanist point of view, Shelley's *Frankenstein* presses readers to consider whether there is any reason to exclude the posthuman person from the rights of the human being. From the far-sighted perspectives of the Creature and Bostrom, the posthuman could simply mean a "certain possible type of human mode of being," which is compatible with other modes of being human.[207]

This new mode of being human might encourage a more cosmopolitan perspective on rights. Seen from this posthuman(itarian) perspective, rights would not be narrowly construed as the exclusive domain of humans but rather broadly understood as expressions of one's humanity or humaneness toward others. Such a posthuman(itarian) perspective on justice would not throw out the human along with rights but rather reformulate rights in light of a new, more fluid, understanding of possible ways of being human. Instead of speaking of the human versus the nonhuman or the posthuman, we would find ways of speaking about being human in relation to the post/human and non/human so as to avoid the exclusion of anyone who does not neatly fit extant categories of the human, the posthuman, and the nonhuman. If humans indeed could find such a way of responding to and, as Haraway puts it, "becoming with" the non/human and the post/human, then we might be well on our way to the realization of a truly ethical posthumanism—which might be best rendered as Post/humanism 3.[208] The use of the slash between "post" and "human(ism)" opens up room for the term to encompass more than solely the posthuman: it places the human alongside the posthuman and humanism alongside posthumanism, treating them at once as distinct and overlapping concepts. The slash after "post" also creates an undefined space for future articulation of what is unknown or unnameable now about the post/human condition. In a recent work of speculative fiction about the rise of "animal symbiont" children—genetically modified hybrids of humans and other "critters," such as monarch butterflies—Haraway points to a near future in which people dispense with the terms "nonhuman" and "human" in favor of "humus," a term that conveys the way that human life lives in synergy and symbiosis with other forms of life and matter.[209]

Such open-mindedness toward the re/conceptualization of the post/human and non/human has tremendous moral and political importance. Yet philosophers continue to avoid the issues raised by the counterfactual case of the Creature and the actual cases of GM children today. In her political reading of the concept of the human, Phillips does not treat the ethical, legal, and political issues raised by the making of post/human children. She dismisses genetic engineering of humans as "science fiction" rather than investigating its actual practice in recent history and its realistic possibilities in the near future.[210] Phillips also draws a bright line between humans and other beings, such as artificially intelligent machines and non/human animals. In defense of this stark demarcation of the human being as distinct from other kinds of being, she argues that only humans have made claims for rights. Until some other being makes such a claim to equal membership in the human community, she sees no reason to draw the line between humans and other beings differently.[211]

Frankenstein affords a more open-minded view of the value of Post/humanism 3 than does Phillips. Shelley's cascade of thought experiments on the rights of the child bridges rather than divides the human, the non/human, and the post/human. The novel accomplishes this important and visionary philosophical task through its systematic exploration of the social and political predicament of a post/human child. Shelley imagines exactly what Phillips presents as almost unimaginable: a new kind of being, made by a scientist, making a claim for a right that belongs to human children. By deducing the bad consequences of denying the Creature the right to share love with another, Shelley also accomplishes an important political task: putting the rights of the child—without discrimination as to origins, social status, or scientific classification—on the agenda for any future legitimate political community.

Children have always had a liminal place in relationship to the state and the human community as a whole. Deemed incapable of the moral agency or reason necessary for adult self-governance, they have been denied for much of history the possibility of holding rights, both in theory and in practice. Much like the Creature, children have been seen and treated as political aliens to human communities. Born of Shelley's thought experiments on the rights of the child, the idea of a post/human(itarian) and truly cosmopolitan justice seeks to rectify this historic injustice toward children of all kinds. Post/human(itarian) justice would thus resist the imperialism of humanistic justice, beginning in the family.

Most presciently, *Frankenstein* leads readers to see that the justification of a fundamental right to love is the same for a post/human child as it is for a child deemed human. The immanent possibility of making post/human children en masse through gene editing and other biotechnologies makes the recognition of this fundamental right all the more urgent. Knoepfler, whose career has focused on making genetically modified mice, has already expressed concern about the unregulated, rogue use of CRISPR-Cas9 to create children in a cold laboratory setting without recognizable parents, let alone the enjoyment of the parental love.[212] This brave new world will become more real with the advent of artificial womb technology but is certainly possible now with unregulated, rogue use of surrogates and gamete donors, without parents or fitting substitutes in place to lovingly care for the GM baby upon birth.[213] Knoepfler powerfully asks, "If people in the real world soon create new types of GM human beings in a laboratory in an asexual manner, an important question is: who would be the new child's parents? Who would care for them, particularly if they turn out to have developmental disabilities, diseases, or deformities? What would be their ultimate fates?"[214]

Without guaranteeing the right to love for post/human children, we run the risk of isolating, disabling, stigmatizing, marginalizing, alienating, or, worst of all, killing them due to their different origins, features, and capacities. Like the Creature, the post/human child has been a specter, lurking at the perimeter of rights theories, eerie for its virtual invisibility yet denied and ignored. There is a need to incorporate a new, almost unimaginable, kind of child into theories of rights in order to truly justify and fully ensure the fundamental rights of all children. What is stunning is that the teenage Mary Shelley saw this issue coming about two hundred years before it became a live one.

NOTES

PREFACE

1. John Vohlidka, "Atomic Reaction: *Godzilla* as Metaphor for Generational Attitudes Toward the United States and the Bomb," in *The Atomic Bomb in Japanese Cinema: Critical Essays*, ed. Matthew Edwards (Jefferson, NC: McFarland, 2015), 56–67, especially 57.

2. Gregory William Mank, *Bela Legosi and Boris Karloff: The Expanded Story of a Haunted Collaboration, with a Complete Filmography of Their Films Together* (Jefferson, NC: McFarland, 2009), 85.

3. Stephen King, *Danse Macabre* (New York: Gallery Books, 1981), 61.

4. Maurice Hindle, ed., "Introduction," Mary Shelley, *Frankenstein, or the Modern Prometheus* (New York: Penguin, 1994), xliv–xlvii.

5. Interestingly, *Classics Illustrated*—which translated "stories by the world's greatest authors" into comic books for children—also depicted the Creature as unintentionally killing William Frankenstein. "*Frankenstein* by Mary W. Shelley," adapted by Ruth A. Roche, *Classics Illustrated* 26 (December 1945), 22.

6. Mary Shelley, *Frankenstein: The 1818 Text*, 3rd ed., ed. D. L. Macdonald and Kathleen Scherf (Peterborough, Ontario: Broadview, 2012), 154–55.

7. Mary Shelley, *Frankenstein: The 1818 Text, Contexts, Criticism*, 2nd ed., ed. Paul J. Hunter (New York: Norton, [1996] 2012), 101.

8. Marvel Comics made such a superhero version of the Creature in *The Frankenstein Monster* series (1973–75).

INTRODUCTION

1. Jon Turney, *Frankenstein's Footsteps: Science, Genetics, and Popular Culture* (New Haven, CT: Yale University Press, 1998), 6.

2. Although the artificial creation (versus assisted reproduction) of human or human-like life is still a fantasy, a living bacterium with "a completely synthetic genome" was made in 2010. Stuart Fox, "J. Craig Venter Institute Creates First Synthetic Life Form," *Christian Science Monitor*, 21 May 2010, accessed 25 June 2016 at http://www.csmonitor.com/Science/2010/0521/J.-Craig-Venter-Institute-creates-first-synthetic-life-form.

3. Shelley, *Frankenstein: The 1818 Text, Contexts, Criticism*, 4.

4. Percy Shelley, "On *Frankenstein*," in *Frankenstein: The 1818 Text, Contexts, Criticism*, 213–15, especially 214.

5. Paul O'Flinn, "Production and Reproduction: The Case of *Frankenstein*," *Literature and History* 9:2 (1983), 194–213, especially 196.

6. I use the term "Creature" to describe the nameless person made by Victor Frankenstein rather than the derogatory term "monster" that his father-scientist ascribed to him. From this point forward, I only use the term "monster" in scare quotes to emphasize the way that it is a harmful slur imposed upon him, not his actual name. In support of this interpretation, the text itself gives the term "the creature" as the first description of Victor's creation after he is brought to life. Also, in his first conversation with his father, the Creature himself begs Victor to see him as "thy creature." Shelley, *Frankenstein: The 1818 Text, Contexts, Criticism*, 35, 68. On the role of reader bias in naming in the nameless Creature, see Charles E. Robinson, "Introduction," in Mary (with Percy) Shelley, *The Original Frankenstein: Two New Versions, Mary Shelley's Earliest Draft and Percy Shelley's Revised Text* (New York: Vintage, 2008), 18.

7. Susan Tyler Hitchcock, "The Monster Lives On," in *Frankenstein: The 1818 Text, Contexts, Criticism*, 263–70.

8. Mary Jacobus, "Is There a Woman in This Text?" *New Literary History* 14:1 (1982), 117–41; Devon Hodges, "*Frankenstein* and the Feminine Subversion of the Novel," *Tulsa Studies in Women's Literature* 2:2 (1983), 155–64; Gayatri Chakravorty Spivak, "Three Women's Texts and a Critique of Imperialism," *Critical Inquiry* 12:1 (1985), 254–59; Anca Vlasopolos, "*Frankenstein*'s Hidden Skeleton: The Psycho-Politics of Oppression," *Science Fiction Studies* 10:2 (1983), 125–36; Stephen Jay Gould, "The Monster's Human Nature," *Natural History* 103 (July 1994), 14–21; Lennard J. Davis, *Enforcing Normalcy: Disability, Deafness, and the Body* (London: Verso, 1995), chap. 6; Denise Gigante, "Facing the Ugly: The Case of *Frankenstein*," *ELH* 67:2 (2000), 565–87.

9. Throughout, I use the terms "rights of children," "rights of the child," and "children's rights" synonymously.

10. Mary Shelley, "Introduction to *Frankenstein*, Third Edition (1831)," in *Frankenstein: The 1818 Text, Contexts, Criticism*, 165–66.

11. Turney, *Frankenstein's Footsteps*, 27.

12. O'Flinn, "Production and Reproduction," 194.

13. Paul Cantor, *Creature and Creator: Myth-Making and English Romanticism* (Cambridge: Cambridge University Press, 1984), xvii.

14. Gordon J. Schochet, *Patriarchalism in Political Thought: The Authoritarian Family and Political Speculation and Attitudes Especially in Seventeenth-Century England* (New York: Basic Books, 1975), 233; Dennis Todd, *Imagining Monsters: Miscreations of the Self in Eighteenth-Century England* (Chicago: University of Chicago Press, 1995); David Armitage, "Monstrosity and Myth in Mary Shelley's *Frankenstein*," in *Monstrous Bodies/Political Monstrosities in Early Modern Europe*, ed. Laura Lunger Knoppers and Joan B. Landes (Ithaca, NY: Cornell University Press, 2004), 200–26.

15. Julia V. Douthwaite, *The Wild Girl, Natural Man, and the Monster: Dangerous Experiments in the Age of Enlightenment* (Chicago: University of Chicago Press, 2002).

16. Cantor, *Creature and Creator*, xvii; Michael J. Sandel, *The Case Against Perfection: Ethics in the Age of Genetic Engineering* (Cambridge, MA: Belknap, 2007), chap. 1 (Kindle edition).

17. Nancy J. Hirschmann, *Gender, Class, and Freedom in Modern Political Theory* (Princeton, NJ: Princeton University Press, 2008), 109.

18. Alan Richardson, "From *Emile* to *Frankenstein*: The Education of Monsters," *European Romantic Review* 1:2 (1991), 147–62.

19. The term "hideous progeny" is one that Mary Shelley invented to describe the story of Frankenstein as a kind of "offspring," which she bequeathed to the world to "go forth and prosper," not once, but twice, with her 1818 and 1831 editions of the text. Shelley, "Introduction to *Frankenstein*, Third Edition (1831)," 169. Betty T. Bennett, *Mary Wollstonecraft Shelley: An Introduction* (Baltimore: Johns Hopkins University Press, 1998), 1–22; Anne K. Mellor, *Mary Shelley: Her Life, Her Fiction, Her Monsters* (New York: Routledge, 1988), 1–8, 13–14, 20–21.

20. Chris Baldick, "The Reception of *Frankenstein*," in Shelley, *Frankenstein: The 1818 Text, Contexts, Criticism*, 245.

21. Ibid., 247.

22. Shelley, *Frankenstein: The 1818 Text, Contexts, Criticism*, 67.

23. Baldick, "The Reception of *Frankenstein*," 245.

24. By the term "feminism" and its variants, I follow Karen M. Offen as meaning arguments or forms of activism that criticize patriarchy and male privilege on behalf of the well-being of women as a group in any epoch or culture. By "organized feminism," I mean formal, public, and collective women's movements, often oriented toward political rights such as suffrage in the nineteenth century but also directed toward other economic or social goals such as education or work opportunities. These formal women's movements emerged in the mid to late nineteenth century, first in the 1840s in the United States, then in Western Europe and Britain, and quickly grew in other regions of the world in the mid to late nineteenth century. As Offen has shown, the term "feminist" was not used to describe such movements until 1870s France, whence it spread quickly around the globe. In some of my past scholarship, I distinguished between Mary Wollstonecraft, John Stuart Mill, and other proto-feminists and the self-identified feminists of the late nineteenth century and beyond. I have since abandoned this distinction in favor of the general use of the term "feminist" as a historiographical and hermeneutical concept that can be fruitfully applied to the analysis of arguments and activism concerning the betterment of women's social status in different historical contexts. Within this general category of analysis, I distinguish between the different historical manifestations of feminist arguments and activism that have developed in past texts and contexts. See Bonnie S. Anderson, *Joyous Greetings: The First International Women's Movement, 1830–1860* (Oxford: Oxford University Press, 2000); Lori Ginzberg, *Untidy Origins: A Story of Women's Rights in Antebellum New York* (Chapel Hill: University of North Carolina Press, 2005); Karen M. Offen, *European Feminisms, 1700–1950: A Political History* (Stanford, CA: Stanford University Press, 2000), 19–20; Karen M. Offen, ed., *Globalizing Feminisms, 1789–1945* (London: Routledge, 2010), xxix–xxxiv.

25. Shelley, *Frankenstein: The 1818 Text, Contexts, Criticism*, 36.

26. Ellen Moers, "Female Gothic: The Monster's Mother," in Shelley, *Frankenstein: The 1818 Text, Contexts, Criticism*, 317–27, especially 324–25; Sandra M. Gilbert and Susan Gubar, "Mary Shelley's Monstrous Eve," in Shelley, *Frankenstein: The 1818 Text, Contexts, Criticism*, 328–44, especially 336; Anne K. Mellor, "The Female in *Frankenstein*," in Shelley, *Frankenstein: The 1818 Text, Contexts, Criticism*, 355–68, especially 363.

27. Mellor, *Mary Shelley*, 54.

28. Shelley, "Introduction to *Frankenstein*, Third Edition (1831)," 169.

29. Mary Shelley, *The Journals of Mary Shelley, 1814–1844*, vol. 2, ed. Paula R. Feldman and Diana Scott-Kilvert (Oxford: Oxford University Press, 1987), 554. I silently correct the spelling, grammatical, or penmanship errors in Shelley's journal for the sake of readability.

30. Mary Shelley, "To Maria Gisborne, 11 June [1835]," in *The Letters of Mary Wollstonecraft Shelley*, vol. 2: *"Treading in Unknown Paths,"* ed. Betty T. Bennett (Baltimore: Johns Hopkins University Press, 1983), 244–48, especially 246.

31. Shelley, *The Journals of Mary Shelley*, vol. 2, 554.

32. "*Frankenstein*—Shelley, Mary Wollstonecraft," Open Syllabus Explorer, accessed 24 May 2016 at http://explorer.opensyllabusproject.org/text/1011454.

33. For two classic literary articulations of how reader responses to texts give meaning(s) to texts across time and place, see Italo Calvino, *If on a Winter's Night a Traveller*, trans. William Weaver (New York: Harvest, [1979] 1981), and Umberto Eco, *The Name of the Rose*, trans. William Weaver (New York: Harvest, [1980] 1983), especially the postscript.

34. Among primates so far, a rhesus monkey—which is a distant relative to humans, with 93 percent of its DNA in common—has been cloned by embryo splitting. There are some obstacles to primate (including human) cloning, due to the special biology of primate eggs. See National Institute of Health, Human Genome Research Institute, "Cloning Fact Sheet," accessed 13 September 2016 at https://www.genome.gov/25020028/cloning-fact-sheet/#al-8; Charles Q. Choi, "Monkey DNA Points to Common Human Ancestor," *Live Science*, 12 April 2007, accessed 13 September 2016 at http://www.livescience.com/1411-monkey-dna-points-common-human-ancestor.html.

35. C. Bulletti, A. Palagiano, C. Pace, A. Cerni, A. Borini, and D. de Ziegler, "The Artificial Womb," *Annals of the New York Academy of Sciences* 1221 (2011), 124–28; Saskia Hendriks, Eline A. F. Dancet, Ans M. M. van Pelt, Geert Hamer, and Sjoerd Repping, "Artificial Gametes: A Systematic Review of Biological Progress Toward Clinical Application," *Human Reproduction Update* 21:3 (2015), 285–96.

36. Hindle, ed., "Introduction," *Frankenstein*, xliv–xlvii.

37. David Collings, *Monstrous Society: Reciprocity, Discipline, and the Political Uncanny, c. 1780–1848* (Cranbury, NJ: Bucknell University Press, 2009), 194.

38. Peter Swirski, *Of Literature and Knowledge: Explorations in Narrative Thought Experiments, Evolution, and Game Theory* (London: Routledge, 2007), 96, 108–9.

39. Ibid.

40. Ibid.

41. Here I adapt and apply Jacqueline Bhabha's typology of stateless children to the case of stateless orphans. I develop this typology of the stateless orphan further in Chapters

1 and 4. See Bhabha, "From Citizen to Migrant: The Scope of Child Statelessness in the Twenty-First Century," in *Children Without a State: A Global Human Rights Challenge*, ed. Jacqueline Bhabha (Cambridge, MA: MIT Press, 2011), 1–42, especially 1–3.

42. S. Matthew Liao, "The Right of Children to Be Loved," *Journal of Political Philosophy* 14:4 (December 2006), 420–40; S. Matthew Liao, *The Right to Be Loved* (Oxford: Oxford University Press, 2015), 85–97.

43. Lawrence Lipking, "*Frankenstein*: The True Story, or Rousseau Judges Jean-Jacques," in Shelley, *Frankenstein: The 1818 Text, Contexts, Criticism*, 416–34, especially 426.

44. For an application of the concept of vulnerability to the justification of children's rights, see Martha Nussbaum and Rosalind Dixon, "Children's Rights and a Capabilities Approach: The Question of Special Priority," University of Chicago Public Law & Legal Theory Working Paper No. 384 (2012), 549–94.

45. Shelley, *Frankenstein: The 1818 Text, Contexts, Criticism*, 67.

46. Costas Douzinas, *Human Rights and Empire: The Political Philosophy of Cosmopolitanism* (London: Routledge, 2007), 7, 292.

47. Robert Nozick, *Anarchy, State, and Utopia* (New York: Basic Books, 1974), 42–45.

48. Liao, "The Right of Children to Be Loved"; Liao, *The Right to Be Loved*, 85–97.

49. Shelley, *Frankenstein: The 1818 Text, Contexts, Criticism*, 101–3.

50. Mary Shelley, *The Journals of Mary Shelley*, vol. 1, November 1816, 149.

51. Shelley, "To Maria Gisborne, 11 June [1835]," in *The Letters of Mary Wollstonecraft Shelley, Volume II*, 244–48, especially 246.

52. Shelley, *The Journals of Mary Shelley*, vol. 2, 557.

53. Shelley, *The Journals of Mary Shelley*, vol. 1, 85–102, 311–13.

54. Sir Walter Scott, "From Blackwood's Edinburgh Magazine (March 1818)," in Shelley, *Frankenstein: The 1818 Text, Contexts, Criticism*, 220.

55. Ibid., 221.

56. Ibid.

57. Shelley, *Frankenstein: The 1818 Text, Contexts, Criticism*, 158.

58. Ibid., 158.

59. Ibid., 160.

60. Ibid.

61. Ibid.

62. Ibid., 161.

63. Robinson, "Abbreviations," in *The Original Frankenstein*, 11, 13, 14.

64. Anne K. Mellor, "Choosing a Text of *Frankenstein* to Teach," in Shelley, *Frankenstein: The 1818 Text, Contexts, Criticism*, 204–11; Susan J. Wolfson and Ronald L. Levao, "Texts and Authorship," in Mary Wollstonecraft Shelley, *The Annotated Frankenstein*, ed. Susan J. Wolfson and Ronald L. Levao (Cambridge, MA: Belknap, 2012), 47–57.

65. Shelley, "Introduction to *Frankenstein*, Third Edition (1831)," 169.

66. Baldick, "The Reception of *Frankenstein*," 147.

67. Robinson, "Introduction," in *The Original Frankenstein*, 18.

68. Shelley, "Introduction to *Frankenstein*, Third Edition (1831)," 169.

69. Shelley, *The Journals of Mary Shelley*, vol. 1, 85–102.

70. Shelley, *Frankenstein: The 1818 Text, Contexts, Criticism*, 38–39; Shelley, "Introduction to *Frankenstein*, Third Edition (1831)," 169.

71. David Archard, *Children: Rights and Childhood*, 3rd ed. (New York: Routledge, 2014), 57–58.

72. Amy Gutmann, *Democratic Education* (Princeton, NJ: Princeton University Press, 1999), 49.

73. Onora O'Neill, "Children's Rights and Children's Lives," *Ethics* 98:3 (April 1988), 445–63.

74. S. Matthew Liao, "Human Rights as Fundamental Conditions for a Good Life," in *Philosophical Foundations of Human Rights*, ed. Rowan Cruft, S. Matthew Liao, and Massimo Renzo (Oxford: Oxford University Press, 2015), 79–101, especially 95–97.

75. Shelley, *Frankenstein: The 1818 Text, Contexts, Criticism*, 4.

76. For the earliest published interpretation of the novel as atheistic and impious, see "Edinburgh Magazine [On *Frankenstein*] (March 1818)," in Shelley, *Frankenstein: The 1818 Text, Contexts, Criticism*, 231–37, especially 236.

77. See James Griffin, *On Human Rights* (Oxford: Oxford University Press, 2008), chap. 4, for an extended argument against infants holding human rights.

78. John R. Strachan, ed., *A Routledge Literary Sourcebook on the Poems of John Keats* (London: Routledge, 2003), 14.

79. Archard, *Children: Rights and Childhood*, 104.

80. In Chapter 3, I examine the social scientific and medical-psychiatric basis for the justification of children's right to share love. See Liao, *The Right to Be Loved*, for the passive formulation of a child's right to love and an extended justification of it, also by way of social scientific and medical-psychiatric evidence.

81. For a gradualist argument for allowing children to "grow into" the full slate of civil and political rights over the course of adolescence, see Andrew Rehfeld, "The Child as Democratic Citizen," *Annals of the American Academy of Political and Social Science*, vol. 633, *The Child as Citizen* (January 2011), 141–66.

82. Shelley, *The Journals of Mary Shelley*, vol. 2, 554; Talal Asad, "Reflections on Violence, Law, and Humanitarianism," *Critical Inquiry* 41:2 (Winter 2015), 390–427.

CHAPTER 1

1. Percy Shelley made very few substantial changes to the characterization of the Creature while working as editor of Mary Shelley's original manuscript. One of the few was his suggestion to say the Creature "muttered some inarticulate sounds while a grin wrinkled his cheeks" rather than, as Shelley originally put it, "muttered some words while a grin wrinkled his cheeks" when he tried to rouse his maker from sleep. Shelley accepted Percy's suggested revision, perhaps because it was more consistent with her overall depiction of the Creature as an abandoned newborn striving to reconnect with his parent. See Shelley (with P. Shelley), *The Original Frankenstein*, 82, 277.

2. Ibid., 80–85.

3. Ibid., 84–85.

4. Shelley, *The Journals of Mary Shelley*, vol. 1, March 1815, 68–70.

5. Ibid.

6. Shelley (with P. Shelley), *The Original Frankenstein*, 80–82.

7. Shelley, "Introduction to *Frankenstein*, Third Edition (1831)," 168–69.

8. Ellen Moers, *Literary Women* (Garden City, NY: Doubleday, [1963] 1976), 93–97; Barbara Johnson, "My Monster/My Self," *Diacritics* 12:2 (Summer 1982), 2–10, especially 6; Mellor, *Mary Shelley*, 31–32; Barbara R. Almond, "The Monster Within: Mary Shelley's "Frankenstein" and a Patient's Fears of Childbirth and Mothering," *International Journal of Psycho-analysis* 79:4 (1998), 775–86, especially 778.

9. Indeed, it is possible for parents to revive prematurely born infants solely through the warmth of touch. See Meg Wagner, "Australian Mom Says Cuddling Premature Baby Declared Dead Brought Him Back to Life," *New York Daily News*, 13 March 2015, accessed 15 February 2016 at http://www.nydailynews.com/news/world/mom-cuddles-bring-premature-baby-declared-dead-life-article-1.2148177.

10. U. C. Knoepflmacher, "Thoughts on the Aggression of Daughters," in *The Endurance of Frankenstein: Essays on Mary Shelley's Novel*, ed. George Levine and U. C. Knoepflmacher (Berkeley: University of California Press, 1979), 88–119, especially 90; Mellor, *Mary Shelley*, 1–15; Anne K. Mellor, "Making a 'Monster': An Introduction to *Frankenstein*," in *The Cambridge Companion to Mary Shelley*, ed. Esther Schor (Cambridge: Cambridge University Press, 2003), 9–25, especially 10–12.

11. Bhabha, "From Citizen to Migrant," 1–3.

12. Carole Pateman, *The Sexual Contract* (Stanford, CA: Stanford University Press, 1989), 76, 84–96, 171–72; Barbara Arneil, *Locke and America: The Defense of English Colonialism* (Oxford: Clarendon, 1996), 30–31; Barbara Arneil, "Disability, Self-Image, and Modern Political Theory," *Political Theory* 37:2 (April 2009), 218–42; Nancy J. Hirschmann, "Gendered Politics: Schochet on Hobbes, Gratitude, and Women," in *Feminist Interpretations of Thomas Hobbes*, ed. Nancy J. Hirschmann and Joanne H. Wright (University Park: Pennsylvania State Press, 2012), 127; Pauline Kleingeld, "Kant's Second Thoughts on Colonialism," in *Kant and Colonialism*, ed. Kathleen Flickschuh and Lea Ypi (Oxford: Oxford University Press, 2014), 43–68, especially 46.

13. Charles Taylor, *Modern Social Imaginaries* (Durham, NC: Duke University Press, 2004), 23, 146–47; Marina Calloni, "Images of Fear in Political Philosophy and Fairy Tales: Linking Private Abuse to Political Violence in Human Rights Discourse," *Journal of International Political Theory* 12:1 (February 2016), 67–89.

14. Hodges, "*Frankenstein* and the Feminine Subversion of the Novel," 155–64, especially 162; Vlasopolos, "*Frankenstein*'s Hidden Skeleton," 125–36; Spivak, "Three Women's Texts and a Critique of Imperialism," 254–59; Mellor, *Mary Shelley*, 44–47; Gigante, "Facing the Ugly," 565–87; Essaka Joshua, "'Blind Vacancy': Sighted Culture and Voyeuristic Historiography in Mary Shelley's *Frankenstein*," *European Romantic Review* 22:1 (2011), 49–69, especially 49–50.

15. Thomas Hobbes, *Leviathan, or the Matter, Forme, & Power of a Common-Wealth*

Ecclesiastical and Civill, ed. Ian Shapiro (New Haven, CT: Yale University Press, 2006), 79–80, 122.

16. Ibid., 53, 80.

17. Ibid., 122.

18. For the earlier version of his thought experiment on whether a mother would care for or expose an infant in the state of nature, see Thomas Hobbes, *On the Citizen*, ed. Richard Tuck (Cambridge: Cambridge University Press, 1998), 107–10. Schochet, *Patriarchalism in Political Thought*, 230.

19. John Locke, *Two Treatises of Government*, ed. Peter Laslett (Cambridge: Cambridge University Press, [1960] 2005), 306.

20. Ibid., 310.

21. Ibid.

22. Ibid., 207.

23. Ibid., 206.

24. Ibid., 211, 315.

25. Ibid., 307, 313, 314, 347.

26. Ibid., 390, 391, 393.

27. Ibid., 393.

28. Ibid., 391, 393.

29. Pateman, *The Sexual Contract*, 96.

30. Locke, *Two Treatises*, 207.

31. Ibid., 315–16.

32. Archard, *Children*, 10, 161.

33. Mary Wollstonecraft, *A Vindication of the Rights of Woman*, ed. Eileen Hunt Botting (New Haven, CT: Yale University Press, 2014), 174 (hereafter *Rights of Woman*).

34. Kate Millet, *Sexual Politics* (Garden City, NY: Doubleday, 1970), 67.

35. Locke, *Two Treatises*, 391.

36. Ibid., 389, 391.

37. Ibid., 385.

38. Ibid., 389.

39. Ibid., 390.

40. Ann L. Kibbie, "The Estate, the Corpse, and the Letter: Posthumous Possession in *Clarissa*," *ELH* 74:1 (Spring 2007), 117–43.

41. Susan M. Okin, *Justice, Gender, and the Family* (New York: Basic Books, 1989), 80–81.

42. Locke, *Two Treatises*, 390.

43. Ibid., 304, 393, 394.

44. Ibid., 392, 394.

45. Ibid., 393.

46. Ibid., 308. On Locke's developmental model of the human capability for consent and its legal and political implications, see Tom Cockburn, *Rethinking Children's Citizenship* (New York: Palgrave, 2012), 54; Sana Nakata, *Childhood Citizenship, Governance and Policy: The Politics of Becoming Adult* (New York: Routledge, 2015), 49–50.

47. Locke, *Two Treatises*, 393.

48. Jean-Jacques Rousseau, *Emile, or on Education*, trans. Allan Bloom (New York: Basic Books, 1979), 474.

49. Jean-Jacques Rousseau, *The Social Contract and the First and Second Discourses*, ed. Susan Dunn (New Haven, CT: Yale University Press, 2002), 100.

50. Ibid., 114.

51. Penny Weiss, *Gendered Community: Rousseau, Sex, and Politics* (New York: New York University Press, 1995), 58.

52. Ibid. For the term "natural woman," see Susan M. Okin, "Rousseau's Natural Woman," *Journal of Politics* 41:2 (May 1979), 393–416.

53. Greg Kucich, "Biographer," in *The Cambridge Companion to Mary Shelley*, 226–41, especially 236–37.

54. Mellor, *Mary Shelley*, 47–48; Douthwaite, *The Wild Girl, Natural Man, and the Monster*, 110, 113; Nancy Yousef, *Isolated Cases: The Anxieties of Autonomy in Enlightenment Philosophy and Romantic Literature* (Ithaca, NY: Cornell University Press, 2004), 10.

55. Rousseau, *The Social Contract and the First and Second Discourses*, 116.

56. Ibid., 113–19.

57. Ibid., 101.

58. Immanuel Kant, *Toward Perpetual Peace and Other Writings on Politics, Peace, and History*, ed. Pauline Kleingeld (New Haven, CT: Yale University Press, 2006), 17–18.

59. Ibid., 45, 46, 49.

60. Ibid., 131.

61. Ibid., 133.

62. Ibid.

63. Pateman, *The Sexual Contract*, 168–71.

64. Nakata, *Childhood Citizenship, Governance, and Policy*, 17.

65. Simone de Beauvoir, *The Second Sex*, trans. and ed. H. M. Parshley (New York: Vintage, 1989), xxiii, 131–32, 239, 269. I thank Colleen Mitchell for this insight and reference.

66. Ibid.

67. Millet, *Sexual Politics*, 88.

68. Nancy J. Hirschmann, "Invisible Disability: Seeing, Being, Power," in *Civil Disabilities: Citizenship, Membership, and Belonging*, ed. Nancy J. Hirschmann and Beth Linker (Philadelphia: University of Pennsylvania Press, 2015), 204–22, especially 213–14.

69. Yousef, *Isolated Cases*, 152.

70. Mellor, *Mary Shelley*, 3–4; Charlotte Gordon, *Romantic Outlaws: The Extraordinary Lives of Mary Wollstonecraft and Her Daughter Mary Shelley* (New York: Random House, 2015), 220 (Kindle edition).

71. Shelley, *The Journals of Mary Shelley*, vol. 1, 38–39, 85–88, 97; Robinson, "Introduction," in *The Original Frankenstein*, 22.

72. Gordon, *Romantic Outlaws*, 651.

73. Shelley, *The Journals of Mary Shelley*, vol. 1, 85, 86, 89–91, 94–96, 101.

74. Ibid., 287, 311–13, 387, 411.

75. Kucich, "Biographer," in *The Cambridge Companion to Mary Shelley*, 234–37.

76. For example, see Lipking, "*Frankenstein*: The True Story," 416–34; Richardson, "From *Emile* to *Frankenstein*," 147–62; Yousef, *Isolated Cases*, 149–69.

77. John Locke, *Essay Concerning Human Understanding* (London, 1690), Book II, chap. 1, §2.

78. Ibid., Book I, chap. 4, §2.

79. Locke, *Two Treatises*, 304.

80. Jean-Jacques Rousseau, *Émile, ou de l'éducation* (Paris: Crapart, Caille, et Ravier, 1802), vol. 1, 15–16. Allan Bloom translated this line from the second paragraph of *Emile* differently than other English translators have done: "In the present state of things a man abandoned to himself in the midst of other men from birth would be the most disfigured of all." While a good literal translation, it fails to capture the poetic quality and rhythm of Rousseau's repeated, metaphoric, synonymous use of the concepts of mutilation, monstrosity, deformity, and disfigurement, beginning from the first paragraph of *Emile*. For Bloom's rendition in context, see Rousseau, *Emile*, 37.

81. Wollstonecraft, *Rights of Woman*, 185.

82. Ibid.

83. Ibid.

84. Richardson, "From *Emile* to *Frankenstein*," 148.

85. Wollstonecraft, *Rights of Woman*, 69.

86. Ibid., 70.

87. Ibid.

88. Ibid.

89. Shelley (with P. Shelley), *The Original Frankenstein*, 122.

90. Ibid.

91. Ibid., 190.

92. Ibid., 191.

93. William Godwin, *Enquiry Concerning Political Justice, with Selections from Godwin's Other Writings*, ed. K. Codell Carter (Oxford: Oxford University Press, 1971), 22 (hereafter cited as *Political Justice*).

94. Ibid.

95. Ibid., 24.

96. Ibid.

97. Ibid.

98. Ibid., 69.

99. Ibid., 217.

100. Rousseau, *Emile*, 37.

101. Ibid.

102. William Godwin, *Enquiry Concerning Political Justice, and Its Influence on Morals and Happiness* (London: G. G. and J. Robinson, 1799), vol. 2, 99. The 1971 Oxford edition of *Political Justice* is abridged and does not contain this passage.

103. Fred Botting, *Making Monstrous: Frankenstein, Criticism, Theory* (Manchester: Manchester University Press, 1991), 139.

104. Wollstonecraft, *Rights of Woman*, 188.

105. Godwin, *Political Justice*, 37.

106. Ibid., 34.

107. Ibid.

108. Rousseau, *Emile*, 62.

109. Gómez U. Reyes, Rico M. P. Hernández, Hernández D. Reyes, Hernández L. Javier, Martínez M. Ortiz, "Mozart's Music in the Prenatal Period," *Ginecología y obstetricia de México* 74:8 (2006), 424–28.

110. Godwin, *Political Justice*, 36.

111. Ibid., 37.

112. E. Simons, T. To, R. Moineddin, D. Stieb, and S. D. Dell, "Maternal Second-Hand Smoke Exposure in Pregnancy Is Associated with Childhood Asthma Development," *Journal of Allergy and Clinical Immunology in Practice* 2:2 (March–April 2014), 201–7.

113. Godwin, *Political Justice*, 35, 28.

114. Ibid., 127–28.

115. Ibid., 130–39.

116. Wollstonecraft, *Rights of Woman*, 69; Douthwaite, *The Wild Girl, Natural Man, and the Monster*, 29–52.

117. Wollstonecraft, *Rights of Woman*, 69.

118. Ibid., 39.

119. Ibid., 39.

120. Ibid., 69.

121. Godwin, *Political Justice*, 33.

122. Ibid., 31.

123. Ibid., 37.

124. Ibid., 99–102.

125. Ibid., 102–3.

126. Ibid., 102.

127. Ibid., 112.

128. Ibid., 103–5.

129. Mellor, *Mary Shelley*, 9.

130. Ibid., 10–11.

131. Scott, "From Blackwood's Edinburgh Magazine," 227.

132. Anne K. Mellor, "Righting the Wrongs of Woman: Mary Wollstonecraft's *Maria*," *Nineteenth-Century Contexts* 19 (1996), 413–24.

133. Moers, *Literary Women*, 99.

134. Shelley (with P. Shelley), *The Original Frankenstein*, 123.

135. Ibid., 125.

136. Ibid., 168–69.

137. Ibid., 169.

138. Isaiah Berlin, "Two Concepts of Liberty," in *Liberty*, ed. Henry Hardy (Oxford: Oxford University Press, 2008), 203. I am grateful to Colleen Mitchell for this insight and reference.

CHAPTER 2

1. Archard, *Children: Rights and Childhood*, 57–58.

2. Ibid., 41–54.

3. Wollstonecraft, *Rights of Woman*, 199.

4. Ibid., 188.

5. Gutmann, *Democratic Education*, 49.

6. Wollstonecraft, *Rights of Men*, 14; Wollstonecraft, *Rights of Woman*, 180–82.

7. Here and throughout I apply Onora O'Neill's typology of obligations, which has become essential to contemporary theories of children's rights, and thus helps to elucidate the similarities and differences between Wollstonecraft's views and the contemporary work on the topic. Onora O'Neill, "Children's Rights and Children's Lives."

8. Elizabeth Frazer, "Mary Wollstonecraft and Catharine Macaulay on Education," *Oxford Review of Education* 37:5 (2011), 603–17, especially 613.

9. Alan Richardson, "Mary Wollstonecraft on Education," in *The Cambridge Companion to Mary Wollstonecraft*, ed. Claudia Johnson (Cambridge: Cambridge University Press, 2002), 24–41.

10. Carol H. Poston speculated that Wollstonecraft was speaking from the perspective of an adult survivor of child abuse, "not necessarily sexual . . . but emotional and physical." Poston, "Wollstonecraft and 'The Body Politic,'" in *Feminist Interpretations of Mary Wollstonecraft*, ed. Maria J. Falco (University Park: Pennsylvania State University Press, 1996), 87. Biographers have disagreed about the extent of Wollstonecraft's experience of neglect or abuse as a child but at least agree that she witnessed her father's violence against her mother. See Lyndall Gordon, *Vindication: A Life of Mary Wollstonecraft* (New York: HarperCollins, 2005), 9.

11. My extended treatment of Wollstonecraft's theological foundations for her moral and political philosophy is found in Eileen Hunt Botting, *Family Feuds: Wollstonecraft, Burke, and Rousseau on the Transformation of the Family* (Albany: State University of New York Press, 2006), 131–88. For an alternative, secular reading of Wollstonecraft's theory of rights in the context of her republicanism yet independent of her theological commitments, see Alan Coffee, "Mary Wollstonecraft, Public Reason, and the Virtuous Republic," in *The Social and Political Philosophy of Mary Wollstonecraft*, ed. Sandrine Bergès and Alan Coffee (Oxford: Oxford University Press, 2016), chap. 10).

12. Wollstonecraft, *Rights of Woman*, 52.

13. Ibid., 87.

14. Wollstonecraft, *Original Stories from Real Life*, in *Works*, vol. 4, 413.

15. Richard Price, *Political Writings*, ed. D. O. Thomas (Cambridge: Cambridge University Press, 1991), 23; Wollstonecraft, *Rights of Men*, 14.

16. Wollstonecraft, *Rights of Woman*, 186; Onora O'Neill, "Kantian Approaches to Some Famine Problems," in *Matters of Life and Death: New Introductory Essays in Moral Philosophy*, ed. Tom Regan (New York: McGraw Hill, 1989), 258–70; Onora O'Neill, *Constructions of Reason: Explorations of Kant's Practical Philosophy* (Cambridge: Cambridge University Press, 1989), 75–77, 188.

17. Wollstonecraft, *Rights of Woman*, 59.

18. John Locke, *Some Thoughts Concerning Education* (London: Printed for A. & J. Churchill, 1693), § 116; Wollstonecraft, *Rights of Woman*, 203.

19. Wollstonecraft, *Rights of Woman*, 203.

20. Out of 116 total uses of the term "rights" in her two major political treatises, Wollstonecraft only used the term "natural rights" two times in the *Rights of Men* and six times in the much longer *Rights of Woman*. Richard Tuck, *Natural Rights Theories: Their Origin and Development* (Cambridge: Cambridge University Press, 1981), 5–31; Brian Tierney, *The Idea of Natural Rights: Studies on Natural Rights, Natural Law, and Church Law, 1150–1625* (Grand Rapids, MI: Eerdmans, [1997] 2001), 43–77; Annabel Brett, *Liberty, Right, and Nature: Individual Rights in Later Scholastic Thought* (Cambridge: Cambridge University Press, [1997] 2003), 49–87.

21. Wollstonecraft, *Rights of Woman*, 39; Wollstonecraft, *Rights of Men*, 7.

22. Price, *Political Writings*, 147.

23. Thomas Paine, *Political Writings*, ed. Bruce Kuklick (Cambridge: Cambridge University Press, 2000), 176, 198.

24. Wollstonecraft, *Rights of Woman*, 185.

25. Mary Astell, *Reflections upon marriage. The third edition. To which is added a preface, in answer to some objections* (London, 1706), preface; Catharine Macaulay, *Letters on education. With observations on religious and metaphysical subjects* (London, 1790), 210.

26. Wollstonecraft, *Original Stories from Real Life*, in *Works*, vol. 4, 359.

27. Wollstonecraft, *Rights of Men*, 14.

28. Ibid.

29. Ibid.

30. Ibid.

31. Ibid.

32. See Mary Wollstonecraft, "To George Blood, 6 October 1791," in *The Collected Letters of Mary Wollstonecraft*, ed. Janet Todd (New York: Columbia, 2003), 188–90.

33. O'Neill, "Children's Rights and Children's Lives," 447.

34. Ibid., 447–48.

35. Wollstonecraft, *Rights of Woman*, 185.

36. Ibid., 92.

37. Although she does not discuss the case of children in an orphanage here, Wollstonecraft's argument for Duties 2a and 2b would apply in the same way to institutional parenting as they do to parenting of biological children, stepchildren, or foster children. Equality of provision of care to children is what matters most, not the particular type of childrearing environment.

38. Wollstonecraft, *Rights of Woman*, 92–93.

39. O'Neill, "Children's Rights and Children's Lives," 447.

40. Wollstonecraft, *Rights of Woman*, 186.

41. Ibid.

42. Wollstonecraft, *Rights of Woman*, 208.

43. O'Neill, "Children's Rights and Children's Lives," 446–47; Immanuel Kant,

Groundwork for the Metaphysics of Morals, ed. Allen W. Wood (New Haven, CT: Yale University Press, [1785] 2002), 38, 41, 47–48, 128, 155.

44. Wollstonecraft, *Rights of Woman*, 224.

45. Ibid., 183.

46. Locke, *Two Treatises*, 306, 381.

47. Wollstonecraft, *Rights of Woman*, 183.

48. Ibid., 180.

49. Ibid., 180–81.

50. Locke, *Two Treatises*, 381.

51. Wollstonecraft, *Rights of Woman*, 183.

52. Ibid.

53. Ibid., 184.

54. Ibid.

55. Ibid.

56. Locke, *Two Treatises*, 381.

57. Wollstonecraft, *Rights of Woman*, 184.

58. Ibid.

59. O'Neill, "Children's Rights and Children's Lives," 452.

60. Wollstonecraft, "To Gilbert Imlay, 1 January 1794," in *Works*, vol. 6, 377.

61. Virginia Sapiro, *A Vindication of Political Virtue: The Political Theory of Mary Wollstonecraft* (Chicago: University of Chicago Press, 1992), 157.

62. Locke, *Two Treatises*, 303–7.

63. Wollstonecraft, *Maria, or the Wrongs of Woman*, in *Works*, vol. 1, 107.

64. Tristan McCowan, "Human Rights Within Education: Assessing the Justifications," *Cambridge Journal of Education* 42:1 (2012), 67–81, especially 73.

65. Amartya Sen, *Development as Freedom* (New York: Anchor, 2000), 195–99.

66. McCowan, "Human Rights Within Education," 170.

67. Rehfeld, "The Child as Democratic Citizen," 141–66.

68. Gutmann, *Democratic Education*, 49.

69. Wollstonecraft, *Rights of Woman*, 199.

70. Wollstonecraft, *Maria*, 168.

71. Wollstonecraft, *Rights of Woman*, 174.

72. Wollstonecraft, *Maria*, 180.

73. Wollstonecraft, *Rights of Woman*, 21–24.

CHAPTER 3

1. Swirski, *Of Literature and Knowledge*, 96, 108–9.

2. Shelley, *Frankenstein: The 1818 Text, Contexts, Criticism*, 101–3.

3. Strachan, ed., *A Routledge Literary Sourcebook on the Poems of John Keats*, 14.

4. Shelley, *The Journals of Mary Shelley*, vol. 2, 554.

5. Beth Lau, "Jane Austen and John Keats: Negative Capability, Romance and Reality,"

Keats-Shelley Journal 55, *Women Writers of the British Regency Period* (2006), 81–110, especially 84–85.

6. Wollstonecraft, *Rights of Woman*, 111, 23.

7. Eileen Hunt Botting, *Wollstonecraft, Mill, and Women's Human Rights* (New Haven, CT: Yale University Press, 2016), 56.

8. Shelley, *Frankenstein: The 1818 Text, Contexts, Criticism*, 101. For dating the milestones in the Creature's life, including his approximate age of one year, nine months at the time of demanding a female companion, see Essaka Joshua, "'Marking the Dates with Accuracy': The Time Problem in Mary Shelley's Frankenstein," *Gothic Studies* 3:3 (December 2001), 279–308, especially 300–303.

9. Shelley, *Frankenstein: The 1818 Text, Contexts, Criticism*, 103–4.

10. Liao, *The Right to Be Loved.*

11. Shelley, *Frankenstein: The 1818 Text, Contexts, Criticism*, 103.

12. Ibid., 101.

13. Ibid., 100–104.

14. Ibid., 103.

15. Ibid., 103–4.

16. Ibid., 102.

17. Ibid., 102–3.

18. Ibid., 84.

19. Joshua, "'Marking the Dates with Accuracy,'" 300–303.

20. John Milton, *Paradise Lost*, Book IV, lines 707–8, accessed 24 March 2016 at http://www.paradiselost.org/8-Search-All.html; Shelley, *Frankenstein: The 1818 Text, Contexts, Criticism*, 103.

21. Botting, *Family Feuds*, 175.

22. Wollstonecraft, *Rights of Woman*, 95.

23. Botting, *Wollstonecraft, Mill, and Women's Human Rights*, 106–7.

24. Wollstonecraft, *Rights of Woman*, 45–46.

25. While parthenogenesis (asexual reproduction from unfertilized eggs) can take place in some species (including "some lizards, insects, and fish"), it does not happen in humans (or other mammals) without "artificial stimulus," such as "an electric shock to the egg," in a laboratory setting. This technique is currently used to make cloned human embryonic stem cell lines but is not used for purposes of human reproduction. Paul Knoepfler, *GMO Sapiens: The Life-Changing Science of Designer Babies* (London: World Scientific, 2016), 51.

26. In the recent case of *The View* talk show host Sherri Shepherd, a court affirmed her legal status as a mother despite her attempt as a litigant to deny parental responsibility for a child born as a result of her choice to use IVF, egg donation, her then-husband's sperm, and a surrogate: "That this child came about through a complicated series of contracts and payments, rather than a sexual act, does not change the fact that Shepherd made sure this child was brought into the world, and she must assume her share of the responsibility for the child's well-being." Joanna L. Grossman, "Baby Mama: Appellate Court Declares Sherri Shepherd Is the Legal Mother of a Child Born to Her via Surrogate," *Verdict: Legal Analysis and Commentary from Justia*, 1 December 2015, accessed 3 March 2016 at https://verdict

.justia.com/2015/12/01/baby-mama-appellate-court-declares-sherri-shepherd-is-the-legal-mother-of-a-child-born-to-her-via-surrogate.

27. Shelley, *Frankenstein: The 1818 Text, Contexts, Criticisms*, 3.

28. James J. McKenna and Jay T. Gettler, "'It's Dangerous to Be an Infant': Ongoing Relevance of John Bowlby's Environment of Evolutionary Adaptedness (EEA) in Promoting Healthier Births, Safer Maternal-Infant Sleep, and Breastfeeding in a Contemporary Western Industrial Context," in *Evolution, Early Experience and Human Development: From Research to Practice and Policy*, ed. D. Narvaez, J. Panksepp, A. Schore, and T. Gleason (New York: Oxford University Press, 2012), 439–52, especially 439.

29. The questions of the basis and extent of a child's duty for self-preservation are ones that stand beyond the scope of my present argument yet merit further consideration in *Frankenstein* scholarship (particularly in regard to the Creature's plan to immolate himself at the end of the novel) as well as in theories of children's rights and duties (particularly the ethics of suicide, assisted or solo).

30. Shelley, *Frankenstein: The 1818 Text, Contexts, Criticisms*, 67.

31. Ibid., 102.

32. Joshua, "'Marking the Dates with Accuracy,'" 295.

33. Adrienne Rich, *Of Woman Born: Motherhood as Experience and Institution* (New York: W. W. Norton, 1976), 11.

34. Knoepflmacher, "Thoughts on the Aggression of Daughters," in *The Endurance of Frankenstein*, 90.

35. Ibid., 101, 109.

36. Mellor, *Mary Shelley*, 4–7, 54.

37. Shelley, "To Maria Gisborne, 11 June [1835]," 246.

38. Shelley, *Frankenstein: The 1818 Text, Contexts, Criticism*, 31.

39. Dianne Long Hoeveller, "Frankenstein, Feminism, and Literary Theory," in *The Cambridge Companion to Mary Shelley*, 45–62, especially 51–52.

40. Barbara Johnson, *A World of Difference* (Baltimore: Johns Hopkins University Press, 1987), 151; Paul Youngquist, "*Frankenstein*: The Mother, the Daughter, and the Monster," *Philological Quarterly* 70:3 (Summer 1991), 339–59, especially 347.

41. Shelley, *Frankenstein: The 1818 Text, Contexts, Criticism*, 33.

42. Ibid., 83.

43. Ibid., 38–39.

44. Ibid., 35–36; Mary Shelley, *Frankenstein; or, the Modern Prometheus* (London: Lackington, Hughes, Harding, Mavor & Jones, 1818), 98 [copy held by the J. P. Morgan Library with annotations by Mary Shelley. Hereafter referred to as "1818 Thomas," following Robinson, "Abbreviations," 13].

45. Shelley, *Frankenstein: The 1818 Text, Contexts, Criticism*, 36.

46. Ibid., 91.

47. Ibid., 84.

48. Ibid., 91.

49. Shelley, "To Maria Gisborne, 11 June [1835]," in *The Letters of Mary Wollstonecraft Shelley*, vol. 2, 246.

50. Laurie Langbauer, "Motherhood and Women's Writing in Mary Wollstonecraft's Novels," in *Romanticism and Feminism*, ed. Anne K. Mellor (Bloomington: Indiana University Press, 1988), 208–19; Botting, *Family Feuds*, 186.

51. Rich, *Of Woman Born*, 13, 42, 212.

52. Andrea O'Reilly, "Introduction," in *From Motherhood to Mothering: The Legacy of Adrienne Rich's Of Woman Born*, ed. Andrea O'Reilly (Albany: SUNY Press, 2004), 1–26, especially 2.

53. Rich, *Of Woman Born*, 85, 128, 211–12; Sarah Blaffer Hrdy, *Mother Nature: A History of Mothers, Infants, and Natural Selection*, 1999), 105; McKenna and Gettler, "'It's Dangerous to Be an Infant,'" 444.

54. Sarah Blaffer Hrdy, "Mothers and Others," *Natural History Magazine*, May 2001, accessed 20 May 2016 at http://www.naturalhistorymag.com/picks-from-the-past/11440/mothers-and-others.

55. Susan M. Okin, *Justice, Gender, and the Family* (New York: Basic Books, 1989), 5.

56. I am grateful to Colleen Mitchell for imagining this alternative ending to the story.

57. Shelley, *Frankenstein: The 1818 Text, Contexts, Criticism*, 84.

58. Ibid., 67.

59. Ibid., 102–3.

60. Ibid., 103.

61. Ibid.

62. Ibid., 102.

63. Ibid.

64. Wollstonecraft, "To Gilbert Imlay, 1 January 1794," in *Works*, vol. 6, 377.

65. Botting, *Family Feuds*, 211.

66. Nikhil Swaminathan, "Strange but True: Men Can Lactate," *Scientific American*, 6 September 2007, accessed 24 March 2016 at http://www.scientificamerican.com/article/strange-but-true-males-can-lactate; Laura Kaplan Shanley, "Milkmen: Fathers Who Breastfeed," accessed 24 March 2016 at http://www.unassistedchildbirth.com/milkmen-fathers-who-breastfeed.

67. Noam Scheiber, "Paid Leave for Moms and Dads: Reporter's Notebook," *New York Times*, 16 September 2015, accessed 24 March 2016 at http://www.nytimes.com/2015/09/16/insider/changing-attitudes-toward-paid-leave-for-moms-and-dads-reporters-notebook.html.

68. Shelley, "1818 Thomas," 98; Shelley, *Frankenstein: 1818 Text, Contexts, Criticism*, 33.

69. Melanie L. Glocker, Daniel D. Langleben, Kosha Ruparel, James W. Loughead, Ruben C. Gur, and Nobert Sachser, "Baby Schema in Infant Faces Induces Cuteness Perception and Motivation for Caretaking in Adults," *Ethology* 115:3 (2009), 257–63. See also Konrad Lorenz, *Studies in Animal and Human Behavior* (Cambridge, MA: Harvard University Press, 1971).

70. Ibid.

71. Jessika Golle, Fabian Probst, Fred W. Mast, and Janek S. Lobmaier, "Preference for Cute Infants Does Not Depend on Their Ethnicity or Species: Evidence from Hypothetical Adoption and Donation Paradigms," *PLoS ONE* 10:4 (2015), e0121554.

72. Glocker et al., "Baby Schema in Infant Faces," 257–63.

73. Gould, "The Monster's Human Nature," 14–21.

74. Ibid.

75. Shelley, *Frankenstein: The 1818 Text, Contexts, Criticism*, 102.

76. Ibid., 103.

77. Ibid., 102.

78. Ibid.

79. Ibid.

80. Ibid.

81. Stanley Greenspan (with Nancy Breslau Lewis), *Building Healthy Minds: The Six Experiences that Create Intelligence and Emotional Growth in Babies and Young Children* (New York: Da Capo Press, 1999), 374.

82. S. Matthew Liao, "The Idea of a Duty to Love," *Journal of Value Inquiry* 40:1 (2006), 1–22; Immanuel Kant, *The Metaphysics of Morals*, trans. Mary Gregor (Cambridge: Cambridge University Press, 1996), 161; Immanuel Kant, *Groundwork of the Metaphysic of Morals*, trans. H. J. Paton (New York: Harper & Row, 1964), 67; Liao, *The Right to Be Loved*, 131.

83. Shelley, *Frankenstein: The 1818 Text, Contexts, Criticism*, 33.

84. Ibid., 33.

85. Ibid., 34. I credit Greg Kucich and Agustín Fuentes with this insight about the Creature's possible status as a "hybrid."

86. Ibid., 35–36; Shelley, "1818 Thomas," 98.

87. Shelley, *Frankenstein: The 1818 Text, Contexts, Criticism*, 93.

88. Ibid., 101.

89. Ibid., 102–3.

90. John Bowlby, *Attachment*, 2nd ed., vol. 1 of *Attachment and Loss* (New York: Basic Books, [1969] 1982), 177–234.

91. Shelley, *Frankenstein: The 1818 Text, Contexts, Criticism*, 89.

92. Liao, *The Right to Be Loved*, 17–25.

93. Shelley, *Frankenstein: The 1818 Text, Contexts, Criticism*, 70–73.

94. Ibid., 67.

95. "Patrick Cotter O'Brien," accessed 13 April 2016 at http://www.thetallestman.com/patrickcotter.htm.

96. "Anton de Franckenpoint," accessed 13 April 2016 at http://www.thetallestman.com/antondefranchepoinct.htm.

97. Syndy McMillen Conger, "A German Ancestor for Mary Shelley's Monster: Kahlert, Schiller, and the Buried Treasure of 'Northanger Abbey,'" *Philological Quarterly* 59:2 (Spring 1980), 216–33; Shelley, *Frankenstein: The 1818 Text, Contexts, Criticism*, 33.

98. Swirski, *Of Literature and Knowledge*, 108.

99. McKenna and Gettler, "'It's Dangerous to Be an Infant,'" 449.

100. Nussbaum and Dixon, "Children's Rights and a Capability Approach," 555, 574.

101. Ibid., 554.

102. Ibid., 584.

103. Shelley, *Frankenstein: The 1818 Text, Contexts, Criticism*, 70.

104. Ibid.

105. Ibid.

106. Ibid., 72.

107. Ibid., 70.

108. Greenspan (with Lewis), *Building Healthy Minds*, 374–77.

109. Shelley, *Frankenstein: The 1818 Text, Contexts, Criticism*, 79–80; Greenspan (with Lewis), *Building Healthy Minds*, 87–88.

110. Joshua, "'Marking the Dates with Accuracy,'" 287; Shelley, *Frankenstein: The 1818 Text, Contexts, Criticism*, 82.

111. Bowlby, *Attachment*, 177–209.

112. Ibid., 302–3.

113. Ibid., 211, 217. John Bowlby, "Attachment and Loss: Retrospect and Prospect," *American Journal of Orthopsychiatry* 52:4 (October 1982), 664–78, especially 667–70.

114. Richard Bowlby and Jennifer McIntosh, "John Bowlby's Legacies and Meanings for the Family Law Field: In Conversation with Sir Richard Bowlby," *Family Court Review* 49:3 (2011), 549–56, especially 556.

115. See Shelley (with P. Shelley), *The Original Frankenstein*, 82, 277. As discussed in Chapter 1, note 3, Percy Shelley suggested that the Creature be "inarticulate" at birth, and Mary Shelley accepted the edit. McKenna and Gettler, "'It's Dangerous to Be an Infant,'" 448–49.

116. Shelley, *Frankenstein: The 1818 Text, Contexts, Criticism*, 84.

117. I am indebted to Greg Kucich for the insight that Mr. DeLacey is a mother figure.

118. Mary Poovey, "My Hideous Progeny: Mary Shelley and the Feminization of Romanticism," *PMLA* 95:3 (May 1980), 332–47, especially 337.

119. Shelley, *Frankenstein: The 1818 Text, Contexts, Criticism*, 93.

120. Ibid., 93–94.

121. John Bowlby, *Separation: Anxiety and Anger*, vol. 2 of *Attachment and Loss* (New York: Basic Books, 1973), 50, 52, 245–48.

122. Shelley, *Frankenstein: The 1818 Text, Contexts, Criticism*, 93.

123. John Bowlby, *Loss: Sadness and Depression*, vol. 3 of *Attachment and Loss* (New York: Basic Books, 1980), 40–41, 214–28.

124. McKenna and Gettler, "'It's Dangerous to Be an Infant,'" 439.

125. Shelley (with P. Shelley), *The Original Frankenstein*, 322.

126. Shelley, *Frankenstein: The 1818 Text, Contexts, Criticism*, 82.

127. Nussbaum and Dixon, "Children's Rights and a Capabilities Approach," 584.

128. Shelley, *Frankenstein: The 1818 Text, Contexts, Criticism*, 158–59.

129. Ibid., 95.

130. Ibid., 91.

131. Godwin, *Political Justice*, 36; Shelley, *Frankenstein: The 1818 Text, Contexts, Criticism*, 160.

132. Hannah Arendt, *The Origins of Totalitarianism* (New York: Harcourt, [1951] 1996), 374.

133. Shelley, *Frankenstein: The 1818 Text, Contexts, Criticism*, 94.

134. Ibid.

135. Liao, *The Right to Be Loved*, 131–50.

136. Plausible imitators include the television series *Lost* (2004–10) and the film *Inception* (2010).

137. Shelley, *Frankenstein: The 1818 Text, Contexts, Criticism*, 102.

138. Ibid., 104.

139. Ibid., 119.

140. Ibid., 102–3.

141. Botting, *Family Feuds*, 102, 111, 151.

142. Wollstonecraft, *Rights of Woman*, 145–46, 182.

143. Ibid.

144. Liao, *The Right to Be Loved*, 74.

145. Greenspan (with Lewis), *Building Healthy Minds*, 49–83, 374.

146. Shelley Burtt, "What Children Really Need: Toward a Critical Theory of Family Structure," in *The Moral and Political Status of Children*, ed. David Archard and Colin M. Macleod (Oxford: Oxford University Press, 2002), 231–52, especially 244–47.

147. An interesting question raised by this thought experiment, which I am unable to explore here, is whether adult children nevertheless have a right to compensation or reparations (such as paid therapy) due to child neglect or abuse suffered during their dependency on parents.

148. Shelley, *Frankenstein: The 1818 Text, Contexts, Criticism*, 119.

149. Ibid.

150. Ibid., 118.

151. Ibid.

152. Ibid., 118–19.

153. Ibid., 118.

154. Ibid., 119.

155. Ibid.

156. Ibid.

157. Ibid.

158. Ibid.

159. Ibid.

160. Ibid.

161. Ibid.

162. Program for "Christening Michael Monsoor (DDG 1001)," 18 June 2016, General Dynamics/Bath Iron Works.

163. Shelley, *Frankenstein: The 1818 Text, Contexts, Criticism*, 120.

164. Ibid., 160.

165. Mellor, "Choosing a Text of *Frankenstein* to Teach," 209–10.

166. Botting, *Wollstonecraft, Mill, and Women's Human Rights*, 92.

167. Robert Lamb, "Was William Godwin a Utilitarian?" *Journal of the History of Ideas* 70:1 (2009), 119–41, especially 120. Lamb argues that Godwin is a utilitarian with a nonhedonic, virtue-oriented conception of "human happiness."

168. Carol J. Adams, *The Sexual Politics of Meat (20th Anniversary Edition): A Feminist-Vegetarian Critical Theory* (New York: A&C Black, 2010), 120, 152, 193.

169. Shelley, *Frankenstein: The 1818 Text, Contexts, Criticism*, 118–19.

170. Liao, *The Right to Be Loved*, 16.

171. Ibid.; David Roden, "Cylons in the Original Position: The Limits of Posthuman Justice," in *Battlestar Gallactica and Philosophy: Knowledge Here Begins Out There*, ed. J. T. Eberl (Malden, MA: Wiley-Blackwell, 2008), chap. 12; Upendra Baxi, *The Posthuman and Human Rights* (Oxford: Oxford University Press, 2009), 197–239.

CHAPTER 4

1. Swirski, *Of Literature and Knowledge*, 108.

2. Turney, *Frankenstein's Footsteps*, 67, 72, 186, 195.

3. Knoepfler, *GMO Sapiens*, xiv, 2, 5; James Kozubek, *Modern Prometheus: Editing the Human Genome with CRISPR-Cas9* (Cambridge: Cambridge University Press, 2016), chap. 5. See also George W. Sledge Jr., "Could You Be Any Cuter? Genome Editing and the Future of the Human Species," *Musings of a Cancer Doctor*, Stanford Medicine Department of Oncology, 14 May 2015, accessed 29 May 2016 at http://med.stanford.edu/oncology/about/chief-s-blog/2015/could-you-be-any-cuter--genome-editing-and-the-future-of-the-hum.html; Kevin McCormack, "Brave New World or Dark Threatening Future: A Clear-Eyed Look at Genome Editing and What It Means for Humanity," *Stem Cellar*, 5 May 2016, accessed 29 May 2016 at https://blog.cirm.ca.gov/tag/gene-editing.

4. Due to their greater size, eggs (not sperm) or a one-cell embryo would be used for germline modification of humans with CRISPR-Cas9. Knoepfler, *GMO Sapiens*, 146. The transhumanist philosopher Nick Bostrom uses the term "healthspan" to describe improvements in longevity and health due to such technological and medical interventions. See Nick Bostrom, "Why I Want to Be a Posthuman When I Grow Up," in *Medical Enhancement and Posthumanity*, ed. Bert Gordijn and Ruth Chadwick (Dordrecht: Springer, 2008), 107–37, accessed 15 June 2016 at www.nickbostrom.com. All references to this paper are to the online version, 1–25.

5. Chris Lake, "Gene Editing Technology Has Scientists Worried About 'Frankenbabies,'" *Inquisitr*, 16 January 2016, accessed 31 May 2016 at http://www.inquisitr.com/2714833/gene-editing-technology-has-scientists-worried-about-frankenbabies.

6. M. K. Joseph, "The Composition of *Frankenstein*," in Shelley, *Frankenstein: The 1818 Text, Contexts, Criticism*, 173; Baldick, "The Reception of *Frankenstein*," 242; Scott, "Blackwood's Edinburgh Magazine," 221; "Edinburgh Magazine [On *Frankenstein*] (March 1818)," 231.

7. Armitage, "Monstrosity and Myth in Mary Shelley's *Frankenstein*," 225–26; Hitchcock, "The Monster Lives On," 263–70; Elizabeth Young, *Black Frankenstein: The Making of an American Metaphor* (New York: New York University Press, 2008).

8. Eduardo Cadava, "The Monstrosity of Human Rights," *PMLA* 121:5 (October 2006), 1558–65.

9. Young, *Black Frankenstein*, 2.

10. Steve Berman, "We Cannot Build a Frankenstein GOP," *Resurgent*, 15 April 2016, accessed 29 May 2016 at http://theresurgent.com/we-cannot-build-a-frankenstein-gop.

11. Martha C. Nussbaum, *Frontiers of Justice: Disability, Nationality, Species Membership* (Cambridge, MA: Belknap, 2006), 1–8.

12. Nussbaum and Dixon, "Children's Rights and a Capability Approach," 593.

13. James Robert Brown and Yiftach Fehige, "Thought Experiments," *The Stanford Encyclopedia of Philosophy* (Spring 2016 ed.), ed. Edward N. Zalta, accessed 29 May 2016 at http://plato.stanford.edu/archives/spr2016/entries/thought-experiment.

14. Swirski, *Of Literature and Knowledge*, 95–97.

15. Ibid., 108.

16. Ibid.

17. Ibid.

18. Richard Holmes, "Mary Shelley and the Power of Contemporary Science," in Shelley, *Frankenstein: The 1818 Text, Contexts, Criticism*, 183–94; D. L. Macdonald and Kathleen Scherf, "Introduction," in Shelley, *Frankenstein: The 1818 Text*, 3rd ed., 19–24.

19. Macdonald and Scherf, "Introduction," 14–18.

20. Joshua, "'Marking the Dates with Accuracy,'" 300–303.

21. Swirski, *Of Literature and Knowledge*, 108.

22. Holmes, "Mary Shelley and the Power of Contemporary Science," 186–87.

23. Macdonald and Scherf, "Introduction," 22.

24. Shelley, "Introduction to *Frankenstein*, Third Edition (1831)," 168.

25. Swirski, *Of Literature and Knowledge*, 108.

26. Ibid.

27. Ibid., 109.

28. It would vastly underestimate the incredibly creative range of interpretations of *Frankenstein*'s projectability into matters of science and politics to attempt to sum up even a mere sample of them in an endnote. Nonetheless, here are two excellent resources for further study on this point: Turney's *Frankenstein's Footsteps* and Esther Schor, ed., *The Cambridge Companion to Mary Shelley* (Cambridge: Cambridge University Press, 2003).

29. Shelley, *Frankenstein: The 1818 Text, Contexts, Criticism*, 36, 38, 50. The *OED* includes "the face" or "countenance" among its primary definitions of "aspect" in usage around the time *Frankenstein* was composed. "Aspect, n.," accessed 4 June 2016 at oed.com.

30. Diego F. Wyszynski, ed., "Glossary," in *Cleft Lip and Palate: From Origin to Treatment* (Oxford: Oxford University Press, 2002), 507.

31. Ibid.

32. Shelley, *Frankenstein: The 1818 Text, Contexts, Criticism*, 35.

33. Ibid., 35–36.

34. Ibid., 36, 38, 50.

35. Ibid., 36.

36. Ibid., 50.

37. The *OED* cites Lord Byron's 1817 poem "Manfred" as an example of the use of the

word "aspect" to mean "face": "Ah! he unveils his aspect: on his brow/ The thunder-scars are graven." "Aspect, n.," accessed 4 June 2016 at oed.com.

38. Shelley, *Frankenstein: The 1818 Text, Contexts, Criticism*, 158.

39. Ibid., 36.

40. Ibid., 35.

41. Ibid., 33, 35, 36, 67.

42. Anne K. Mellor, "Frankenstein, Racial Science, and the Yellow Peril," in Shelley, *Frankenstein: The 1818 Text, Contexts, Criticism*, 481–90.

43. Young, *Black Frankenstein*, 27. In showing the legacy of the story for African American struggles against white power, Young makes a case that the Creature's skin could be black or brown because its "color" is like a "mummy."

44. Shelley, *Frankenstein: The 1818 Text, Contexts, Criticism*, 36.

45. John A. Nackashi, E. Rosellen Dedlow, and Virginia Dixon-Wood, "Health Care for Children with Cleft Lip and Palate: Comprehensive Services and Infant Feeding," in Wyszynski, ed., *Cleft Lip and Palate*, 303–18, especially 305; Lynna Y. Littleton-Gibbs and Joan Engebretson, eds., *Maternity Nursing Care*, 2nd ed. (Boston: Cengage Learning, 2012), 882.

46. Littleton-Gibbs and Engebretson, eds., *Maternity Nursing Care*, 882.

47. Shelley, *Frankenstein: The 1818 Text, Contexts, Criticism*, 35.

48. Gigante and Davis focus on the skin in general as the primary site of the Creature's deformity or ugliness, not specifically the skin around the facial area between the eyes and the mouth. Gigante, "Facing the Ugly"; Davis, *Enforcing Normalcy*, chap. 6.

49. Littleton-Gibbs and Engebretson, eds., *Maternity Nursing Care*, 882–83.

50. Ibid.

51. Glenn Cohen, *The Globalization of Health Care: Legal and Ethical Issues* (Oxford: Oxford University Press, 2012), 424.

52. Ravi A. Malhotra, "Justice as Fairness and Critical Theory," in *Critical Disability Theory: Essays in Philosophy, Politics, Policy, and Law*, ed. Dianne Pothier and Richard Devlin (Vancouver: University of British Columbia Press, 2006), 70–86.

53. Eileen Hunt Botting, "Wollstonecraft, Hobbes, and the Rationality of Women's Anxiety," in *Disability and Political Theory*, ed. Barbara Arneil and Nancy J. Hirschmann (Cambridge: Cambridge University Press, 2016), chap. 5.

54. Malhotra, "Justice as Fairness and Critical Theory," 72.

55. Botting, "Wollstonecraft, Hobbes, and the Rationality of Women's Anxiety."

56. Malhotra, "Justice as Fairness and Critical Theory," 72.

57. Eva Feder Kittay, "When Caring Is Just and Justice Is Caring: Justice and Mental Retardation," in *The Subject of Care: Feminist Perspectives on Dependency*, ed. Eva Feder Kittay and Ellen K. Feder (New York: Rowman & Littlefield, 2002), 257–76, especially 264–65.

58. Operation Smile is a worldwide charitable organization that uses such "before" and "after" photos to show the positive impact of the corrective surgeries it arranges for children with cleft lip/palate. To its credit, the organization does not feature "after" photos on the

front page of its website but rather files them under "patient spotlights." See "Patient Spotlights," *Operation Smile*, accessed 4 June 2016 at http://www.operationsmile.org/profile/14.

59. Littleton-Gibbs and Engebretson, eds., *Maternity Nursing Care*, 883.

60. Ibid., 882–83.

61. Lucy Le Mare, Karyn Audet, and Karyn Kurytnik, "Protecting the Rights of International 'Orphans': Evaluating the Alternatives," in *Children's Rights: Multidisciplinary Approaches to Participation and Protection*, ed. Tom O'Neill and Dawn Zinga (Toronto: University of Toronto Press, 2008), 39–68, especially 51; Kieran Guilbert, "Cleft Surgery Boosts Economy, Gives Developing Nations Reason to Smile," *Reuters*, 24 March 2016, accessed 31 May 2016 at http://www.reuters.com/article/westafrica-health-idUSL5N16U3IE; "Alejandro's Story," *Operation Smile*, accessed 4 June 2016 at http://www.operationsmile.org/alejandros-story.

62. "Danila's Story," *Operation Smile*, accessed 4 June 2016 at http://www.operationsmile.org/patient-stories/danilas-story; "Marcilene's Story," *Operation Smile*, accessed 4 June 2016 at http://www.operationsmile.org/patient-stories/marceline-patient-story.

63. Shelley, *Frankenstein: The 1818 Text, Contexts, Criticism*, 67.

64. Mark W. J. Ferguson, "Facial Clefting in Antiquity," in *Cleft Lip and Palate: Long-Term Results and Future Practice*, vol. 1, ed. A. G. Huddart and M. W. J. Ferguson (Manchester: Manchester University Press, 1990), 3–5, especially 3.

65. Gigante, "Facing the Ugly," 565, 582. Gigante notes that Shelley used the term "u[n]-namable" to describe the Creature in her journal, after she watched with approval the 1823 stage production of *Presumption* and its representation of the Creature in the theater program as a blank.

66. Le Mare, Audet, and Kurytnik, "Protecting the Rights of International 'Orphans,'" 51.

67. Ibid.

68. Guilbert, "Cleft Surgery Boosts Economy."

69. The Reconstructive Surgery Act of 2007 (H.R. 2820, 110th Congress) is legislation that would "cover cleft/craniofacial patients of all ages." It has not yet been reintroduced to Congress. See "Stop Insurance Denials for Cleft and Craniofacial Patients in the United States!" accessed 4 June 2016 at http://www.thepetitionsite.com/1/craniofacial.

70. See "David vs. Goliath—Fighting the Insurance Company," *cleftAdvocate*, accessed 4 June 2016 at http://www.cleftadvocate.org/insurance.html.

71. Preterm birth can be related to birth defects. See Richard E. Berhman and Adrienne Stith Butler, eds., *Preterm Birth: Causes, Consequences, and Correction* (Washington, DC: National Academies Press, 2007), 150. Sometimes "late fetal deaths" due to birth defects are included in the analysis of their prevalence. Adolfo Correa and Larry Edmonds, "Birth Defect Surveillance Systems and Oral Clefts," in Wyszynski, ed., *Cleft Lip and Palate*, 117–27, especially 120.

72. Shelley, *The Journals of Mary Shelley*, vol. 1, March 1815, 68–70; Shelley, *Frankenstein: The 1818 Text, Contexts, Criticism*, 36.

73. Shelley, *The Journals of Mary Shelley*, vol. 1, March 1815, 68–70.

74. Gigante, "Facing the Ugly," 569.

75. Nussbaum and Dixon, "Children's Rights and a Capability Approach," 554, 584.

76. Shelley, *Frankenstein: The 1818 Text, Contexts, Criticism*, 101.

77. For historical background on the evolution of child welfare policy in the United States and its foreign relations, see Theda Skocpol, *Protecting Soldiers and Mothers: The Political Origins of Social Policy in the United States* (Cambridge, MA: Harvard University Press, 1992), 424–540; Lori Askeland, ed., *Children and Youth in Adoption, Orphanages, and Foster Care: A Historical Handbook and Guide* (Westport, CT: Greenwood, 2006); Catherine Ceniza Choy, *Global Families: A History of Asian International Adoption in America* (New York: New York University Press, 2013), 15–74.

78. Jennifer Kwon Dobbs, "Baby Scooping 'Stateless' Children," *Foreign Policy in Focus*, 21 September 2012, accessed 8 June 2016 at http://fpif.org/baby_scooping_stateless_children.

79. See Chapters 2 and 3 for the development of this distinction between a child's "growing out of" some rights, such as to love, and "growing into" other rights, such as to vote.

80. Bhabha, "From Citizen to Migrant," 1–3.

81. Dobbs, "Baby Scooping 'Stateless' Children."

82. Bhabha, "From Citizen to Migrant," 1–3.

83. UNICEF, "Refugee and Migrant Crisis in Europe," September 2015, accessed 1 July 2016 at http://www.unicef.org/publicpartnerships/files/Refugee_and_migrant_children_in_Europe_-_Sept_2015.pdf.

84. Louise Osborne and Ruby Russell, "Refugee Crisis Creating Stateless Generation of Children in Limbo," *Guardian*, 27 December 2015, accessed 1 July 2016 at https://www.theguardian.com/world/2015/dec/27/refugee-crisis-creating-stateless-generation-children-experts-warn.

85. Dobbs, "Baby Scooping 'Stateless' Children"; Madison Park, "U.S. Law Aimed at Helping North Korean Orphans," *CNN*, 27 January 2014, accessed 8 June 2016 at http://www.cnn.com/2013/05/13/us/north-korea-adoption.

86. Pamela Collis, "The Stateless Surrogate Orphan," *International Academy of Matrimonial Lawyers, 25th Anniversary Meeting, Educational Programme*, 9 September 2011, 1–2, accessed 8 June 2016 at https://www.iafl.com/cms_media/files/session_6.pdf?static=1.

87. "Australia Child Protection Agency Probes Gammy's Father," *BBC News*, 5 August 2014, accessed 9 June 2016 at http://www.bbc.com/news/world-asia-28654831.

88. Collis, "The Stateless Surrogate Orphan," 3–4.

89. "Stateless Child Wins Home Ruling," *Los Angeles Times*, 11 March 1993, accessed 8 June 2016 at http://articles.latimes.com/1993-03-11/news/vw-1297_1_japanese-citizenship.

90. Shelley, *Frankenstein: The 1818 Text, Contexts, Criticism*, 93.

91. Seyla Benhabib took such a critical and cosmopolitan approach in rethinking the citizenship of migrants (including children) in *The Rights of Others: Aliens, Residents, and Citizens* (Cambridge: Cambridge University Press, 2004).

92. Bhabha, "From Citizen to Migrant," 3.

93. Ibid., 1–3.

94. Frances Robles, "Wave of Minors on Their Own Rush to Cross U.S. Border," *New York Times*, 4 June 2014, accessed 8 June 2016 at http://www.nytimes.com/2014/06/04/world/americas/wave-of-minors-on-their-own-rush-to-cross-southwest-border.html; Sonia Nazario, "The Children of the Drug Wars: A Refugee Crisis Not an Immigration Crisis," *New York Times*, 11 July 2014, accessed 8 June 2016 at http://www.nytimes.com/2014/07/13/opinion/sunday/a-refugee-crisis-not-an-immigration-crisis.html.

95. Nazario, "The Children of the Drug Wars."

96. Julia Preston, "New U.S. Effort to Aid Unaccompanied Child Migrants," *New York Times*, 2 June 2014, accessed 8 June 2016 at http://www.nytimes.com/2014/06/03/us/politics/new-us-effort-to-aid-unaccompanied-child-migrants.html; Michael D. Shear, "Obama Approves Plan to Let Children in Central America Apply for Refugee Status," *New York Times*, 30 September 2014, accessed 8 June 2016 at http://www.nytimes.com/2014/10/01/us/obama-approves-plan-to-let-children-apply-for-refugee-status-in-central-america.html.

97. See Article 8 of the Convention on the Rights of the Child, accessed 9 June 2016 at http://www.ohchr.org/en/professionalinterest/pages/crc.aspx.

98. Arendt, *Origins of Totalitarianism*, 372–84.

99. Judith Butler, *Toward a Performative Theory of Assembly* (Cambridge, MA: Harvard University Press, 2015), 73.

100. Jake Silverstein, "The Displaced: An Introduction," *New York Times*, 5 November 2015, accessed 9 June 2016 at http://nyti.ms/1kcnJfc.

101. Ibid.

102. Arendt, *Origins of Totalitarianism*, 374.

103. Ibid., 375.

104. Ibid., 375, 357, 387.

105. Jyothi Kanics, "Realizing the Rights of Undocumented Children in Europe," in Bhabha, ed., *Children Without a State*, 131–50, especially 140.

106. Elena Rozzi, "Unaccompanied and Separated Children in Spain: A Policy of Institutional Mistreatment," in Bhabha, ed., *Children Without a State*, 151–76, especially 163.

107. Stephen H. Legomsky, "Undocumented Students, College Education, and Life Beyond," in Bhabha, ed., *Children Without a State*, 217–36, especially 222.

108. See Chapter 1 for an extended analysis of the willful blindness of the Kantian state toward children and their rights.

109. Dana Villa, *Arendt and Heidegger: The Fate of the Political* (Princeton, NJ: Princeton University Press, 1995), 147.

110. The Editorial Board, "10,000 Child Refugees Are Missing," *New York Times*, 10 February 2016, accessed 9 June 2016 at http://www.nytimes.com/2016/02/10/opinion/10000-child-refugees-are-missing.html.

111. Ibid.

112. Shelley, *Frankenstein*, 93–94.

113. Ian Shapiro, *Democratic Justice* (New Haven, CT: Yale University Press, 1999), 73.

114. Elizabeth F. Cohen, "Neither Seen nor Heard: Children's Citizenship in Contemporary Democracies," *Citizenship Studies* 9:2 (May 2005), 221–40, especially 221.

115. Ibid., 234.

116. UNICEF, "Refugee and Migrant Crisis in Europe."

117. Colene Bentley, "Family, Community, Polity: Theorizing the Basis and Boundaries of Political Community in *Frankenstein*," *Criticism* 47:3 (2005), 325–51, especially 335.

118. Ibid.

119. Arendt, *Origins of Totalitarianism*, 376.

120. Ibid., 377.

121. For an extended critique of the social contract tradition's banishment of the stateless orphan to the very edges of the state of nature, see Chapter 1.

122. Arendt, *Origins of Totalitarianism*, 576. The question of the relationship between the right to love and the right to life is beyond the scope of this study but would be a profitable topic to explore in relationship to *Frankenstein.*

123. Shelley, *Frankenstein: The 1818 Text, Contexts, Criticism*, 158.

124. McCowan, "Human Rights Within Education," 170.

125. Arendt, *Origins of Totalitarianism*, 375.

126. Knoepfler, *GMO Sapiens*, 90, 93.

127. Ibid., 91.

128. Ibid., 87, 89–90, 92.

129. Ibid., 92–93.

130. Ian Sample, "World's First Baby Born from New Procedure Using DNA of Three People," *Guardian*, 27 September 2016, accessed 5 October 2016 at https://www.theguardian.com/science/2016/sep/27/worlds-first-baby-born-using-dna-from-three-parents.

131. Stephen Castle, "Britain Set to Approve Technique to Create Babies from 3 People," *New York Times*, 3 February 2015, accessed 15 June 2016 at http://www.nytimes.com/2015/02/04/world/europe/britain-nears-approval-of-fertilization-technique-that-combines-dna-of-three-people.html.

132. Sample, "World's First Baby Born from New Procedure."

133. Knoepfler, *GMO Sapiens*, 91.

134. Ibid., 87.

135. Ibid., 4.

136. Shelley, *Frankenstein: The 1818 Text, Contexts, Criticism*, 38–39.

137. This definition of the posthuman is partly inspired by Bostrom's "Why I Want to Be a Posthuman When I Grow Up," 1–2.

138. Gigante, "Facing the Ugly," 582. Gigante quotes from Shelley's 9–11 September 1823 letter to Leigh Hunt, describing her favorable response to the representation of the Creature as a blank space in the theater program for *Presumption*, the first stage adaptation of *Frankenstein.*

139. Ben Golder, "What Is an Anti-Humanist Human Right?" *Social Identities* 16:5 (2010), 651–88, especially 656.

140. Anne Phillips, *The Politics of the Human* (Cambridge: Cambridge University Press, 2015), 131–32.

141. Golder, "What Is an Anti-Humanist Human Right?" 656–59.

142. Phillips, *The Politics of the Human*, 107.

143. Cynthia Pon, "'Passages' in Mary Shelley's *Frankenstein*: Toward a Feminist Figure of Humanity?" *Modern Language Studies* 30:2 (2000), 33–50, especially 33.

144. Ibid. Although often cited as the leading theorist of a posthumanist or posthuman feminism because of groundbreaking essays such as "Ecce Homo, Ain't (Ar'n't) I a Woman, and Inappropriate/d Others: The Human in a Post-Humanist Landscape" (1989), Haraway has since rejected the labels of "posthuman" or "posthumanist" for her work. See Donna J. Haraway, *When Species Meet* (Minneapolis: University of Minnesota Press, 2008), 17, and Donna Haraway, "Ecce Homo," in *The Haraway Reader* (London: Routledge, 2004), 47–61.

145. Phillips, *The Politics of the Human*, 111.

146. Golder, "What Is an Anti-Humanist Human Rights?" 659–64; Baxi, *Human Rights in a Posthuman World*, 197–239.

147. Samuel Moyn, *Human Rights and the Uses of History* (London: Verso, 2014), 146.

148. Golder, "What Is an Anti-Humanist Human Right?" 661.

149. Baxi, *Human Rights in a Posthuman World*, 204–5.

150. Golder, "What Is an Anti-Humanist Human Right?" 656, 664.

151. Knoepfler, *GMO Sapiens*, 52.

152. Phillips, *The Politics of the Human*, 113.

153. Nick Bostrom, "A History of Transhumanist Thought," *Journal of Evolution and Technology* 14:1 (2005), 1–30, especially 14–15, accessed 20 June 2016 at http://www.nickbostrom.com/papers/history.pdf.

154. Transhumans are already mobilized as a political group. See the Transhumanist Bill of Rights (2015), accessed 20 June 2016 at http://www.transhumanistparty.org/TranshumanistBillofRights.html. In 2004, Neil Harbisson, a colorblind performance artist who had an antenna mounted in his skull to enable him to "hear" colors as sound waves, gained a kind of formal recognition as a cyborg when he was allowed to take a U.K. passport photo with his antenna in full view. See David Wolfe, "This Is the First Human Cyborg Who Is Colorblind But Can Hear Color," accessed 20 June 2016 at http://www.davidwolfe.com/first-human-cyborg-colorblind-can-hear-color.

155. Baldick, "The Reception of *Frankenstein*," 245.

156. Marshall Brown, "*Frankenstein*: A Child's Tale," *NOVEL: A Forum on Fiction* 36:2 (Spring 2003), 145–75, especially 151; Theodora Goss and John Paul Riquelme, "From Superhuman to Posthuman: The Gothic Technological Imaginary in Mary Shelley's *Frankenstein* and Octavia Butler's *Xenogenesis*," *Modern Fiction Studies* 53:3 (2007), 434–59.

157. See Brown's "*Frankenstein*: A Child's Tale" for a view of the novel as a "regressive" or "infantile" text that interprets the world from a child's imaginative perspective. For a broader look at children's literature as a kind of posthuman literature, see Zoe Jacques, *Children's Literature and the Posthuman: Animal, Environment, Cyborg* (New York: Routledge, 2015).

158. Bostrom, "Why I Want to Be a Posthuman When I Grow Up," 1–2.

159. Knoepfler, *GMO Sapiens*, 153.

160. Ibid., 92.

161. Bostrom, "Why I Want to Be a Posthuman When I Grow Up," 2.

162. Castle, "Britain Set to Approve Technique to Create Babies from 3 People"; Ewen

Callaway, "U.K. Scientists Gain License to Edit Genes in Human Embryos," *Nature* 530:7588 (2016), accessed 13 September 2016 at http://www.nature.com/news/uk-scientists-gain-licence-to-edit-genes-in-human-embryos-1.19270.

163. Sandel, *The Case Against Perfection*, chaps. 3 and 4.

164. Ibid., 742–45, 810–13.

165. Ibid., 322–33.

166. Francis Fukuyama, *Our Posthuman Future: Consequences of the Biotechnology Revolution* (New York: Picador, 2003), 70, 74, 90.

167. Ibid., 5, 10, 205–14.

168. Ibid., 85, 157; Baxi, *The Posthuman and Human Rights*, 208–20.

169. Such a fundamentalist religious point of view on cloning and other forms of human genetic modification as the making of "abominations" is grippingly represented by the "Prolethean" cult on the BBC America television series *Orphan Black* (2013–17).

170. Knoepfler, *GMO Sapiens*, 1, 228–31.

171. Lake, "Gene Editing Technology Has Scientists Worried About 'Frankenbabies.'"

172. Knoepfler, *GMO Sapiens*, 223.

173. Fukuyama, *Our Posthuman Future*, 85, 157.

174. Knoepfler, *GMO Sapiens*, 33, 223.

175. Ibid., 223.

176. Ibid., 252.

177. Ibid., vi.

178. Ibid., 90.

179. Shelley, *Frankenstein: The 1818 Text, Contexts, Criticism*, 69.

180. Diana Reese, "A Troubled Legacy: Mary Shelley's *Frankenstein* and the Inheritance of Human Rights," *Representations* 96:1 (2006), 48–72, especially 57–59.

181. Shelley, *Frankenstein: The 1818 Text, Contexts, Criticism*, 101.

182. Ibid., 104.

183. Ibid., 100.

184. Joshua, "'Marking the Dates with Accuracy,'" 301.

185. Shelley, *Frankenstein: The 1818 Text, Contexts, Criticism*, 103.

186. Bostrom, "Why I Want to Be a Posthuman When I Grow Up," 11.

187. Martha Nussbaum, *Political Emotions: Why Love Matters for Justice* (Cambridge, MA: Harvard University Press, 2013), 15.

188. Shelley, *Frankenstein: The 1818 Text, Contexts, Criticism*, 91, 158.

189. Ibid., 99.

190. Ibid., 161.

191. Ibid., 67.

192. Ibid., 94–95.

193. Asad, "Reflections on Violence, Law, and Humanitarianism," 390–427.

194. Bentley, "Family, Community, Polity," 332.

195. Knoepfler, *GMO Sapiens*, 90–91.

196. "Human plus" is a term commonly used to describe transhumans and the transhumanist movement.

197. Phillips, *The Politics of the Human*, 124.

198. Phillips treats the work of Jane Bennett as exemplary of Posthumanism 3 due to her work on the active interrelation between organic and inorganic matter, even though Bennett does not label herself this way. See Jane Bennett, *Vibrant Matter: A Political Ecology of Things* (Durham, NC: Duke University Press, 2010), 6; Phillips, *The Politics of the Human*, 126. I follow suit in my consideration of Haraway as a pioneering, though not self-identifying, representative of the burgeoning school of thought on Posthumanism 3.

199. Haraway, *When Species Meet*, 17.

200. Haraway, "A Manifesto for Cyborgs: Science, Technology, and Socialist Feminism in the 1980s," in *Haraway Reader*, 8.

201. Ibid., 9; Haraway, *When Species Meet*, 17.

202. Haraway, "A Manifesto for Cyborgs," 37.

203. Ibid., 9.

204. Ibid., 8–9.

205. Cohen, "Neither Seen nor Heard," 224.

206. Phillips, *The Politics of the Human*, 109.

207. Bostrom, "Why I Want to Be Posthuman When I Grow Up," 24.

208. Haraway, *When Species Meet*, 23.

209. Donna Haraway, *Staying with the Trouble: Making Kin in the Chthulucene* (Durham, NC: Duke University Press, 2016), 140.

210. Phillips, *The Politics of the Human*, 113, 116.

211. Ibid., 132.

212. Knoepfler, *GMO Sapiens*, 14, 208.

213. Ibid., 13.

214. Ibid., 208.

INDEX

ACKNOWLEDGMENTS

This book has been cooking on a back burner in my mind since I was an undergraduate at Bowdoin College. My professors have been instrumental in bringing this work to life, even decades after I first discussed *Frankenstein,* feminism, and the social contract tradition with them. I especially thank Ann Kibbie and Paul Franco for their mentorship, but also Denis Corish, David Collings, Bill Watterson, and the late John Ambrose for encouraging my interest in mapping the intersections of politics, philosophy, and literature.

I am indebted to the American Council of Learned Societies for awarding me a fellowship to complete this book in 2015–16. For one, it allowed me the opportunity to fulfill a longtime intellectual dream of mine. In a tremendous stroke of luck, I received word that I was awarded the fellowship about two weeks after my son Jacob's birth. His inspiration is writ on every page, for he reminded me each day of the fundamental entitlements of infants and other children.

At the University of Notre Dame, the Institute for Scholarship in the Liberal Arts supported this project all the way to its completion, including a generous subvention for its publication. I am extremely grateful to Associate Dean Mark Schurr of Notre Dame, who arranged not only for my research leave to follow my maternity leave but also for additional research funding. The generosity of Notre Dame's College of Arts and Letters allowed me to visit the J. P. Morgan Library in New York, where I saw Mary Shelley's own annotations to the 1818 edition of *Frankenstein,* known as the "Thomas Copy."

There are many students, scholars, and colleagues whose critical engagement with my ideas over the years made this book far better than it would have been if I had worked alone in a secret laboratory like Victor Frankenstein. Sparking this project into a long process of composition, de-composition, and re-composition, Greg Kucich invited me to present a paper on *Frankenstein* and feminism at a conference on "Cosmopolitanism" at Notre Dame's London Center in May 2009. Gordon Schochet, Nancy J. Hirschmann, and Steven B.

Smith have been indefatigable supporters of this book, from providing scholarly feedback to writing letters for fellowship applications. Gordon was a true champion of my ideas. I kept every single email he sent me with historical, philosophical, film, and pop cultural references to *Frankenstein*. Charles Beitz, Ann Kibbie, Catherine Zuckert, Julia Douthwaite, Neil Delaney, and Ken Garcia made insightful comments on my fellowship application. Sandrine Bergès and Alan Coffee read a version of Chapter 2 that has been published as "Mary Wollstonecraft, Children's Human Rights, and Animal Ethics" in their edited volume, *The Social and Political Philosophy of Mary Wollstonecraft* (Oxford University Press, 2016). Their editorial suggestions, along with some by Neil Delaney, enabled me to see that a revised and expanded version of the chapter belonged in my Frankenstein book project. I also benefited from questions and comments on Chapter 2 from participants in the University of Pennsylvania Political Theory Workshop in November 2014, in particular Jeffrey Green, Nancy J. Hirschmann, and Rogers Smith. Devi Snively and Agustín Fuentes organized some unforgettable Frankenstein-themed parties and film festivals, plus directed and produced their own amazing short film based on the novel. Their initiative and example gave me the artistic courage to go forward with a project that others might have thought crazy in its very inception. Conversations with my colleagues in the Political Science Department at Notre Dame shaped the book at pivotal points in the composition process: Dave Campbell, Naunihal Singh, Sue Collins, and Monika Nalepa, among others. Essaka Joshua invited me to take part in the Disability Studies Forum at Notre Dame, which introduced me to the field of critical disability studies. Many conversations with Essaka about *Frankenstein,* Romanticism, and disability studies, along with her scholarship, informed the arguments of this book. My friends in the field of physical anthropology—Agustín Fuentes, Blaine Maley, Jim McKenna, and Jonathan Marks—answered all my questions about evolution, genetics, and attachment theory, while expressing genuine interest in Mary Shelley and her Creature. A fellow traveler in feminist philosophy, Jennifer Dragseth helped me think through the meaning of motherhood and motherlessness in *Frankenstein*. My colleagues in the Glynn Family Honors Program at Notre Dame—Neil Delaney, Alex Hahn, Holly Goodson, Wendy Wolfe, Richard Cross, and Paul Weithman—provided good-humored support of my creative enterprises, like the Honors "Frankenfilm" festivals. Dozens of students in the Honors Program took my "Wollstonecraft and Shelley" seminar over the past decade. It was my discussions with them about the Creature that led me to see him as a child who had been deprived of the most important thing any young person can have—love. Maureen Williams stands out among them for her collaboration with me on a paper on Wollstonecraft, Shelley, and evolutionary theory—co-presented at the 2009 Midwest Political Science Association Meeting while she was finishing her senior thesis in biology. Proving that Frankenstein projects don't always go wrong, she now has a career in research biology.

During the ACLS fellowship year, I had the opportunity to present my work in several forums. I thank Brooke Ackerly for inviting me to co-organize a conference within a conference on "Responsibility, Human Rights, and Global Justice" for the Southern Political Science Association Meeting in Puerto Rico in January 2016. The feedback from participants was essential for my crafting of the arguments of this book. I especially thank Nancy J. Hirschmann and Jeff Spinner-Halev, whose criticisms of a draft of the introduction led me to return to the idea of relating *Frankenstein* to ethical issues surrounding disabled infants and artificial reproductive technology. Regina Kreide, Brooke Ackerly, Marina Calloni, Lorna Bracewell, Karie Cross, Michael Goodhart, and Pablo Gilabert will also see the impact of their comments on the final product. At the Midwest Political Science Association meeting in April 2016, I had the honor of being part of "Frankenstein at (almost) 200: A Mary Shelley Roundtable" with Devi Snively, Greg Kucich, Marina Calloni, and Colleen Mitchell. As part of her work as section chair, Jane Gordon very graciously organized this roundtable. I benefited immensely from comments and questions from her and the other participants. After the conference, Maria Calloni provided an in-depth critique of a draft of Chapter 3, which also helped me to develop the format for the conclusion. Colleen Mitchell has been a meticulous research assistant for this book in addition to writing and presenting her own compelling work on Shelley. I also appreciate that a number of my Notre Dame graduate students, including Colleen Mitchell and Karie Cross, discussed a version of Chapter 1 for a session of the Gender and Politics Working Group in February 2016. At the 2016 American Political Science Association Meeting, Michaele Ferguson gave insightful commentary on Chapter 1 that clarified my presentation of the typology of the stateless orphan that I find to be implicit within the social contract tradition. In the Fall of 2016, the graduate students in my seminar on Locke, Rousseau, Wollstonecraft, and Shelley helped me to see *Frankenstein* in a fresh light. Garrett Fitz-Gerald's idea that the Creature's ideal familial community would have been a school for the blind made it into the final product.

As I went through the process of writing and circulating a book proposal, feedback from several editors—Bill Frucht, David Armitage, Damon Linker, Alexandra Dauler, and Elaine Fan—was crucial. I owe a special debt to Elaine Fan for arranging for an external review of my proposal so enthusiastic that it galvanized my commitment to complete the book in time for the bicentennial of the novel. At Penn Press, Damon Linker showed such a strong interest in the proposal that I chose to work with him, a good colleague since graduate school. He arranged for two reader reports that were invaluable sources of advice for the polishing of the manuscript. I entrusted the book to him—may it go forth and prosper.

Finally, this book would not have happened without my family. Although he shares the name Victor, my husband bears no resemblance to Victor Frankenstein. He is a great father who gave me the time I needed to write a book while we raise our son together. I thank him for tolerating my obsession with *Frankenstein*, despite his firm, no-nonsense belief in the superiority of nonfiction over fiction. My mom and dad helped take care of Jacob and me during his first year of life and my first year of motherhood. Their constant companionship has been a muse for my defense of a child's right to parental love. In my hometown of Island Falls, Maine, my father sponsored the "Frankenstein Book Club" in the back room of his law office in the spring and summer of 2015. To all the participants in the book club, especially Dad and his friend Ralph, I credit you for giving me the community support I needed. For it takes a village to write a book, as to raise a child.

CPSIA information can be obtained
at www.ICGtesting.com
Printed in the USA
JSHW010440021019
1722JS00001B/13